The Deans

THE DEANS

Trevor Beeson

scm press

British Library Cataloguing in Publication data

A catalogue record for this book is available
from the British Library

0 334 02987 2

First published in 2004 by SCM Press
9–17 St Albans Place, London N1 0NX

www.scm-canterburypress.co.uk

SCM Press is a division of
SCM-Canterbury Press Ltd

Printed and bound in Great Britain by
Biddles Ltd, www.biddles.co.uk

Contents

Preface

The cordial reception accorded to my book *The Bishops* included the suggestion that I might write a companion volume on the deans. At first I thought not, for whereas the cathedrals now provide one of the most vibrant expressions of the Church of England's life, they were for most of the nineteenth century, and in some instances until comparatively recently, largely dormant. What would there be to write about their leaders?

On further reflection, however, I recognized more clearly than before that the undemanding character of cathedral life encouraged the appointment to deaneries of a remarkable body of men whose interests and achievements belonged to a wide variety of other spheres. Eccentricity was never regarded as a disqualification.

In now seeking to offer brief lives of some of these deans and their successors who led the revival of cathedral life in the twentieth century, I was grateful for the further suggestion that they should each be allocated more space than I had considered necessary for the bishops.

It was my own great privilege and joy to spend 20 years in the service of Westminster Abbey, as a canon, and Winchester Cathedral, as dean, and in this volume my concern is not simply to provide portraits of 22 fascinating churchmen, but also to indicate how the role of the dean has changed almost beyond recognition since the Barchester era. I cannot believe that this process has ended.

Esmé Parker, my former Winchester secretary and friend, who used her computer skills to turn the semi-legible manuscripts of my four previous books into documents fit for a publisher's eyes, sadly died, far too young, when she had completed only three chapters of this present volume. My gratitude to her is unbounded. I am grateful to Sheila Burns for completing this task with no less skill and, once again, to Fiona Mather for miraculously tracking down essential research material.

TB

I

Introduction

'Flagships of the spirit', 'Shopwindows of the Church of England', 'Supermarkets of religion'. These are just three of the descriptions of England's cathedrals coined by their deans during recent years. Leaving aside the triumphalist note that some in other spheres of Christian witness understandably find offensive, the descriptions point to the reforming zeal that radically altered the life of the cathedrals during the second half of the twentieth century. It is a transformation that many of the deans whose lives are chronicled in this book would have found incredible, though some would have enthusiastically approved, and their astonishment would have been heightened by the discovery that the revival of cathedral life took place during a period when the rest of the Church was in serious numerical and financial decline. There is nothing comparable in any other part of Western Europe.

A discussion of England's 42 cathedrals must begin, however, with the recognition that no two of them are alike and that generalizations are dangerous. The differences of size and architecture are obvious, but each has its own particular history, extending sometimes over more than nine centuries, and each has developed its own particular ethos and style, encouraged by the degree of independence they have enjoyed almost from their beginnings. The differences are most marked in the contrast between those of great size which look back to the Middle Ages, or even earlier, and the so-called parish church cathedrals which were created in response to the huge expansion of population that took place in the industrial towns of the nineteenth and early twentieth centuries. The life of Durham Cathedral, standing proudly on a high cliff and conscious of the fact that once it was, in the words of Sir Walter Scott, 'Half church of God, half castle 'gainst the Scot', is altogether different from that of Blackburn, an enlarged nineteenth-century parish church standing humbly in the streets of what was once the cotton-weaving centre of the world. This is not to say that one is more important than the other: simply that each is different and each has an equally important part to play in the Christian mission in its region. In some years Canterbury has over two million visitors and provides the setting for the enthronement of Archbishops and other magnificent ceremonies, whereas Bradford is lucky to have as many as 30,000 visitors and occupies an island in a Muslim/Hindu sea. Yet who dare claim that Canterbury deserves higher regard?

Differences acknowledged – joyfully – the heart of every cathedral's life is the same. It offers a daily round of worship; it is the church of a bishop and a place which offers a focus of unity to a diocese; it is governed by a chapter consisting of a dean, a number (usually four) of residentiary canons, and since 1999 up to three laypeople; it employs many others in a variety of subsidiary roles – musicians, vergers, masons, administrators and the like – and relies heavily on volunteers for a great deal of additional activity; it acknowledges a responsibility not only to the diocese but also to the civic life of its county or region.

Thus all are exceedingly busy and the day is long past when a scholar could move from a university post to a deanery in order to find more time for his studies or a distinguished parish priest, wearied by years of unceasing labour in a tough town, could move to a cathedral close to end his days in rest and peace. During the mid-1990s the number of visitors to English cathedrals was of the order of 14.5 million annually. Canterbury and York shared 4.5 million of these, while St Paul's claimed 1.4 million, Chester 1 million, Salisbury and Norwich each half a million, and eleven others each 3–400,000.

The number visiting the most popular cathedrals declined dramatically during the early years of the twenty-first century but remains high and the visitors contribute substantially to their finances. For most of the 1990s donations from visitors and, in a few cases, admission charges exceeded a total of £4.5 million, while profits from shops and the recently opened refectories brought in another £1 million. Canterbury's impressive shop has a thriving mail-order business which offers its customers, world-wide, Canterbury Cathedral fudge at £2.99 a box and teddy bears of the Archbishop and the dean at £69.99 each.

Another substantial source of income is provided by Friends organizations. Started by Dean George Bell at Canterbury in 1927, these spread to most of the other large cathedrals during the 1930s and now have a total membership of about 55,000. Some have as many as 3–4,000 Friends and a special secretariat to administer subscriptions, newsletters and Christmas cards. The original intention, largely maintained, was to provide additional money for the repair and embellishment of the fabric (never for day-to-day running costs) but the annual subscription has always been low enough to encourage the recruitment of members who may be relatively poor, yet ready to provide support by prayer. Nonetheless, Friends' financial contributions now total well over £1 million per annum, with some deans and chapters receiving in excess of £150,000.

Many Friends also make a very important contribution through voluntary work as welcoming stewards, guides, cleaners, library, shop and refectory assistants. A number of cathedrals have 500 or more of these, and everywhere their efforts reduce running costs as well as presenting visitors with the institution's human face. The total number of volunteers now stands at about 10,000, to which may be added about 190 salaried clergy, and about 1,800 full- and part-time paid lay staff – an average of 300 people involved in the running of every cathedral.

Among the full-time staff of the older cathedrals there is always plenty of work for masons and other craftsmen on the repair and conservation of the fabric. Although this task is unending, it is fair to say that these great buildings are now in better condition than they have been for many years past. This is due mainly to a new concern for ancient buildings which developed during the second half of the twentieth century in reaction against the wanton destruction and bankrupt architecture that wreaked havoc in English towns and cities in the 1950s and '60s. Deans and chapters discovered that well-organized appeals drew a generous response from their counties and regions. Ely led the way with a surprising £4 million in the 1980s. Worcester and Salisbury then raised £5 million, Winchester topped £7 million, Norwich and Southwark asked for £10 million and St Paul's, never to be outdone, is now engaged in raising £33 million for a massive programme of restoration and refurbishment to mark the 300th anniversary of the completion of Wren's great building in 1708. Another significant factor was a change of attitude by the Government in the early 1990s. In return for submission to the architectural judgement of a national Cathedrals Fabric Commission, state funding was offered to deans and chapters prepared to help themselves and by the end of the century about £20 million had been allocated.

Within the restored buildings, it is hard to believe that the standard of worship has ever been higher. The twentieth-century Liturgical Movement did much to enhance the visual aspect of worship and the dramatic potential of good ceremonial. Some cathedrals, most notably Chichester, have enlisted the aid of the modern artist. A wider appreciation of great music, encouraged by concerts, radio and recordings offered a challenge to cathedral musicians which brought an immediate response in enlarged repertoires and higher standards. Thus the daily offering of worship led by choirs and organists performing in most cathedrals at the best professional level is a unique religious phenomenon. It attracts many who, for a variety of reasons, do not feel at home in their parish churches, and their number is increasing.

Unfortunately, the same cannot be said of cathedral preaching which, with honourable exceptions, has suffered the general lack of regard for the sermon as a means of communicating the gospel. But in many places high quality educational work of another sort is being undertaken. Schools officers, fostering close relations with both church and state schools, encourage the use of cathedrals as an educational resource and attract many thousands of children every year to study programmes and specially devised acts of worship. Courses of theological education, sometimes shared with local academic institutions, provide stimulating intellectual fare for thoughtful laypeople, and those cathedrals fortunate enough to have working libraries offer important theological resources in their dioceses.

These manifestations of new life have been accompanied by a new openness to the world outside the cathedral close and a new readiness to share a rich heritage with other churches and the community at large. Roman Catholic and Free Church services are common, ecumenical acts of worship frequent and youth events attract their thousands. Curiously in a society apparently becoming more secular, community organizations commemorating something or other in their corporate life invariably turn to a cathedral for a special service. National emergencies and celebrations also find a natural focus of expression in a cathedral. The devising of appropriate acts of worship for these occasions can occupy a good deal of a precentor's time and the larger cathedrals usually have a special music and liturgy office to handle production and administration. At Christmas and Easter when attendances are numbered in many thousands they can be exceedingly busy. Concerts, recitals and, sometimes, drama all contribute to full cathedral diaries throughout the year.

Not everyone is convinced, however, that frenetic activity is the true vocation of the cathedral and there are those – not all of them elderly – who yearn for the tranquillity of most French cathedrals, neglected and unloved though these often seem to be. The opportunity for prayer and reflection undisturbed by tramping feet and the chink of money is not lightly to be dismissed and this and some other questions about the future of cathedral life in England will be discussed in the final chapter. But before then an outline history of cathedrals since their earliest days is offered, followed by brief lives of 22 of the most interesting characters who occupied the deaneries during the period of reform which began during the Victorian era and shows no sign of ending.

2

Change and Continuity

The first English cathedrals were modest affairs, located wherever a bishop chose to establish the base for his missionary work. The name cathedral indicates the place that houses a bishop's *cathedra* (chair), this being the symbol of his teaching authority. As bishops were driven from place to place by either external hostility or strategic need, so the location of their cathedral changed. Thus in Saxon England the missionary bishops in Wessex had their *cathedra* in Dorchester before settling in the seventh century in Winchester. The Celtic bishops in Northumbria moved from Lindisfarne to Chester-le-Street, then finally to Durham in the tenth century.

Another common factor was the presence with the bishop of a small residential community of priests who constituted his *familia*. They worshipped with him, served as his counsellors, and shared in his missionary work. Sometimes these communities consisted of monks, but often they were secular priests bound together by a simple rule and therefore known as canons. The distinction between the two categories of cathedral clergy was not as great then as it became later.

During the eleventh and twelfth centuries the Saxon cathedrals, some of them now fairly substantial buildings, were replaced by massive Norman structures, often standing alongside a formidable castle, and the leading Saxon churchmen were replaced by Normans. At Winchester, William the Conqueror appointed his chaplain as bishop and his brother as prior of what had developed into a sizeable Benedictine monastic community, well organized in accordance with the Cluniac reforms of the tenth century. At London, Maurice, the Archdeacon of Le Mans and the Conqueror's royal chaplain, became the bishop and reorganized the college of secular priests after a well-tried Norman pattern with a dean at its head and senior canons in the offices of precentor, chancellor and treasurer. In collegiate cathedrals of this sort – Salisbury was a notable example – it became customary to allocate portions of land, known as prebends, to the financial support of members of the college who subsequently became known as prebendaries, rather than as canons.

In the monastic cathedrals the bishop was the titular abbot but since he was not always himself a monk and was busy about many other things, including administrative functions at the Court, the leadership was in the hands of the prior. The constitution was provided by the Benedictine Rule, except at Carlisle, which was Augustinian, and the community's income came from substantial land-holdings, augmented by gifts and, where there was the shrine of a saint, the offerings of pilgrims.

Thus by the thirteenth century the English cathedrals were being organized on two distinct lines – collegiate at Chichester, Exeter, Hereford, Lichfield, Lincoln, London, Salisbury, Wells and York; monastic at Canterbury, Carlisle, Durham, Ely, Norwich, Rochester, Winchester and Worcester. But there was no marked difference in their buildings inasmuch as all had their great churches, cloisters, chapter houses, refectories, libraries and schools. At the collegiate cathedrals, however, the prebendaries lived in separate houses, rather than dormitories, and some were married. The monastic communities normally had 40–70 monks, though this could be substantially fewer during times of plague, and there were usually about 30 prebendaries in the collegiate bodies.

Throughout the Middle Ages the cathedrals were busy places. The builders were never away for long – disastrous fires were common, the central tower of virtually every cathedral collapsed when the aspirations of architects, urged on by ambitious deans and priors, exceeded their skill. Changes in architectural fashion, the need for more chapels, and the erection of an ever-increasing number of chantries, as well as the repair and enlargement of buildings in the precincts, provided plenty of work for contracted teams of stonemasons, carpenters and metal-workers. By the beginning of the sixteenth century St Paul's had no fewer than 39 chantry chapels served by 54 priests, many of them semi-literate, offering Masses for the dead. Wealthy patrons commissioned painters and sculptors to adorn the buildings and encourage devotion. At the time of Mass the murmuring of the priests at the many altars and the light of hundreds of candles created a numinous atmosphere that could never be recovered today. Most cathedrals had a school, many ran hospitals, and some monks were required to supervise and collect rents and fines from their community's extensive estates.

The major shrines of Canterbury and Winchester attracted huge numbers of pilgrims, and most of the other cathedrals offered a focus of devotion that brought in the crowds. The medieval cathedrals were just as much centres of tourism as are the cathedrals of today. Those that were monastic had a special obligation to offer hospitality to all comers, in accordance with the Rule of St Benedict which decreed that the visitor must be welcomed as if he were Christ himself. At Winchester the prior's lodging, located apart from the common quarters of the rest of the community, included a lofty hall where 100 or more could be entertained, and of the monastery's total income of £1,508 in 1356 no less than £1,055 was allocated to the prior for hospitality. At Canterbury the prior had a household of 25 servants.

It was normal to find the poorest of the poor dining with the prior, as well as some of the other monks, but sometimes the highest in the land were received and Winchester, because of its royal associations in Saxon times, had more than its share of excitement. Yet not everything was sweetness and light, and even the monastic cathedrals, whose chapters were committed to poverty, as well as to chastity, obedience and stability, were not without their problems – some of them financial. In 1331 Prior Alexander of Winchester was accused by one of his monks of selling to outsiders food and clothing due to the destitute parents of monks who were being cared for in a small hospital nearby. The prior denied this and managed to clear his name, while the accusing monk was said to have made off with large amounts of gold and silver. When later he was arraigned before a papal court he was described as, 'not merely as an erring sheep but as a stinking goat, trying to butt the prior and convent with his horns'.

Disputes between communities and their bishop were frequent, particularly over the appointment of priors. From the twelfth century onwards the bishops became more and more isolated from their cathedrals, except at Canterbury where the shrine of Thomas à Becket kept the Archbishop at home. The monastic communities thereupon asserted their independence and their right, in accordance with the Rule of St Benedict, to elect their own priors. It was at the time of such elections that the bishop was inclined to assert his right as abbot to have a say in the choice. Lawyers were employed by both sides in order to reach a settlement. Similar problems arose in the collegiate cathedrals over the appointment of deans and other great officers, and in the major cathedrals the wishes of the King had to be accepted.

On the whole, however, the monastic cathedrals were less open to corruption than their collegiate counterparts. The provisions of the Benedictine Rule exerted some degree of discipline, there were annual meetings of monks at Northampton, later transferred to London, to discuss mutual problems, and abbots were sometimes instructed to carry out Visitations of neighbouring monasteries where discipline was known to be slack. A major, and what became a long-standing, problem in the collegiate cathedrals was the absence of the prebendaries. The truth is that in those institutions there was not enough work to keep 30 or more able-bodied senior priests fully occupied. There was, therefore, the temptation to seek employment elsewhere, sometimes in the parish church of the prebend. It also needs to be remembered that not all the prebends yielded a high income. One of the prebendaries of St Paul's in the second half of the fourteenth century received fixed rents to the value of £2 5s 11d (less 12s in allowances) plus a great quantity of firewood, ten hens and 202 eggs. By the time these had been transported to London they were worth next to nothing. Fortunately, the prebendary was also the dean and it was frequently necessary for a prebendary to hold several appointments in order to secure a reasonable annual stipend.

On the other hand there were certainly many prebends that yielded very substantial incomes and, unsurprisingly, these were greatly coveted and brought much scandal to the cathedrals. Royal and episcopal favourites and relatives were given stalls – at one time Salisbury numbered on its chapter three cardinals living in distant Avignon – and eventually the scale of absenteeism was so large that it became difficult for many cathedrals to maintain their life. In theory a prebendary was required to spend a few months in every year in residence at his cathedral in order to discharge certain responsibilities, but a system of deputies was devised and the office of sub-dean was created to enable even the dean to be away for long periods.

Various attempts were made to bring at least some of the prebendaries into residence, the first of which was an appeal to self-interest. While the income from the prebends could not be touched, it was decreed that the income due to the dean and chapter as a whole would in future be shared only among those prebendaries who had kept a prescribed period of residence. A typical requirement was eight months for the dean, the precentor, the chancellor and the treasurer, and six months for an ordinary prebendary. At Wells there was also a daily distribution of money and bread for everyone present. The new arrangement worked like magic – the prebendaries flocked back to their closes. So much so that there was insufficient work for all, and some had forsaken major responsibilities in the parishes of the diocese. A division was, therefore, made between residentiary and non-residentiary prebendaries, creating a distinction in cathedral chapters that has remained ever since.

This necessary action soon led, however, to another abuse. The increased number of residentiary prebendaries each entitled to a share of the dean and chapter's surplus revenue, meant inevitably that the dividend was lower for all. Steps were taken, therefore, to reduce the number of residentiaries and this was achieved by the crude method of making those who aspired to residence to lay on substantial entertainment, lasting perhaps two or three days, sometimes extending over a whole year, for all who were associated with the cathedral. The cost of this was so high that admission to residence became restricted to those rich enough to pay the entry charge. This practice was forbidden by a Papal Bull in 1392. Yet corruption remained in some places and when in 1505 Henry VII appointed John Colet, the friend of Erasmus and Thomas More, to the deanery of St Paul's with firm instructions to reform the life of London's cathedral, it proved impossible for this man of great courage and personal integrity to make any progress. The residentiary prebendaries, he said, 'cast aside their care for the Church; they pursue their own private gains; they contravert the common property to their private uses. In these unhappy and disordered times residence in the cathedral is nothing less than seeking one's own advantage and, to speak more plainly, robbing the Church and enriching oneself. O abominable crime! O detestable iniquity!' When the chapter rejected his proposed new statutes, and the bishop refused to support him, Colet turned to Cardinal Wolsey who produced alternative new statutes but, in spite of his authority as papal legate, these too were rejected. Colet thereafter concentrated his attention on the refounding of St Paul's School and on his death entrusted this to the Mercers' Company, believing that it would not be safe in the hands of the corrupt Church.

When reformation came 20 years later it was violent. The monastic cathedrals were most affected inasmuch as all religious houses were suppressed, but as institutions they survived and were given a form of government very close to that of the collegiate cathedrals. In many cases there was continuity of personnel: seven of the eight priors – Canterbury was the only exception – became the first deans and remained in their lodgings. Royal charters granted in 1541 provided for the appointment of twelve prebendaries and most of these came from compliant former monks who were academically qualified. Provision was also made for six minor canons, twelve lay clerks and ten choristers.

Mass continued to be celebrated in accordance with the Sarum rite, but with the Epistle and Gospel in English, and the Canonical Hours were also recited until replaced by mattins and evensong in the First English Prayer Book of 1549. At Canterbury and Winchester the shrines were dismantled and everywhere the treasury of ornaments and vestments was either confiscated or destroyed. Some of the sources of revenue were also seized, but it was recognized that substantial endowments would be required to maintain the buildings and pay the cathedral's servants and at the end of the day the dean and chapter of Winchester's estates were hardly less than those held by the monks prior to 1541. The same provisions were made for all the other former monastic cathedrals and in 1544–5 three diocesan bishops, probably with some input from Archbishop Cranmer, drew up their statutes.

These became known as cathedrals of the new foundation in distinction from the collegiate cathedrals which retained their existing statutes, and were thereafter regarded as of the old foundation. They, too, lost most of their precious possessions but they were permitted to retain at least twelve prebends and much other agricultural land to sustain their worship and buildings. Henry VIII saw the cathedrals as playing an increasingly important role in the reformed Church of England as centres of learning and providers of education. So much so that he created new cathedrals at Chester, Peterborough, Oxford, Gloucester, Bristol and Westminster, endowing these with some of the spoils of the suppressed religious houses. The deans of these cathedrals were all former superiors of monasteries.

It is not to be supposed, however, that the changes imposed on the cathedrals in the 1540s were achieved without pain and difficult personal adjustments. An unbroken tradition extending over five centuries was being radically transformed and, after the death of Henry VIII in 1547, those surrounding the young Edward VI were bent on a more Protestant reformation. Cranmer, who described a prebendary as a clergyman who is, 'neither a learner nor a teacher, but a good viander', was no lover of cathedrals and a period of even greater instability followed. At Winchester the death of Dean Kingsmill, the former prior, led to the appointment of a layman, Sir John Mason, to the deanery, his task being to manage the estates.

During the reign of Mary Tudor (1553–8) Roman Catholic priests, some of whom had changed their allegiances, were reintroduced into the cathedrals, along with the Latin Mass, but no attempt was made to re-establish the religious orders. Mary was herself married to Philip II of Spain with full Catholic ceremonial in Winchester Cathedral in 1554. In December of the following year the Archdeacon of Winchester, John Philpot, was burnt at the stake for his Protestant convictions, while the Bishop of Winchester, who preached at Mary's funeral in 1558, caused so much offence to the new Queen Elizabeth that he was committed to the Tower where he died two years later. Elizabeth, a traditionalist and ever loyal to her father's church policy, soon restored the deans and prebendaries to the cathedrals, but the Protestant bishops she appointed often caused more damage to the interiors of those great buildings than anything achieved by Thomas Cromwell and his henchmen 20 years earlier.

By the time James I reached the throne in 1603 cathedral life had settled into a pattern which, apart from the Commonwealth interlude, remained undisturbed for almost another two and a half centuries. A vivid picture of how this was experienced during the reigns of James I and Charles I came to light in 1918 with the discovery of the diaries of John Young who was Dean of Winchester from 1616 to 1645. Young, a Scot, owed his appointment to the fact that his father, Sir Peter Young, had been a tutor of King James, and moved to England with him in 1603 to serve in his Court. At the age of 26 the future dean was the Chancellor of Wells Cathedral, as well as a royal chaplain, none of which appointments he felt the need to relinquish when five years later he was preferred to Winchester. Indeed, soon after settling in the deanery he acquired the rectory of the Hampshire parish of Over Wallop and a prebendary's stall at York. Pluralism on this scale was normal among privileged churchmen.

The chief impression created by his meticulously kept diaries is of an enormous amount of time devoted to financial matters, in particular to the administration of the dean and chapter's estates, located in many different parts of the south of England. Young usually spent the summer months on one or other of his own estates – he acquired three more during his Winchester years – and apart from time (quite a lot) spent in London on royal or church business, hardly a day passed without his having to deal with rents, leases and fines, settling disputes between tenants, sealing documents and a host of other matters arising from a huge land-holding.

This labour was not, however, without its rewards. Young became very rich. His share of the chapter's surpluses was set at eight times that of each of the twelve prebendaries. Thus he lived in considerable style and on 29 October 1619 paid £18 12s for liveries in velvet and silk with gold buttons for eight manservants. Occasional problems with cooks suggest a large domestic staff. He travelled by coach, rather than on horseback. Relatives and friends turned to him for loans.

Another striking feature of Young's time at Winchester was the calibre of the twelve prebendaries. All royal appointees, most of them were men of distinction – heads of Oxford and Cambridge colleges, professors, deans of royal chapels, and a number of future bishops – who often enough had other subsidiary posts. Winchester, St Paul's and Westminster Abbey were, for historical and geographical reasons, probably untypical in this respect, but prebendal stalls in many other cathedrals often went to royal and episcopal favourites or relatives. Hence the continuation of the absenteeism which had so blighted the life of the pre-Reformation collegiate cathedrals.

This gave Dean Young one of his greatest and most intractable problems and led to clashes between himself and his chapter. Sometimes it proved impossible to elect a suitable vice-dean or a treasurer. In 1624 the receiver was also Dean of Wells. Young's exhortations to his colleagues to keep their residences and fulfil their preaching duties – four Sundays a year – were often met with hostility and on one occasion the complaint that he was treating them like schoolboys. His suggestion that fees should be withheld for non-attendance at statutory services caused an almighty row and a letter of protest to Archbishop Laud from one of the prebendaries.

Contact between the dean and his bishop was infrequent. Enthronements were low-key events, involving only proxies, and Bishops of Winchester generally occupied their London house in order to discharge state responsibilities, or Farnham Castle in the Surrey part of the diocese. Yet opportunities for conflict were not entirely lacking. After a Court dinner in London in December 1630 Young attempted to have conversation with his bishop (Richard Neile) – 'I spoke with my Lord Bishop who used me so harshly that we had but little discourse. I saw him the following Tuesday and tried to reason, but he answered, frowning as before, that he would have nothing to do with me. We parted abruptly.' The disagreement concerned leases.

From time to time there was conflict between the dean and chapter and Winchester's civic authorities, and when the mayor imprisoned two of the choir men, having falsely accused them of failure to pay Ship Money, the matter went before King Charles. The King was also drawn into a dispute concerning the right of the mayor to be preceded by his three maces when attending the cathedral. These contretemps were perhaps warning signs of the coming clash between the Crown and its supporters and the new democratic tendency that was to lead to Oliver Cromwell's Commonwealth.

Cromwell's troops reached Winchester in 1645 when the dean and the prebendaries were deprived of their houses and incomes. The Parliament of the Major Generals suppressed all deans and chapters whose estates were then sold to supporters of the new regime. Dean Young retired to the rectory at Over Wallop, where he remained, a virtual exile, until his death in 1654. He had been a diligent dean who had served his cathedral well. But too much of his time and energy was taken up with trying to make the best of a system of governance which for over three centuries had shown itself to be unworkable. The new statutes devised by Archbishop Laud and imposed on all the cathedrals in 1638 came too late to make a reforming impact. During the Commonwealth the cathedrals were stripped of the remaining vestiges of their Catholic past and used for a variety of secular purposes. In some places their ancillary building provided a useful quarry of materials for the erection of houses by the new gentry. There is, nonetheless, evidence that worship of some sort continued to be offered and at Winchester three ministers were appointed to preach in the cathedral.

Following the restoration of the monarchy in 1660 the deans and chapters were quickly re-established, estates were recovered, cathedrals repaired, houses in the closes rebuilt, new Communion plate and furnishings commissioned, and Archbishop Laud's statutes brought out of libraries. A final revision of the *Book of Common Prayer* was enforced as the sole expression of the Church of England's liturgy. It was a busy and exhilarating time. But the intense activity did not last; neither did it need to do so, at least not in terms of the eighteenth-century view of the role of the Church of England, which was to support the restored monarchy and the hierarchical ordering of society, to offer worship free from the taint of Roman Catholicism or Dissent, and to promote charitable work in education and among the poor. Such a task had its attractions to the sons of the aristocracy, not least if it could be undertaken from a fine house and sustained by a comfortable stipend. Membership of a cathedral chapter became, therefore, an enviable occupation.

Once again, however, problems arose from the fact that there was simply not enough to do to keep thirteen priests usefully occupied. Edmund Pyle, who was a prebendary of Winchester from 1756 to 1776, wrote, 'The life of a prebendary is a pretty easy way of dawdling away one's time: praying, walking, writing and as little study as your heart would wish.' Avarice and idleness combined to revive with a vengeance the old scandals of absenteeism and pluralism, reducing the cathedrals to bastions of privilege and backwaters of religious life. Sometimes, however, the deaneries and prebendal stalls were put to good use and the tradition of scholarship revived and developed. Fine libraries were created, financed sometimes by the admission fees charged for entry to the cathedral. At St Paul's the deanery was used to subsidize (£2,000 per annum) poor bishoprics, usually Bristol or Llandaff, and between 1727 and 1849 eleven successive deans were also diocesan bishops, the most notable of these being the great philosophical theologian Joseph Butler during his time as Bishop of Bristol. A similar arrangement obtained at Westminster Abbey where the deanery was combined with the bishopric of Rochester.

While the complacency and corruption of the eighteenth-century Church has often been exaggerated – Edward White Benson called it, 'the siesta century' – the cathedrals provided ample evidence to support this description and during the early years of the nineteenth century their life reached its nadir. After attending Winchester Cathedral on Sunday 30 October 1825 in the course of one of his celebrated *Rural Rides*, William Cobbett wrote, 'The "service" was now begun. There is a dean and God knows how many prebends belonging to this immensely rich bishopric and chapter, and there were at this "service" two or three men and five or six boys in white surplices, with a congregation of fifteen women and four men.'

The days of this somnolent regime, replicated in cathedrals the length and breadth of England were, however, numbered. The evangelical revival and the rise of the Tractarian Movement both offered a religious critique, but far more significant was the burst of social and economic energy and institutional reform that started in the 1820s and continued throughout the Victorian era. There was no possibility of the Church of England escaping this and the first problem to be tackled was the gross inequality in the distribution of its financial reserves and its consequent inability to provide an effective ministry to the masses now living in the new industrial towns. Since the bishoprics and the cathedrals held the chief concentrations of wealth it was only to be expected that they would be the chief targets of the reformers.

In 1834 the Prime Minister, Sir Robert Peel, urged on by the Bishop of London, Charles James Blomfeld, appointed a commission to make proposals for the re-arrangement of dioceses, the equalization of episcopal stipends, the augmentation of poor benefices and an increase in the number of clergy. This body was permanently constituted as the

Ecclesiastical Commission in 1836 and became responsible, with increasing power, for the administration of the Church of England's financial assets. Its attention soon turned to the cathedrals and in 1840 an Act of Parliament required deans and chapters to turn over to the commission the greater part of their estates and reduce significantly the number of clergy on their books. Each was to have a dean and four canons residentiary who would constitute the chapter and be responsible for the day-to-day life and witness of the cathedral. The dean was to be paid £1,000 per annum and required to reside for at least eight months of the year, the canons £500 per annum in return for at least three months' residence. In cathedrals of the old foundation the offices of precentor, chancellor and treasurer were to be retained. The number of minor canons had to be reduced to between three and six (twelve at St Paul's) depending on the history and status of the cathedral. Beyond the resident community was to be a greater chapter that included 20 or more honorary canons (prebendaries in most old foundation cathedrals) who would meet at least twice a year to offer opinion and advice, and additionally whenever a new bishop had to be elected. It was not long before this office, at the disposal of the bishop, became a coveted honour among the parish clergy of the diocese, but in most cathedrals their influence was slight.

The chapters fought these developments but their position in the public eye was weak and the legislation was devised and implemented with such speed that there was little opportunity to mobilize effective resistance. The changes were effected gradually but relentlessly by the deaths of office-holders and, since their purposes were purely administrative, no one supposed that they would, in the short term anyway, lead to the renewal of cathedral life. Neither did they. Sir Arthur Phelps reported of Winchester in 1854: 'The cathedral is somewhat of a sad sight. You have Grecian monuments cutting into Gothic pillars; the doors shut for the greater part of the day; only a little bit of the building used; beadledom predominant; the chink of money here and there . . . the singing indifferent; the sermons bad.' Another financial blow fell in 1868 when the Ecclesiastical Commissioners took a further large slice of the cathedrals' reserves. This, combined with an agricultural depression in the 1880s, left many of them with scarcely enough to pay their deans and chapters, and nothing to maintain their fabrics. The deans and canons of Winchester, Salisbury and Gloucester went on to half-pay. Dean Burgon of Chichester (one of the poorest deaneries) wrote, 'I never knew the sense of being really poor until I came hither'.

Meanwhile there was talk of cathedral reform. In 1869 the Archbishop of Canterbury and York convened a meeting of deans at Lambeth Palace, 'to consider the best mode of introducing certain salutary changes in our cathedral system'. A liaison committee was formed and the deans were asked to submit statements about the reforms most urgently needed in their own cathedrals. The Dean of Norwich, E. M. Goulburn, published his statement, and followed this with a collection of sermons on *The Principles of the Cathedral System* (1870). He emphasized the importance of, 'sacred learning, study, devotion, retirement from the world, and the maintenance of the perpetual worship of God'. He said that deans and canons should be required, 'to make some contribution to theological literature once every five years'.

A book of essays published in 1872 contained many suggestions for reform but first its editor, J. S. Howson, who was Dean of Chester, felt obliged to deal with what was apparently a frequently asked question – Are cathedrals really needed? Harvey Goodwin, a reforming Dean of Ely before he became Bishop of Carlisle, said that cathedrals should maintain daily worship, 'on a grand scale' and be open from sunrise to sunset; lay clerks should also be lay readers; the encouraging of the parish clergy to feel at home, and the housing of ordinations, diocesan conferences and choir festivals would enable cathedrals to become the mother churches of their dioceses; the deans and canons should publish an annual account of their cathedral activities and also undertake useful work in the diocese. At York the Honourable Augustus Duncombe, who was dean from 1858 to 1880 and managed to secure also the offices of precentor and chancellor, had already raised the worship to a high standard, while at St Paul's and Westminster Abbey there were popular Sunday evening services that attracted thousands. By the end of the 1870s Edward White Benson had seized the opportunity provided by the building of a new cathedral at Truro to initiate a fresh approach to cathedral life reflecting more closely its primitive origins.

It was not until well into the twentieth century, however, that all the deans and chapters recognized the inevitability of substantial change. By this time many more cathedrals had been created from parish and collegiate churches to serve the new bishoprics established in heavily populated industrial areas. Liverpool and Guildford had newly built cathedrals, and Coventry – rebuilt after wartime bombing – became the spearhead of dynamic renewal. The process of change continues.

Westminster Abbey has always been unique. It was a cathedral for only ten years during the reign of Henry VIII but it has a special place in the life of the English Church and nation and been served by some of the most notable and interesting deans. Hence their inclusion in this book.

Founded in 1065 by Edward the Confessor, the last but one of the Saxon kings, as a royal church served by Benedictine monks, it immediately became the place for coronations. All but two of England's kings and queens were crowned there and during the Middle Ages many of them were buried as near as possible to the Confessor's shrine. These other royal associations inevitably distinguished the Abbey from all the other Benedictine houses in England and it was once described as, 'the noisiest church in Christendom'. There was another distinction: in common with Monte Cassino and some other major monasteries in Europe, it was exempted from episcopal jurisdiction and made answerable only to the Pope.

At the Reformation Henry VIII retained this exemption and placed the new collegiate community under his own jurisdiction. It was governed by a dean (the former abbot) and twelve prebendaries (six of these, former monks), after the manner of the other collegiate churches, until Mary Tudor replaced them with Benedictine monks and restored the papal prerogative.

This proved to be, however, an interlude of just under three years as the monks were immediately turned out by Elizabeth I in 1558. The restored collegiate body was granted a Royal Charter (unsigned and therefore a source of future contention), which confirmed the Abbey as a Royal Peculiar with, in effect, a Presbyterian polity and no bishop – a status and style it still enjoys. Lancelot Andrewes was dean from 1601 to 1605 and the translation of the Authorized Version of the Bible was masterminded in the Jerusalem Chamber. As elsewhere, the Commonwealth brought much destruction to the interior of the building, though a Board of Governors appointed by Parliament carried out extensive repairs to the general fabric and the royal tombs. Seven Presbyterian divines were appointed to conduct some sort of daily worship at 7 a.m., and what became known as the Westminster Assembly of Divines held 1,163 sessions between 1643 and 1649 compiling Calvinist documents which became the doctrinal basis of English-speaking Presbyterianism. Within a fortnight of the Restoration of the monarchy in 1660, Charles II had appointed a new dean, and with hardly less speed Elizabeth's Charter was rehabilitated. The Abbey's restored collegiate life developed along more or less the same lines as those of the cathedrals, experiencing painful but necessary reforms and the late twentieth century's renewal.

Note: the heads of the Cathedral foundations created in parish churches during the late nineteenth and twentieth centuries were known as provosts, but under the 1999 Cathedrals Measure all became deans.

3

The Geologist
William Buckland, Westminster

William Buckland, Dean of Westminster from 1845 to 1856, was undoubtedly the most extraordinary of all the holders of this historic office. He was in fact active at Westminster for little more than four years, being obliged in 1849 to retire with a serious brain disease to the Abbey living of Islip in Oxfordshire. But during those four years he achieved a number of important improvements to the Abbey's environment that would not at the time have been possible to anyone lacking his scientific skill.

Buckland was one of Britain's earliest geologists and, although some of his pioneering work was subject to later correction, he helped to change the way in which the origin and history of the universe was understood. He was born in 1784 at Axminster in Devonshire where his father was the rector of two rural parishes. He was educated at Blundell's School, Tiverton, then at Winchester College where he began to collect fossils. At Corpus Christi College, Oxford, to which he was admitted as a scholar, he read classics and, having been elected to a fellowship in 1808, was ordained to the priesthood. His outlook was that of a liberal latitudinarian.

But his chief interest was in minerals and during the next four years he travelled on horseback over a large part of south west England collecting specimens. This was the beginning of what became a very large collection, donated eventually to the Oxford Museum. In 1813 he was appointed Reader in Minerology at Oxford and in the same year became a Fellow of the Geological Society of London, of which he was later to be the President. In 1818 he was elected to the Royal Society and in the following year, at the instigation of the Prince Regent, and in order to augment his small salary, a Readership in Geology was established at Oxford, with Buckland as its first occupant.

A paper on the slate and greenstone rocks of Cumberland and

Westmoreland was followed by another on the plastic clay at Reading. He then embarked on the excavation, the first ever in England, of the Kirkland Cave in Yorkshire. This led to the discovery of animal bones, of the sort that provided the basic diet of hyenas, and he concluded from this that Yorkshire had once been a sub-tropical land inhabited not only by hyenas, but also by elephants, tigers and the like. Their disappearance was, he believed, caused by a climatic change, creating a catastrophic flood, and this he linked with the Flood story in Genesis.

All of this he expounded in a book *Reliquiae Diluvionae* (Relics of the Flood) published in 1824 and, although his suggestion that the Genesis six days of creation was best regarded as six ages of creation caused a certain amount of controversy, the biblical literalists were happy to use his thesis to support their arguments. In the scientific world the publication of the book won him a European reputation, but in 1840 a young Swiss naturalist demonstrated that the deposits in caves were the result not of flood but of ice. Buckland, who had greatly encouraged the young man, was ready to acknowledge the error of his own hypothesis when he recognized that the scratching and smoothing of rocks in the Yorkshire cave might have been caused by glacier ice. He was now led to believe that Scotland and much of the north of England had once been submerged in ice.

Meanwhile Buckland had resigned his Fellowship in order to marry and in 1825 was appointed a canon of Christ Church, Oxford, combining this with the rectory of the country parish of Stoke Charity in Hampshire. He continued to lecture in Oxford, however, and for about 15 years was the university's star turn, attracting large audiences in spite of a two-guineas entrance fee. Another geologist testified to his engaging style:

Cheery, humorous, bustling, full of eloquence; seldom without his famous blue bag, whence even at fashionable evening parties he would bring out and describe with infinite drollery, amid the surprise and laughter of his audience, the last 'find' from a bone cave.

Another geologist, the distinguished Sir Roderick Murchison, expressed doubts about the appropriateness of Buckland's style to a Bristol meeting of the British Association for the Advancement of Science of which he was the first President:

The fun of one of the evenings was a lecture of Buckland's. In that

part of his discourse which he treated of ichnolites, or fossil foot-
prints, the Doctor exhibited himself as a cock or a hen on the
edge of a muddy pool, making impressions by lifting one leg
after another. Many of the grave people thought our science was
unsuited to buffoonery by a Oxford don.

The truth is that Buckland had a passionate desire to share his dis-
coveries with others and to explain their significance to people for
whom geology offered exciting revelations such as are associated in
the modern mind with the exploitation of distant planets. The intellectual implications of the discourses were no less radical than those in
astronomy that brought about the Copernican Revolution in the sixteenth century. In his much-noticed *Bridgewater Treatise*, published
in 1836 after six years in preparation and titled 'The Power, Wisdom
and Goodness of God as manifested in the Creation', Buckland sought
to explain the history of the earth as discussed by geologists and
palaeontologists. 'Their studies', he declared, 'indicated a super-
natural design and were not contrary to the Bible since this was a book
of religion, not of science.' This caused some concern among the
extreme evangelicals in the Church, and not least to the Dean of York
who wrote several letters of protest. Tractarian objections would later
cause Buckland to leave Oxford.

His interests moreover extended beyond geology to the world of
living animals and here the eccentric side of his personality became
even more evident. His house at Christ Church was not only a fossils
museum but also a menagerie containing an extraordinary variety of
live and stuffed animals and birds. Snakes and guinea pigs were
confined to cages, and toads to bowls, but jackdaws and owls were
free to fly from room to room. A stuffed hippopotamus served as the
children's rocking horse. When the Duke of Wellington was installed
as Chancellor of the University Buckland allowed the live turtle sent
for the banquet a swim in the fountain of Tom Quad with his son,
Frank, as its rider. After the reptile's head was severed in the kitchen,
the kitchen boy noticed, to Buckland's satisfaction, that it was still
capable of biting his finger.

Buckland's research involved him in the sampling of the flesh of the
creatures he was studying and he claimed to have eaten his way
through the whole of the animal creation. At one point he believed the
worst taste to be that of a mole, but he revised his judgement when he
consumed a handful of horseflies, which he declared to be horrible.
His guests at Christ Church, and later at the Westminster deanery,

were sometimes horrified to be served mice in batter or giraffe for breakfast. None of which could quite match his behaviour when being entertained in the manor house at Islip. His host was a descendant of the British Ambassador in Paris at the time when the royal tombs were despoiled, and had inherited from him the heart of Louis XIV. This, having turned to powder was kept in a silk handkerchief which after the dinner was passed round the table. When it reached Buckland he held the handkerchief to his lips, put the contents into his mouth and said solemnly: 'See I am eating the heart of *le roi soleil* before whom all Europe trembled.' The reactions of the host and other guests were not recorded.

Buckland owed his appointment to Westminster to Sir Robert Peel, with whom he enjoyed a lifelong friendship, and he succeeded Samuel Wilberforce, who had departed for the bishopric of Oxford after less than twelve months at the deanery. His decision to become a dean was much influenced by the growth in Oxford of the High Church Tractarian Movement. Its leaders believed that the argument from design for the existence of God might be accepted by the members of a variety of religious denominations and must therefore be false. What is more, the holding in Oxford of the inaugural meeting of the British Association, attended by all sorts of people, threatened the Anglican dominance in the university. And when Buckland identified the alleged bones of a saint as those of a goat, and a saint's blood as bat's urine their worst fears were confirmed. Neither did it help when the British Association supported the appointment of the liberal Renn Dickson Hampden to the Regius Professorship of Divinity. As support for the Tractarians increased, so attendance at scientific lectures declined, and in a letter to a friend and colleague, Henry Acland, Buckland wrote: 'Some years ago I was sanguine, as you are now, as to the possibility of Natural History making some progress in Oxford, but I have long come to the conclusion that it is utterly hopeless.'

Buckland always relished the opportunity to apply his scientific knowledge to practical issues, and was at one time Chairman of the Oxford Gas and Coke Company. At the Abbey there were plenty of practical matters to keep him occupied and it was to these that he now turned. The quality of the stone and cement being used for the restoration of the building concerned him and he took over the supervision of the stonemasons. And when in 1848 he and his two daughters contracted typhoid he decided to investigate the source of the disease. Known locally as Westminster fever, it had previously been confined to the Abbey's precincts, but on this occasion it spread wider and claimed several lives in the city. Once he was recovered Buckland investigated the sewers in the precincts and found these to be silted up. Four hundred cubic yards of foul waste were removed and piped drainage – the first ever in London – was installed.

As an active member of the Institution of Civil Engineers he then proposed a scheme for extending this form of drainage to other parts of London and also investigated the possible source of a supply of pure water for the capital. The need for this had become urgent since the outbreak of typhoid in Westminster was accompanied by a much larger and more serious outbreak of cholera in many other districts. When this ended in 1849 a service of thanksgiving was held in the Abbey and provided Buckland with the opportunity to preach one of his forthright sermons. Taking as his text 2 Kings 5 v.13, 'Wash and be clean', he declared,

> The greater number of the poor who perish are the victims of the avarice and neglect of small landlords and owners of the filthy, ill-ventilated habitations in which the poorest and most ill-fed and helpless are compelled to dwell. Fatal diseases are continually engendered from lack of adequate supplies of water, withholden from the dwellings of the poor by the negligence of the owners, . . . it will be the fault of Parliament if we do not instantly begin to remedy these crying evils, if in two or three years our city is not duly supplied with water. Above all things cleanse your hearts and not your garments only, and turn unto the Lord your God.

Buckland was no socialist, however, and in a sermon preached at the reopening of the choir and the transepts after a major reordering of the building, and at a time when the Chartists were making their voices heard, he said:

> There never was and, while human nature remains the same, there never can be a period in the history of human society when inequalities of worldly conditions will not follow the unequal use of talents and opportunities originally the same . . . . Equality of mind or body, or of worldly condition is an inconsistent with the order of nature as with the moral laws of God.

On his appointment to Westminster Buckland gave up most of his research and lecturing, though he investigated the cause and the cure of potato disease, the temporary suspension in the growth of fleas, and made various recommendations for the improvement of farming methods. By this time he had done more than his bit, for the catalogue of the Royal Society included over 50 research papers he had published and he belonged to over 50 scientific societies in Britain and North America. In 1848 he was awarded the Wollaston Medal – the highest honour in geological research. Moreover he kept open house at the deanery and leading scientists and others who could face the taxing cuisine came for conversation about their subjects. Mrs Buckland, a woman of considerable intellect, opened a coffee shop in Pye Street, Westminster, and this was combined with an industrial school where boys were taught to make paper bags and to print. Modelled on a similar enterprise in Edinburgh, it was the first of its kind in London. The parish of St Matthew, which later became a leading Anglo-Catholic centre, was created to enable the church to minister to the huge slum population of the neighbourhood.

Besides his work at the Abbey, Buckland undertook responsibility for the attractive dean and chapter parish of Islip in Oxfordshire – the place of Edward the Confessor's birth. He spent every autumn there, conducting the services and visiting the parishioners. He also provided the labourers with allotments on dean and chapter land and instructed them on their best use. A cottage constructed at the end of an old tithe barn had a room set aside for the recreation of the village boys. Returning from Islip to London on horseback one year and in the company of a friend, darkness and mist descended before the journey was completed. They seemed to be lost until Buckland dismounted, knelt down to smell the ground, and then announced 'Uxbridge'.

In 1850, however, Buckland was struck down by a mysterious illness, which left him unable to work and subject to fits of depression. He retired to Islip, attended no more chapter meetings, and the sub-dean, Lord John Thynne, presided over the Abbey's affairs until death came in 1856. An autopsy revealed that the base of his skull had degenerated, probably as a result of an accident on the Continent many years earlier when his carriage overturned.

He was buried at Islip and on his granite gravestone were incised some words composed by Lord John Thynne:

> Endued with a superior intellect,
> He applied the Power of his Mind
> To the Honour and Glory of God,
> The advancement of Science
> And the welfare of Mankind.

4

The Plantsman
Thomas Garnier, Winchester

Thomas Garnier, Dean of Winchester from 1840 to 1872, was not among the liveliest Victorian deans but he was one of the best loved and, most unusually, was held in high regard by his chapter. An archdeacon, who served with him for many years, said, 'It was impossible for the chapter to quarrel with or disagree with the dean when present', and for much of his long reign – he did not retire until he was 96 – he was referred to in Winchester and throughout Hampshire as 'the good old dean'. The local weekly newspaper frequently described him on its news pages as, 'our venerable and much beloved dean'.

His other claim to fame was as a gardener and plantsman. Before his appointment as dean he had already been a prebendary of the cathedral for ten years, but more significantly had spent 33 years as rector of the South Hampshire parish of Bishopstoke – a benefice he held for a further 28 years. There he developed a celebrated garden, said to rival the national showpiece at Chiswick. Rare shrubs and trees were his speciality and he grew over 50 varieties of rhododendrons. He also won the silver medal of the Royal Horticultural Society for his strawberries and the fame of the garden drew the Prince Consort to make a special visit in 1848. He was an early Fellow of the Linnaean Society and lived long enough to become Father of the Society. A copy of his *Herbarium* is in the Natural History Museum.

As a dean, however, Garnier was in no sense a pioneer, though he tried hard to improve the standard of the cathedral's music and was brave enough to appoint Samuel Sebastian Wesley as organist. In many ways he would have been more at home in the century in which he was born than in the Victorian age when his leadership of Winchester Cathedral was exercised. What was for him a bewildering process of change came, not through a perceived need to adjust to radical social change, but because of the legal requirement to meet the financial demands of the newly formed Ecclesiastical Commission.

When Garnier took office in 1840 the capitular estates supported in considerable style a dean and twelve prebendaries – all of whose incomes were augmented substantially by the revenues of other benefices. Besides Bishopstoke, Garnier himself held the Hampshire parishes of Froyle, Southwick and Hinton Ampner (served by poorly paid curates) and his total income, which included inherited family money, made him one of Winchester's richest ever deans. By 1868, however, the golden years were ended. A large portion of the estates had been surrendered to the Commissioners, the number of prebendaries (now renamed canons) had been reduced by natural wastage to five and instead of six minor canons there were now four. The dean had vacated all his parish benefices, having reached the age of 92.

The layout of the close was also markedly different, for, as the size of the chapter declined and some of the fine houses ceased to be occupied, Garnier took the opportunity to redraw the boundaries and also to plant more trees. Generally, this was to good effect, though future generations would deplore the destruction of the historic house once occupied by the godly Thomas Ken. It was Ken who refused to take in Nell Gwynn when Charles II was occupying the deanery and was later rewarded by appointment as Bishop of Bath and Wells – 'Give it to the little dark man at Winchester', ordered the King, 'he was the man of integrity who wouldn't give Nelly a lodging.'

Apart from about ten years spent in Oxford during the closing years of the eighteenth century, Thomas Garnier spent the whole of his life in Hampshire. He was born in 1776 into a family of Hugenot origin who lived at Rooksbury Park – a large country house at Wickham, not far from Portsmouth. His father, who later became High Sheriff of Hampshire, succeeded his own father as Apothecary General to the Army – a highly paid sinecure office which was eventually denounced as a scandal. The London family house was a fashionable social centre, frequented by the celebrities of the day, and the Hampshire house was also a place to which invitations were eagerly sought. At Hyde Abbey School, Winchester, young Thomas had George Canning, the future statesman, as a fellow pupil.

He entered Winchester College in 1789 at a time when William of Wykeham's foundation was particularly corrupt and in 1793 became aware of the repercussions in England of the French Revolution when the ringleaders of a scholars' rebellion against the headmaster raised the Gallic Red Cap of Liberty on the college tower. The headmaster resigned. Soon after this Garnier went to Worcester College, Oxford, where he stayed long enough to take a postgraduate degree in law and also to acquire from his tutor what was to become a lifelong love of flowers. When only 22 he published a paper on *The Rare Flowers of Hampshire*. In 1796 he was elected to a Fellowship of All Souls but, because of a French invasion scare, left immediately for Hampshire to command 50 volunteers from among his father's tenants at Rooksbury Park. Four years later he was ordained. About this time, however, he contracted a fever which led to the loss of sight of an eye.

During 1802–03 Garnier took advantage of a brief cessation of hostilities to travel on the Continent, in the course of which he was presented to Napoleon, whom he described as, 'smiling and very gracious'. Fortunately, he was able to get away from France just before the resumption of war and thus escape internment. In 1804 he left Oxford to become rector of the family living at Wickham but after four years moved to a more lucrative post at nearby Bishopstoke. There he replaced the old rectory with a new house fit for bringing up children, but sadly it did not ward off the maladies of the time: two daughters died before they were three and another in her early teens. Tragedy struck again when a young sailor son perished at sea in a hurricane. Besides building the house, Garnier bought some nearby fields to add to the one-acre garden and this made possible his notable work as a plantsman. Later, at his own expense, the old parish church was replaced.

Appointment as a prebendary of Winchester came in 1830 and may have owed something to the fact that his brother was already on the chapter, having married a daughter of Bishop Brownlow North, one of the most notorious nepotists of all time. But there can be little doubt that Lord Melbourne, the Prime Minister in 1840, nominated him to the deanery because he was a Whig. Garnier also suited Bishop Charles Sumner, who had a general rule that only evangelicals were to be given senior posts in the diocese, and throughout Garnier's decanate the chapter was, apart from a brief spell when Samuel Wilberforce held a prebendal stall, uncompromisingly evangelical in its outlook. So much so that when the saintly John Keble, who was for 30 years vicar of nearby Hursley, preached what was deemed to be a High Church sermon in the cathedral he was never again invited to occupy its pulpit. Within the chapter itself, however, Garnier always favoured generosity and reconciliation, and after a disagreement with a colleague was heard to say, 'His heart is all right, it is his liver that is at fault.'

In common with the other cathedrals, the dean and chapter of Winchester protested strongly against the administrative reforms that would play havoc with their tranquil way of life. They informed the Commission:

> We do not make light of our daily services of prayer and praise . . . neither would we depreciate the value of our Sunday services . . . . But we beg leave state it as our entire conviction that the utility of cathedral institutions is not to be measured by considerations of this nature alone . . . . Cathedrals are retreats of learned leisure, free from the anxieties attendant upon a narrow income and from the incessant cares which belong to the cure of souls, they can give themselves more entirely to the higher walks of literature and theology.

This is not how it seemed to those living outside the close who were not on the dean and chapter's payroll and by the time Garnier moved into the deanery the changes had begun with a vengeance. One unforeseen effect of the reform was that little money became available for the repair of the cathedral itself. At the beginning of the century the architect reported that the interior of the building was in a deplorable condition with the walls defaced by obscene writing, some windows unglazed, many of the galleries and staircases choked with rubbish of every description. This was then taken in hand and over £40,000 was spent on repairs and alterations under the vigorous direction of prebendary George Knott – an authority on Italian art and poetry. Unfortunately he fell from a ladder while supervising the work and died soon after Garnier became dean, having never fully recovered from his injuries. No further substantial work, apart from the restoration of the west front, was undertaken until the end of the century, by which time huge cracks had appeared in the rest of the walls and the eastern part of the cathedral was in danger of total collapse.

A great effort was made, however, to raise the standard of the music and to this end Samuel Sebastian Wesley was appointed organist in 1849. He moved to Winchester from the recently rebuilt Leeds Parish Church, having previously been at Hereford and Exeter Cathedrals, and having just published *A Few Words on Cathedral Music and the Musical System of the Church with a Plan of Reform*. There was ample scope for reform in his new sphere. But although Wesley was later said to have done for English cathedral music what Chopin did for the piano, his performance at Winchester was in many ways disappointing. He was essentially a very fine organist and a great composer of choral music but, like some other outstanding musicians, before and since, he lacked the patience to make the most of relatively modest local material.

Wesley waged constant war on the deans and chapters of his time for what he regarded as their failure to provide the money necessary to the employment of competent musicians. 'The religious musician should no longer rank as a Lazarus', he declared in a long memorandum to a national enquiry into the music of cathedrals and collegiate churches, and he also believed that music publishers were robbing composers like himself of their due. One of his finest anthems, 'The Wilderness', failed to find a publisher because it was deemed to be unsuitable for performance in churches. Wesley also hated precentors.

At Winchester he negotiated a good salary for himself, then got the dean and chapter to purchase for £2,500 the organ used at the 1851 Great Exhibition. His first volume of anthems, published in 1853, was dedicated to Garnier who did his best to defend in chapter his erratic behaviour. He was not respectful and often discourteous to the canons. More seriously, the choir's performance was not improving and in 1857 the chapter ordered an enquiry into the reasons for this. These were not difficult to find: of the 780 choral services held during the previous year, Wesley had been present at only 397. He was a prima donna who preferred a national to a local stage and, when not away from Winchester, was often to be found casting a fly on the river Itchen. The organ was left in the hands of a 14-year-old pupil and, through lack of training, the choristers were well below an acceptable standard. Some of the lay clerks were drunkards, others were insolent and rude and sometimes deliberately sang wrong notes.

The dean and chapter admonished Wesley for neglect of duty, but this made little difference and further censure was required two years later. He moved to Gloucester in 1865. His successor, G. B. Arnold, who had been one of Wesley's pupils and when only 20 became the youngest ever recipient of an Oxford Doctorate of Music, lacked his master's gifts as a composer but raised the standard of the choir. He also started a diocesan choral festival – the first of which attracted to two services a total of 956 singers and almost 4,000 people in the congregations. Of Garnier's personal contribution to the cathedral's worship it was recorded that he imported 'much life and energy' to the services when he intoned. One of Wesley's more reasonable complaints had been that members of the chapter, lacking real skill, insisted on officiating at choral services. Garnier initiated in 1864 a choral Eucharist on the great festivals of the Christian year and earlier decreed that the choir should enter in procession on weekdays, as well as on Sundays. Special services marked important national or local occasions and the installation of gas lighting and heating stoves made the building less inhospitable in the winter.

None of this represented major reform, but beyond the cathedral Garnier remained true to his Whig principles and was stimulated by his friendship with Lord Palmerston whose country house was at nearby Romsey. He strongly believed in the education of working men and served for many years on the committee of the Mechanics' Institute. He also spoke out against poverty, unemployment and poor housing, as well as other forms of social injustice, and was much involved in the foundation of the Royal County Hospital in Winchester. Sixty old people were given a 2s 6d weekly pension and parties for children were often held in the deanery. When he walked from the deanery to the city he was reported to have always been 'followed by applicants for relief, none of whom, deserving or undeserving, went away empty-handed. If he had a full purse in the morning, it would be empty by the evening.'

Another of his special local interests was a newly founded city museum to which he contributed a remarkable number of exhibits. These included a two-toed sloth, an armadillo and a Canadian lynx, as well as collections of Indian birds – all of which were probably acquired for him by his brother-in-law, Sir Edward Parry, who was an intrepid explorer. Bullets and military ornaments from Waterloo had been given to him by returning local soldiers.

In 1867 Garnier marked his ninety-first birthday by planting in the deanery garden an acorn said to have come from an oak planted during the time of William the Conqueror. This grew to be a fine tree which still stands. He also marked the occasion by climbing at a fast pace the nearby St Catherine's Hill, but his health soon declined and, because of failing sight and general infirmity, he was eventually dispensed from attending cathedral services. By the time he was 96 he knew little of what was taking place around him and the problem of getting him to leave the deanery after his retirement was solved by taking him for an afternoon drive in his carriage and returning him to another house in the cathedral close which he believed to be his own.

There he stayed, cared for by his only surviving child, until his death in June 1873 when he was almost 98. He had had four daughters and four sons, one of whom, also named Thomas, rowed in the first university boat race and subsequently became Dean of Ripon, then of Lincoln. Garnier's death was reported with deepest regret by the *Hampshire Chronicle* which attributed his demise to the prescription of over-strong medicine, though this was hotly denied by his physician in a letter published the following week. Ten years later an elderly verger told a visitor to the cathedral that Garnier was 'the best dean we ever had or ever will have'.

5

The Hymn Writer
Henry Alford, Canterbury

Henry Alford, who was at Canterbury from 1857 to 1871, was unique among nineteenth-century deans in that he died of overwork – and at the early age of 60. The doctors said that his brain and body were worn out and a close friend declared that for what he had accomplished in 60 years others would have needed twice as long. He was certainly an unusually active dean for his time, but the cathedral occupied only part of his life, for he was also a scholar, a poet, a musician, a water-colourist and an intrepid traveller, as well as an outstanding preacher in constant demand for a sermon or an address. A bibliography of his published works occupies 15 pages, detailing 48 volumes, at the end of the biography compiled by his widow.

Some of these works are quite slight, but others are substantial, including the edited works of John Donne in seven volumes. Most notable was his *Commentary on the Greek Testament*, in four volumes, which occupied him for 18 years and won high praise both for its scholarly handling of the Greek text and its helpful exegesis of the message. Alford was one of the first Englishmen to recognize the validity of the work of German scholars in their attempts to find agreement over a critical text of the New Testament earlier and more accurate than that used for the traditional European translations. In 1847 when he was the vicar of a small country parish, he spent three months in Bonn mastering German and this enabled him to compile his own version of the text, based largely on the work of four leading German scholars.

This dependence on their work led to some criticism from other English scholars who, as the years went by, were developing their own expertise in the field and, as one of them, C. J. Ellicott, put it, Alford was an instinctive scholar, rather than a punctilious researcher. Nonetheless, it was widely recognized as a very remarkable personal achievement – the best of its time – and ran to several editions. For the remainder of the nineteenth century no New Testament scholar could handle the Greek text without asking 'What does Alford say about this?' Characteristically, he went on to produce an English version for the benefit of those who were without Greek and it came to be very highly regarded in America, as well as in Britain, not least by preachers. It was Alford's idea that there should be an official revision of the Authorized Version of the Bible and, although there were those who regarded his suggestion as rash and potentially dangerous, a Company of Revisers was eventually formed and, until ill health required him to withdraw, he was a leading member of the group that met in the Jerusalem Chamber of Westminster Abbey to deal with the New Testament. His presence reassured the doubters among the parish clergy.

As a dean, Alford was among the early cathedral reformers and accomplished a good deal at Canterbury, but shortly before his death he sadly concluded, 'The office of dean is, in many of our cathedrals, practically useless; the dean, while nominally head of the cathedral body, is almost without employment and absolutely without power to act.' By this time he believed that cathedrals should be more closely integrated with the life of their dioceses and that this required the bishop to be also the dean. In response to the objection that the bishops were already overworked, he said, 'They are not likely to have much more work added by becoming dean.'

His own problems as a dean started immediately after his arrival in Canterbury when he discovered to his astonishment that sermons were preached only at the Sunday morning service and that he was allowed into the pulpit only on Christmas Day, Easter Day and Whit Sunday. For someone whose great gifts as a preacher were an integral part of his ministry this was intolerable, so he proposed that a sermon should be preached also at the Sunday afternoon service, with himself responsible for providing the preacher. The chapter objected on the grounds that the Eucharist was the Church's central act of worship and that this was the only proper place for a sermon. There was, in their view, no place for other services with popular sermons. In the end, however, Alford went ahead and himself undertook all the Sunday afternoon preaching. The canons refused to stand in for him when he was abroad, so he recruited the warden of St Augustine's College, the headmaster of the King's School and some other good preachers. Before long a large congregation was packing the cathedral choir and overflowing into other parts of the building and in 1866 Alford noted, 'the great majority of the congregation consists of occasional attendants and strangers. These latter flock in crowds during the summer when Ramsgate and Margate are full.' Canterbury was now feeling the effects of the Kent coast's accessibility by means of the new railways.

Much time was devoted to major restoration of the cathedral's fabric and the rebuilding of the King's School, as well as to repairing and strengthening relations between the cathedral and the city which had been at a low ebb. But his chief concern, and it was one that brought him many disappointments, was that the cathedral – all cathedrals – should be radically changed, so that they might become an effective element in the mission of the whole Church.

Henry Alford's birth in London in 1810 was accompanied by the death in childbirth of his mother. His devastated father, a successful lawyer, decided thereupon to abandon his practice and seek holy orders, eventually becoming vicar of Ampton, near Bury St Edmunds. The dislocation and vicissitudes of family life led to young Henry spending long periods in the care of relations, the most influential of whom was his uncle, Samuel Alford, who was vicar of a parish near Taunton. At the age of nine he went to a school kept by a Congregationalist minister in Charmouth, Dorset, and this was followed by spells at schools in Hammersmith, Ilminster and, finally, Aston, in Suffolk, which was within reach of his father's vicarage.

From the earliest years he seemed drawn to ordination. When he was only eight he wrote, doubtless with help from his uncle, a 50-page chronological history of the Jews. Two years later he produced a sermon and also a four-chapter book on, 'Looking unto Jesus or the believer's support under trials and afflictions'. At 15 he wrote a long and serious letter to his cousin Fanny (whom he was later to marry) about her forthcoming Confirmation. All displayed signs of the evangelical influence of his home and school life. In 1829 he entered Trinity College, Cambridge, where he read both classics and mathematics with some distinction and, encouraged by his friendship with Tennyson and other Cambridge poets, published his first volume of poems when he was 21. These were highly commended by William Wordsworth who discerned in Alford what he described as a poetic temperament.

In 1833 he became a curate in his father's parish and, to please his father, took an examination to win a Fellowship of Trinity College. He had, however, no intention of becoming an academic and resigned after twelve months in order to be free to marry and to take the College living of Wymeswold. This small, rural parish on the borders

of Leicestershire and Nottinghamshire had been declined by several
other Fellows because of its remoteness and the dilapidated condition
of the church and the vicarage. It suited Alford well enough, however,
for the starting of his marriage and the rearing of a family. Moreover
the pastoral work, at which he excelled, was light enough to leave him
free to pursue his literary work and many other interests, though in
order to make ends meet he was obliged to take in pupils who occupied seven hours of his day. He was there from 1835 to 1853. Trinity
College and other local landowners were persuaded to provide £3,500
for what turned out to be more of a rebuilding than a restoration of
the church. This was carried out by the celebrated Victorian architect,
A. W. Pugin, whose interior re-ordering and furnishings led to accusa-
tions that the vicar was a High Churchman. He had, however, done no
more than outgrow his evangelical upbringing and, although he flirted
briefly with the Tractarians, he was and remained for the rest of his life
a liberal, middle-of-the-road Anglican. A school and a spacious new
vicarage were erected and three services were held in the church every
Sunday.

Alford brought to the worship a new sense of dignity and fine
preaching, though his sermons were often over the heads of his ill-
educated congregation. More to their liking was his small collection of
*Hymns for Sundays and Festivals throughout the Year, with some
occasional Hymns; adapted for use in Churches where the Psalms of
David are Sung*, published a year after his arrival in the parish and
brought into immediate use. His poetic gifts and ability as a composer
came together to make him a prolific hymn writer and a much larger
collection of over 300 hymns, *A Year of Praise*, was published during
his Canterbury years. Most of his hymns were too strongly marked by
the religious ethics of their time to survive far beyond the nineteenth
century, though 'Come ye thankful people, come' remains a firm
Harvest favourite and 'In token that thou shalt not fear', described by
Dean Stanley as 'The Baptismal canticle of the English Church', was in
common use until almost the end of the twentieth century.

He was Hulsean Lecturer at Cambridge in 1841/2 and this resulted
in two volumes on *The Consistency of the Divine Conduct in
Revealing the Doctrines of Redemption*. In 1846 he began work on
his Greek commentary, the first volume of which, occupying 664
pages, appeared three years later. The edited works of John Donne
also belong to his Wymeswold period and no year passed without
something appearing from his pen – often several items – and the
happiness of his 18 years in the parish were marred only, but

tragically, by the deaths in childhood of his two sons. Two daughters survived.

In 1838 he was sounded out for appointment as a missionary bishop in New Zealand, but quickly dealt with this by pointing out that canonically he was too young to become a bishop. Seven years later he was offered the Bishopric of New Brunswick, in America but declined on the grounds that he did not feel called to missionary work. He was not, however, to be allowed to stay at Wymeswold for ever and in 1853 there came an offer that he felt unable to refuse. The vicar of St Mary's, Bryanston Square in London's fashionable West End had acquired the lease of a disused chapel in Quebec Street, so named after General Wolfe's heroic death while capturing the Canadian stronghold in 1759. He decided to turn the Quebec Chapel into an independent proprietary chapel to provide music and preaching of the highest quality for those of his parishioners who would value such an offering.

Alford, who was already spending an increasing amount of time in London on literary matters and preaching at St Paul's, Westminster Abbey, and the Chapel Royal, eagerly accepted the opportunity to become the minister of this chapel and rejected the suggestion that he should at the same time retain Wymeswold – 'I have a decided objection to pluralities myself; where a man's duty is, there should be his residence, and one cure of souls is sufficient for one man.' Soon he was preaching to packed congregations and recognized as one of London's leading preachers. At the morning service he delivered a carefully scripted sermon, but in the afternoon he gave extempore expository sermons on the New Testament and in the congregation there were always some with their Greek Testaments open. On Wednesday afternoons there was a ladies' class in New Testament Greek, and on another afternoon Alford conducted a singing class. He also undertook some pastoral work, though the bulk of this was carried out by a curate. It was an important ministry but too good to last and after only four years the Prime Minister, Lord Palmerston, offered Alford the deanery of Canterbury.

He took to the mother church of the developing Anglican Commission the presuppositions and experience of a highly industrious scholar parish priest and it was hardly surprising that he quickly became exasperated with a lethargic institution which seemed to regard the great cathedral as the dean and chapter's private chapel. Among the many letters he received at the time of his appointment was one from a friend who was Bishop of Ripon – 'It seems the very post for which you are fitted and in the occupation of it abundant leisure will be afforded for the prosecution of the studies which you pursue with so much advantage to others.' The leisure turned out to be less than abundant because Alford was determined to be an agent of change, so although he continued his studies and indeed took on new literary responsibilities, the cost to his health was in the end too high.

Only slightly built, his intellectual, domed forehead, bushy eyebrows and flowing white beard combined, nonetheless, to give him a distinguished appearance. Unfortunately, a fall from his horse at Wymeswold left him with a permanent facial scar. He was a generous, humorous man, and an engaging conversationalist whose wide interests gave him an unusually wide circle of friends. Wherever he ministered he became much loved and he had not been at Canterbury long before being referred to as, 'our good dean'. But there were battles to be fought with the chapter, which was dominated by men of strong conservative views, and these caused pain. Outside the cathedral itself, his study – a beautiful square room, with every wall and many other spaces filled with books – was what he described as his 'workshop'. After 8 a.m. family prayers, the rest of the morning was spent there, engaged on literary work, during the afternoon he went for a walk – he had a great love of the countryside – and after evensong and dinner the evening was spent in reading and conversation. He went back to his 'workshop' after 10 p.m. prayers, and it was this highly disciplined timetable, inevitably interrupted from time to time by other commitments, that enabled him to achieve so much.

One of these commitments was *The Contemporary Review*, of which he became the first editor in 1866. A pioneering venture in independent, rather than partisan, literary criticism, this 150-page monthly magazine inevitably involved its editor in a great deal of work. It covered religion, literature and the arts and was launched with a team of over 50 contributors and production staff. Alford was himself a regular contributor but his main task was to match books with reviewers, having first made his choice from the large number of newly published volumes. At the end of 1866 he told a friend that the previous two months had been the busiest of his busy life. Surprise was often expressed at the wide range of his choice and the magazine was an immediate success. It survives today as one of the oldest publications in the English-speaking world, though it is now chiefly concerned with current affairs.

After his initial clash with the chapter over Sunday afternoon sermons, Alford soon found himself in another conflict, this time over so-called 'State Services'. These had been appended to the *Book of*

Common Prayer towards the end of the seventeenth century and were designed to commemorate on appropriate dates the Gunpowder Treason and Plot, the death of King Charles I, the Restoration of the monarchy, and the accession of William and Mary of Orange. By the middle of the nineteenth century the continuation of these commemorations was increasingly regarded as anomalous and Alford wished to see them ended. Strong objections to this were voiced by conservative members of the chapter, who believed that Church–State relations were in danger of being undermined, but Alford stood his ground and the matter was settled once and for all when, soon after his decision, it was decreed officially that the commemorations should cease. It was hardly a matter of earth-shattering importance, but in the Canterbury precincts it was enough to raise blood pressure to dangerous levels and to create painful conflicts.

Further problems arose when Alford publicly identified himself with the cause of cathedral reform. In 1869 the Archbishops of Canterbury and York proposed a further reduction in the number of cathedral canonries and the abolition of non-residence. They believed that the 1840 reforms had not gone far enough and that the cathedrals still provided too many resting places for unproductive clergymen. Their proposal was hotly resisted by virtually every chapter, but not by Alford who indicated his support and his belief that, in the absence of an episcopal dean, a cathedral could be run effectively by a full-time dean and two archdeacons. His colleagues were furious and responded to the suggestion that they might undertake diocesan duties by pointing out that they had been appointed to pursue their studies. Alford did not, however, believe that cathedrals should have parochial ties, since this would hinder them fulfilling their proper ministry of music and preaching. He was himself an accomplished pianist and organist, and a beautiful baritone voice enabled him to sing the services at the same level as the precentor.

His years at the deanery were a period of considerable restoration of the cathedral fabric and also of the enlargement of the King's School in the precincts which, in consequence, began to receive many more boarders from other parts of Britain and overseas. Unfortunately the work of the cathedral's architect was widely criticized as shoddy and wanting in judgement, but there was praise for Alford's decision that individuals should be commemorated in the cathedral by stained-glass windows, rather than by monuments and memorial tablets. He financed two windows in memory of his infant sons who had died at Wymeswold. He also initiated a scheme which involved the placing of

56 statues in vacant niches in the west front. These were of people whose fame, over the centuries, was connected with the cathedral and soon after his death he joined their company – the statue being paid for by the Canterbury Harmonic Union.

This Union, which performed oratorios, was just one of Alford's many contributions to the life of the city. He supported the charities and schemes for social improvement, as well as the hospital and dispensary and two national schools. He also paid for a curate to serve in the city's most populous and poorest parish, and got on very well with the Nonconformists, including the Unitarians. Official guides were appointed to take parties round the cathedral. In these ways, and not least through his warm, outgoing personality, relations between the cathedral and the city became very cordial. He also enjoyed the friendship of successive Archbishops of Canterbury, J. B. Sumner, C. T. Longley, and A. C. Tait, though he regretted that he saw all too little of them and, in a sermon in Lambeth Palace chapel at the consecration in 1870 of the Archdeacon of Canterbury as Suffragan Bishop of Dover, ventured to suggest that Canterbury was, 'more cut off from episcopal ministrations than any other diocese in the realm'. Two years earlier, however, he got Archbishop Longley to hold the first ordination in the cathedral for 50 years and persuaded him to stay on to give the first address at a week's mission to the city. This proved to be what Alford described as a 'most kindly and fatherly address' to working men in the National School Room. Before the year was out Longley was dead and Alford had enthroned his successor, at the cathedral's morning service, attended by over 200 robed clergy and more than 2,000 people in the nave.

It was while making the arrangements for this great occasion that Alford began to show clear signs of strain. Eight years earlier, when just past his fiftieth birthday, doctors had warned him that he was doing too much and ought to slow down. His response to this was not to reduce his workload, but rather to increase his holidays. Throughout his life he was a great traveller and particularly enjoyed continental journeys which he described in letters to members of his family. He now began to spend several weeks, sometimes a few months, away from Canterbury but the beneficial effects of these breaks were quickly negatived by the accumulation of work awaiting his return. In January 1871 he took a chill from which he was not strong enough to recover and died within three days. The cathedral was crowded for the simple funeral he had requested and at the committal in St Martin's churchyard one of his hymns was sung – the opening verse being

Ten thousand times ten thousand,
In sparkling raiment bright,
The armies of the ransomed saints
Throng up the steeps of light:
'Tis finished – all is finished,
Their fight with death and sin;
Fling open wide the golden gates
And let the victors in.

In the final year of his life he had embarked on what was to be a massive commentary on the whole of the Old Testament, but it was left unfinished at Exodus 25.

6

The Old Mastiff
Walter Farquhar Hook, Chichester

'The old mastiff of the Church of England'. This was how Walter Hook described himself and it represented a perceptive understanding of his special contribution to the religious life of mid-Victorian England. He saw himself as a watchdog protecting the true vocation of the Church from the assaults of, on the one hand, the more extreme Tractarians who would take it Romewards, and on the other the dissenting evangelicals who sought to undermine its historic Catholic tradition. His own position was that of a High Churchman in the seventeenth-century Laudian tradition and he was tenacious in upholding this as the Church of England's one, true, faith.

Amid the controversies of his time Hook was a stalwart and vociferous defender of this line and often found himself under attack from different directions, but his mastiff-like tenacity extended to the development of parish life in accordance with the Anglican tradition. By the time he became Dean of Chichester (1859–75) his greatest work lay behind him and, exhausted by his work as vicar of Leeds for 20 years, his defence of the Church of England, rudely interrupted by the collapse of the cathedral spire, took the form of 12 volumes of biographies of the Archbishops of Canterbury, designed to demonstrate the essential continuity of the Church's life from its earliest days.

By any standard Hook's work at Leeds was phenomenal and made him one of the two greatest parish priests of the nineteenth century, the other being W. J. Butler of Wantage. But whereas Butler ministered in the relative stability and tranquillity of a Berkshire country town and had enough time to found a women's religious community, Hook was called to tackle a large and fast developing Northern manufacturing town to which the Church of England had thus far failed to offer an effective ministry.

The centre of the woollen trade, the population of Leeds had grown from 53,000 in 1801 to 123,000 in 1831, and four years after Hook's arrival in 1837 it had gone well past 150,000. Many of the people lived in the most squalid of slums in which robbery and prostitution were rife and where further population growth was frequently checked by outbreaks of Asiatic cholera and what was known as Irish fever. The whole of the town and a large part of the suburbs were within the boundaries of a single parish, served from the ancient parish church of Leeds and 17 chapels of ease by 18 clergy. When Hook left in 1859 the number of clergy had increased to 60, there were 17 endowed parishes with their own vicarages and 21 schools with houses for their masters. The old parish church had been replaced by a new building, with room for nearly 3,000 people, and in the chancel was the first of the parish surpliced choirs. All of which was achieved by a priest of wide vision and an iron will that was never daunted by obstacles.

He rose every morning at 5 o'clock, sometimes earlier, and after two hours of reading, writing and meditation embarked on a routine of activity that sometimes threatened his health, but in the end brought him to a position of pre-eminence in the civic as well as the religious life of Leeds. Before the creation of the new parishes in 1844, when all the 'occasional' services were held in the parish church, the vicar and two curates were in church from 8 a.m. to 11.30 a.m. every day dealing with weddings (1,000 a year), twice a day for baptisms (2,000 a year), twice a day for churchings, twice a day in winter and three times in summer for funerals (1,500 a year). Little time remained for any other work.

The mastiff image went further and embraced his appearance. When he was a child a little girl cousin declared frankly that, 'Walter is not pretty' and his looks did not improve with age, though his flaming red hair eventually became pure white. With a low brow, a heavy jowl, a large mouth and occasional twitching of the face he bore some resemblance to Dr Johnson. As a young man he had been tall, muscular and agile but in middle age, and especially after he became an abstainer, he grew stout and massive. He admitted to a 'diabolical temper'. Those who were unaware of these and other mastiff-like qualities, but knew of his detestation of foreigners, often likened him to John Bull and both images were employed in the context of admiration and affection. When he left Leeds 't'owd Doctor' was presented with a casket containing 2,000 guineas and among many other gifts was a pair of boots from a poor bootmaker.

Walter Farquhar Hook was born in 1798 in the Mayfair home of his maternal grandfather, Sir Walter Farquhar, Bt. His paternal grandfather, a musician, was the composer of the once-popular song 'The Lass of Richmond Hill', and his father was the Rector of Hertingford-bury, near Hertford. Young Walter attended the local grammar school and went from there to Blundell's School, Tiverton, where he learned practically nothing. The appointment of his father to a canonry of Winchester provided, however, a means of escape and he was enrolled as a commoner of Winchester College. This was in the days before public school reform when the College was financially corrupt and discipline maintained by sheer brutality. Walter was very unhappy and wrote to his brother, 'I hate this place more and more every day. I was licked yesterday more severely than ever before. I cannot run or hollow out even now without hurting my side.' It did not help that he preferred history, biography and poetry to classics, the standard fare, but he worked hard and thanks to the Prince Regent, whose patronage the family enjoyed, secured a place at Christ Church, Oxford.

Once again, he did not like the prescribed classics course and pre-ferred to study Shakespeare. He led a somewhat lonely life and was disappointed when he failed by a narrow margin to win the Newdigate Prize for English verse. In the end he was as glad to get away from Oxford as he had been from Winchester – 'I long to escape from this odious place: I am disgusted with Oxford and my heart leaps with joy at the thought of quitting it.' He was in London to witness in Westminster Abbey the Coronation of King George IV – an unedify-ing ceremony from which Queen Caroline was excluded.

His father had added to the Winchester canonry the archdeaconry of Huntingdon, a royal chaplaincy and the rectory of Whippingham on the Isle of Wight, from which he was mostly absent. He was, how-ever, there long enough to prepare his son for ordination at the rectory and in 1821 Walter Hook was ordained privately in Winchester College chapel by the Bishop of Hereford, who was also warden of the college. The idea was that he should become curate of Whippingham and, in the absence of his father, run the parish. While still a deacon he deputized for his father, who was ill, as the preacher at the Bishop of Winchester's Visitation at Newport and the bishop was so impressed with the sermon that he asked for it to be published. Its subject was *The Peculiar Character of the Church of England Independently of its Connexion with the State* and this revealed him as a High Churchman of the Laudian school – a position later reinforced by a visit to Scotland and an encounter with the Scottish Episcopal Church.

Besides running his father's parish, Hook decided to remedy the defects in his education and erected in the churchyard a wooden hut, to which he repaired every morning to study the early Fathers of the Church and the writers of the Reformation period. The appointment of his father to the deanery of Worcester in 1825 required, however, resignation from Whippingham, which left the curate without a job, but after a short period he was appointed vicar of Moseley – at that time a small country parish about four miles from Birmingham. He took this in his stride and, having founded a village school and secured the services of a curate, augmented his modest stipend of £150 per annum by taking on the lectureship of St Philip's Church, Birmingham, which gave him an extra £230. There his preaching was greatly admired and he also established a penitentiary for 'fallen women' and superintended the city's schools.

When the parish of Holy Trinity, Coventry, fell vacant in 1828 some of its people were keen to have Hook as their vicar, so his uncle, Sir Thomas Farquhar, approached the Lord Chancellor, the patron, who readily appointed him. This glorious church with its tall fifteenth-century spire, standing alongside St Michael's Church, which later became Coventry's first cathedral, offered formal, uninspiring worship on Sunday morning, leaving the more enthusiastic members of the congregation to attend Dissenting chapels in the evening. The town, in which weaving was the chief industry, was in a period of severe depression with a large number of its citizens in receipt of relief and many paupers in the workhouses. It was the kind of challenge that Hook relished.

First, however, there was the matter of marriage. Within a year of moving into the vicarage he had married 17-year-old Delicia Johnson – the daughter of an eminent Birmingham physician. Their very happy marriage extended over 42 years and Delicia not only provided her husband with the strong support he needed but also wrote widely used books of devotion, dutifully published under his name. Their honeymoon was spent in Paris but a letter to his curate indicated that it was not entirely blissful: 'I am heartily sick of Paris. I hate France and think Frenchmen the most detestable of human beings.'

Returning to Coventry he started in the summer of 1830 a Sunday evening service which attracted congregations of nearly 2,000 and led to a request that it should continue in the winter. This required the installation of gas lighting and thus Holy Trinity became the first Coventry church to have an evening service. A course of sermons on St Matthew's Gospel lasted for several years and this was augmented by Lent lectures and Holy Week addresses. But the strain of reviving parish life proved to be too great and in 1831 he suffered a serious breakdown of health. Epileptic fits caused the loss of consciousness for 5–10 minutes and these recurred for the next three to four years – the prescribed treatment of a shaven head led him to wear a wig, though he often regarded this as an object of mirth. At one point he wondered whether he ought to move to a small, untaxing parish but the fits gradually abated and his dynamic ministry continued unchecked.

It was during his time at Coventry that the Tractarian Movement was started in Oxford but Hook had already initiated more frequent celebrations of holy communion and his regular expositions of the *Book of Common Prayer* indicated that his insights predated those of Keble, Pusey and Newman. With them he maintained the most cordial relations, but he never identified himself with their movement and he was hostile to some of its later developments. These known friendships and the character of much of his works brought Hook fierce opposition from Coventry evangelicals and Dissenters whose description of him as 'the Reverend Autocrat of Coventry' was more polemical than untrue. His community work was, however, beyond all criticism. A dispensary, founded to provide medical attention for the working classes eventually had 13,000 members. A savings bank was opened to encourage thrift, while the Religious Society for Useful Knowledge offered a library, education classes and lectures. The Bishop of Lincoln, a friend of his father's, expressed approval by making him a prebendary and life was proceeding sweetly until 1836 when his first child died in infancy.

In the following year came appointment to Leeds. This was in the hands of 25 local trustees who had first offered it to Samuel Wilberforce, the future reforming Bishop of Oxford. When he refused, some friends suggested Hook and, although his election was resolutely opposed by seven evangelicals, he secured sufficient votes and gradually won them over to his side. He marked his election by returning to the Oxford he once hated to take a DD and to preach twice in the university church to crowded congregations. He was soon brought down to earth, however, when, soon after his arrival in Leeds, an angry mob, some 3,000 strong, attended a meeting to protest against the levying of a church rate. They had not foreseen the mastiff-like character of the new vicar who spoke powerfully of the Church's place in the community and its needs, and in spite of some continuing opposition, secured agreement to a half-penny rate to finance, among other things, the purchase of surplices and service books.

Appointment as a chaplain to the Queen took him in 1838 to London to preach to a handful of courtiers in the Chapel Royal, but the sermon caused a sensation. Published under the title 'Hear the Church' it was a revamped version of a sermon he had preached in Holy Trinity, Coventry, and in which he had argued that the Church of England was not a creation of the sixteenth-century Reformation but had a venerable Catholic ancestry dating back to the earliest days of Christianity in these islands. Over 100,000 copies of the sermon were sold and its influence was strengthened by the knowledge that Hook was, beyond doubt, not looking Romewards.

The replacement of the old parish church was for him an absolute priority. The medieval building had been much altered and packed with ugly pews and galleries. Although it provided for 1,500 worshippers there was often, since Hook's arrival, 'standing room only', and he rejected the suggestion that the decaying structure should be restored and enlarged – 'I loathe it', he declared, 'I cannot preach comfortably in it, I cannot make myself heard. The dirt and the indecorum distress me.' He was not, in fact, an outstanding preacher and speaker, and tended to be unimpressive in small meetings, but he could rise to the great occasion and always spoke with a burning conviction that drew people to hear him. He was also blessed with a rich, deep voice and it was said that to hear him read a lesson was a sermon in itself. He chaired a 16-strong building committee that worked incessantly to raise the required £28,000 and, aided by gifts from all parts of the country as well as from Leeds, the new cathedral-like church was completed, consecrated and paid for in 1841. A choir was formed to lead choral services under the direction of Samuel Sebastian Wesley, the greatest of the nineteenth-century church musicians, who was between cathedral appointments at Exeter and Winchester.

By now the 50 elderly people, mainly women, who attended the monthly holy communion had been augmented by many others of all ages, at a weekly celebration. On Easter Day there were as many as 4–500 communicants – a figure that was doubled by the time that Hook left. In 1837, 1,000 carefully prepared candidates had been presented for Confirmation, then enrolled in Communicants' classes to develop further their discipleship. Upwards of 1,000 children attended Catechism classes on Sunday afternoons. Twenty-two assistant clergy joined the vicar at a monthly breakfast and reported to him regularly on their activities. An extensive programme of teaching was initiated, and reinforced by the publication of pamphlets, one of which – on the Creed – sold 5,000 copies almost immediately and remained in use for the rest of Hook's ministry. A substantial parish magazine was so successful that a London edition was demanded and this was published as *The Englishman's Magazine*. Pastoral work was another high priority and a Society for the Friends of the Sick was formed to enable laypeople to share with the clergy in this aspect of the Church's ministry. Hook believed it to be the responsibility of the vicar to build a team of competent curates. They in turn would in their districts build a community of committed and instructed laity. Thus the Church would be organized, and through worship and prayer empowered for its mission. He counselled his curates never to tyrannize over the laity – 'talk talk talk write write write' – and criticized young clergy in other parishes who did not consult their congregations over changes to services and buildings.

The division of the town into 17 separate parishes came about as a result of an 1844 Leeds Vicarage Act which was strongly opposed by the mill owners and merchants who feared that it would lead to the loss of their church privileges. But it was equally strongly supported by the Prime Minister, W. E. Gladstone, who greatly admired Hook and could now count on him as one of his own supporters, since the experience of ministry in the slums of Coventry and Leeds had led him to abandon the Tory party and become a Liberal. An extraordinary amount of work went into the decentralization of Church life and the drafting of the Bill, and Hook found the Ecclesiastical Commissioners generally collaborative over its financial ramifications. Whenever they became difficult over detail the sound of the mastiff's growl from Leeds was sufficient to bring a speedy settlement. They were left in no doubt as to the importance of the scheme:

> So convinced am I that unless the Church of England can be made in the manufacturing districts the church of the poor, which she certainly is not now, her days are numbered, and that her very existence would be scarcely desirable, that I am willing to make any sacrifice to accomplish my object, even to the resignation of my living, but I certainly am not prepared to make any sacrifice whatever if the great principle to which I have alluded be not conceded.

Some financial sacrifice – £500 per annum, plus substantial fees – became necessary in order to provide stipends for the additional clergy, but this was eventually recovered through the sale of some valuable church property. More troublesome during his early years in Leeds was the opposition of the evangelicals and Dissenters who, like their Coventry counterparts, feared that he was a Romanizer and were also jealous of his increasing influence in Leeds. He faced this with his customary pugnacity.

Besides his deep involvement in the urgent social problems of Leeds, Hook played an important part in the tackling of two other issues which were also of national concern. The first of these related to the exploitation of child labour – some of the worst examples of which were to be found in Leeds. Children of only six or seven were compelled to work 12–14 hours a day in the mills, with appalling consequences for their health and general wellbeing. In many cases it was a form of industrial murder. One of the main driving forces in a campaign to eliminate this evil was George Bull, the vicar of a parish near Bradford who became known as the Ten Hour Parson since the aim was to get working hours reduced to a daily ten. This took 15 years to achieve and in the end owed much to the Parliamentary work of Lord Shaftesbury, but Hook was always a strong supporter of the struggle – to the great displeasure of the mill owners – and in 1846 told a mass meeting in Leeds, 'I come here to tell you that I am ready, in this righteous cause, to press forward with you to the last gasp, and if a collision should occur between your interests and the interests of a higher social class, you may depend on finding me on your side.' He also supported the early-closing movement and proposed arbitration to settle a coal-miners' strike near Leeds.

His other special concern was education and, besides much local school building and adult education, he turned his mind to national policy. He was one of the first to recognize that, although the Church had been in the forefront of providing schools and would continue to invest considerable resources in the education of the nation's children, it could not possibly meet the needs of all of them. In 1846 he addressed a letter on the subject to Bishop Thirlwall of St David's, the most able academic mind on the episcopal bench at the time, and this was subsequently published as a pamphlet. It contained four propositions. (1) All children should receive elementary education. (2) The State alone can enforce education. (3) Religion is essential to education but the State cannot enforce this because there is no common set of beliefs. (4) The State should therefore establish in every school certain classrooms where Church of England clergy and Dissenting ministers can teach their own children. Expressed in Hook's usual forthright language and blunt in its criticism of the existing church schools, the letter created a storm of protest and aroused national interest. Although welcomed by the Liberal Party and supported by a large section of the Press, any prospect of it providing the basis of Government policy was ruled out after vigorous attacks by various church interests.

It can only be a cause for astonishment that, in spite of a seemingly impossible burden of parochial and civic work, Hook was able between 1844 and 1848 to complete five volumes of an eight-volume *Dictionary of Ecclesiastical Biography*. The remaining three volumes were completed by 1853. A *Church Dictionary* published in 1842 ran to 14 impressions. Less surprising is the fact that from time to time he endured periods of ill health and at the end of 1848 broke down through overwork and was off duty for several weeks. Ten years later, feeling worn out, he applied to Lord Carnarvon for a small country living in Hampshire but this had already been promised to another priest. At various times it had been rumoured that he was about to be offered a bishopric, but in truth none was ever forthcoming and the work he was doing in Leeds was far more significant than anything being undertaken by most of the bishops. In any case, he had no desire to join the bench and his ambitions were confined to a canonry at Westminster or St Paul's, or possibly the Mastership of the Temple – posts that would have given him an opportunity to preach, for the first time, to the educated. Whenever deaneries were talked about he said that he was now too old to take on an institution in need of major reform.

But it was to the deanery of Chichester – the most poorly paid of the English deaneries – that he went in 1859. At first the prospect of a quiet life in a Sussex cathedral close, with ample leisure for literary pursuits, seemed attractive to him. In the event the contrast between the hectic life of Leeds and the somnolent ways of Chichester was too great for him to bear and he became very depressed. He had never known a Sunday when he was free of preaching, but now he had got to take his turn with the canons, the archdeacons and the bishop, so his appearances in the cathedral pulpit were fairly infrequent. He was also used to making personal decisions about church affairs and ensuring that they were carried out speedily and efficiently, but now everything, no matter how small, had to go through the tedious procedure of the chapter. It was an experience endured by many others who were translated from a parish to a cathedral, but in Hook's case the frustration was compounded by the fact that for 20 years he had dominated the life of a great town. There was also the problem that he did not find it easy to relate to colleagues and employees who were not in a pastoral relationship with him.

Nonetheless, there was some work to be done at Chichester and he soon made more. His predecessor had set in hand a scheme for re-ordering the interior of the cathedral, and bequeathed £2,000 towards the cost. A public subscription appeal brought in the rest and the project was deemed to be a fitting memorial to the late dean. The aim was to facilitate corporate worship by removing the massive early fifteenth-century stone screen that separated the nave and the choir. Hook could raise but little enthusiasm for the scheme, and argued, characteristically, that it was important to create a need before making new space. To this end he persuaded the chapter to start a Sunday afternoon service, with himself the preacher, and before long the cathedral was filled to capacity.

The re-ordering went ahead as planned, the screen was removed, and Hook got on with writing the lives of the Archbishops of Canterbury. His character seemed to have changed – the hyperactive pastor was now a careful, meticulous scholar. But his peace was soon to be violently disturbed. Concern for the stability of the cathedral's fourteenth-century tower and spire had been expressed in the eighteenth century, but the money secured for their restoration had been used for more pressing repairs. In January 1861 cracks appeared in the tower and surrounding fabric. It was then noticed that the piers supporting the tower were beginning to bulge. Throughout the rest of January and early February an attempt was made to shore up the piers with timber, struts and braces, but to little avail. On 20 February mortar began to crumble and flakes of stone began to fall. Work continued until 3.30 the following morning, and after a break for sleep 70 men struggled in gale-force winds to bring more timber to shore up the now moving structure. At about midday they gave up, since the shores were starting to fall. At 1.30 p.m. the spire seemed to incline slightly to the north west, and then both spire and tower collapsed, telescope fashion into the cathedral's central crossing. No one was hurt and surprisingly little damage was caused to the rest of the building.

Unperturbed, Hook announced, 'I will rebuild the spire, if I beg my bread.' The estimated cost was £50,000 and he thought it right to contribute one year of his own income – £1,000 – which, added to the cost of his removal and the still incomplete repair of the deanery, left him heavily dependent upon his literary earnings. For the remainder of the £50,000 he travelled all over Britain preaching and lecturing; all of which he found tiresome and exhausting. But in November 1867 the cathedral was re-opened and Sir George Gilbert Scott's new spire reckoned to be one of the most elegant in the country.

By this time, however, his wife's health was seriously declining and, once again, he was himself acutely depressed: 'My life has been a failure. I have done many things tolerably; but nothing well. As a parish priest, as a preacher and now as a writer I am quite aware that I have failed, and the more so because my friends contradict the assertion. I am quite the old man and wish for peace and quiet at the end: but I cannot help feeling what a fool I am, and what foolish things I have done.' One of the many who was a long way from regarding him as a failure was the Prime Minister, W. E. Gladstone, who believed that Chichester was an inadequate reward for his labour and in 1870 offered him the deanery of Rochester, which was promptly declined. Early in 1871 came the offer of the deanery of Canterbury which he declined on the grounds that he was now 74 and, 'should be looking for preferment in another country, that is an heavenly'. In May of that year his wife, aged 59, died – worn out by her involvement in his ceaseless activity. Before the year was out he had declined the deaneries of St Paul's and Winchester, thus leaving the persistent Gladstone in no doubt as to his intentions.

These offers were, in any case, too late to be sensible. Hook's own health was now failing and his sermons, having substituted length for depth, no longer attracted large numbers. He continued to write but, though he completed the eleventh volume of his series on the Archbishops, the signs of decline were now only too plain. He did not fear death, but had a lifelong and almost obsessive dread of dying – possibly because he could not bear the thought of losing control. Death came as a friend in 1875 and the Chichester shops were closed on the day of his funeral. A clock and chimes were placed to his memory in the cathedral's bell tower, and a new bell was named 'Great Walter'.

At Leeds a recumbent effigy of him in marble was placed on an alabaster altar tomb in the parish church, and a large church was built in his memory. It was at Leeds that his great work was accomplished, and there he established a pattern of ministry for the Church's work in urban areas that was to become the norm in the Church of England for over a century. But even at its best this failed to fulfil his aim that the Established Church should become 'the church of the poor', and part of the explanation is that it was based on a 1,000-year-old system devised for a world that no longer existed.

7

The Liberal
Arthur Penrhyn Stanley, Westminster

Arthur Penrhyn Stanley was Westminster Abbey's greatest nineteenth-century dean and an eminent Victorian. Under his leadership the Abbey ceased to be a closed community of high privilege, jealous of its royal status, and became a national shrine, open to all, and providing a spiritual heart for the English-speaking world. It was an extraordinary achievement.

Stanley, who was at the Abbey from 1864 until his death in 1881, was ideally suited to this deanery. A scholar good enough to hold an Oxford chair, and an eloquent preacher, he was also a man of supremely liberal mind. Amid the ecclesiastical and political turmoil of his time, he stood out as a religious leader who detested dogmatism and promoted Christianity as a simple, uncomplicated faith – 'What makes a man a Christian is to have the character of Christ – a Master worth living for, worth dying for, whose spirit is the regenerating power of the whole world.' He expressed powerfully the optimism of the Victorian era and, noting in the installation service that he was required to work for 'the enlargement of the Christian Church', he interpreted this as meaning that he was to make the Abbey 'more and more the centre of religious and national life in a truly liberal spirit'. It was to become the material embodiment of a comprehensive national Church. Paradoxically, his deep commitment to freedom of thought and speech and intense desire for harmony and peace caused him to be for most of his life, and for all his time at Westminster, involved in controversy.

His early experience at the Abbey was not encouraging. Christopher Wordsworth, a High Church scholar who later became Bishop of Lincoln, was a member of the chapter and strongly objected to the appointment. He preached against it from the Abbey's pulpit and published a pamphlet condemning Stanley's views. Stanley's response was characteristic of the man: he told his wife, 'Perhaps the sermon is to be answered by a calm reply, certainly by an invitation to dinner at the first opportunity.' Wordsworth, who became a friend, refused to attend the installation but appeared at a chapter meeting held soon afterwards. This gathering filled the new dean with unusual gloom and he wrote to his wife, who was on duty as a lady-in-waiting at Court:

> I confess that I felt no elation, nothing but depression, at the prospect before me. It seemed to me as if I were going down alive into the sepulchre. I had a long conversation with Lord John Thynne [the sub-dean], very courteous and sensible, but opening a vista of interminable questions of the most uninteresting kind . . . . As far as the actual work of the dean is concerned, it is far more unsuited to me than that of a bishop. To lose one's time in conversation is bad, but to lose it in leases and warming [i.e. central heating] plans is worse. However, the deed is done, and my useful life I consider to be closed, except so far as I can snatch portions from the troubles of the office.

Stanley was in fact neither an administrator nor a financier. His failure at an early age to grasp the essentials of arithmetic, combined with an other-worldly view of life, would have mattered less had not the Abbey been faced, for the first time, with some of the problems of the modern world. Weakness in dealing with these had serious long-term consequences, but Stanley's priorities were different and he used the power of the Dean of Westminster, which are much greater than those of a cathedral dean, to put them into effect.

The doors of the Abbey were opened to the public without payment of fees, except for entry to the royal chapels located at the east end of the building, behind the high altar. He would have liked these to be free, too, but attendants were needed for security purposes and these had to be paid. The entire building could, however, be visited without charge on Mondays and Stanley left £3,000 in his will to enable this to be extended to Tuesdays. The public response was enormous, especially on Bank Holidays, and on Easter Monday 1870 an estimated 9,000 people passed through the Abbey's doors. On these occasions and at other busy times Stanley walked about the building and talked to the visitors about its historical and religious significance. On most Saturdays in spring and summer he conducted special tours for 'working men', the popularity of which was increased by the provision of tea in the Jerusalem Chamber afterwards.

The Abbey's tombs and monuments always had a special fascination for him and he saw these as a means of bringing the building's history vividly to life. This led to the publication in 1867 of *Memorials of Westminster Abbey*, in which he provided a history with special reference to the memorials. Over 500 pages long, it was a remarkable piece of work, accomplished in only four years, and ran to eight editions. It was not a work of exact scholarship to meet the demands of later historians, the method and style being nearer to that of a chronicler. The chapters on the architecture were rather weak but he wrote eloquently of those who were buried in the Abbey, especially Edward the Confessor, its founder:

> His appearance was such as no one could forget. It was almost that of an Albino. His full-flushed rose-red cheeks strangely contrasted with the milky whiteness of his waving hair and beard. His eyes were always fixed to the ground. There was a kind of magical charm in his thin white hands and his long transparent fingers, which not unnaturally led to the belief that there resided in them a healing power of stroking away the diseases of his subjects. His manners presented a singular mixture of gravity and levity.

Of particular interest to historians, then and since, was the account of his investigation of the royal vaults beneath the chapel of King Henry VII. His purpose was to find the final resting place of King James I whose burial in the Abbey had been recorded, but without any indication of its location. Aided by a member of the works staff, equipped with a shovel, a few tools and a plentiful supply of candles, he crept into the vault where he was vouchsafed many unforgettable, albeit macabre, sights:

> It was with a feeling of breathless anxiety amounting to solemn awe, which caused the humblest of the workmen employed to whisper with bated breath, as the small opening at the apex of the arch admitted the first glimpse into the mysterious secret which had hitherto eluded this long research. Deep within the arched vault were dimly seen three coffins lying side by side – two of them dark and grey with age, the third somewhat brighter and newer . . . . The vault was entered and the detailed examination of the vault at once commenced. The third coffin on the northern side was immediately found to be that of King James I, as indicated beyond question in the long inscription engraved on a copper plate soldered to the lead

coffin . . . . The two other coffins were as indisputably those of Henry VII and his Queen.

Before reaching this vault Stanley had peered into the narrow vault where the coffin of Queen Elizabeth I was seen to be reposing, as she had requested, on that of her sister Mary Tudor – 'Consorts both in throne and grave, here rest we two sisters, Elizabeth and Mary, in the hope of one resurrection', says the striking Latin inscription on the tomb above.

The opening of the Abbey to visitors was accompanied by the encouragement of institutions of national importance to celebrate significant occasions of their life in the context of worship. Stanley's predecessor, Chenevix Trench, had already made a move in this direction, but he made the Abbey's availability more widely known, and soon there were several of these special services every year. Stanley usually occupied the pulpit himself and extended a warm welcome to those who came, but his hospitality was not without some qualification and this led in 1867 to a serious controversy which echoed throughout the Anglican world.

In that year the Archbishop of Canterbury convened at Lambeth a Pan-Anglican Synod which was attended by 76 bishops and, although the agenda covered a number of matters of mutual concern, the primary purpose of the gathering was to consider and condemn the teaching of the Bishop of Natal, John William Colenso. This bishop, who was exercising a heroic missionary ministry in South Africa, had been charged with heresy and deposed by the Archbishop of Cape Town – an action strongly supported by virtually all of the Church of England's leaders, but not by Stanley who stood almost alone in defending the bishop's freedom to express his beliefs. Stanley did not in fact approve of Colenso's books but he believed passionately in his right to publish them, and spoke strongly in his support in the Convocation of Canterbury and at a meeting of the Society for the Propagation of the Gospel. When therefore the Archbishop of Canterbury requested that his Synod might conclude with an act of worship in the Abbey, Stanley felt bound to refuse because he believed that the illiberality of its condemnation of Colenso was incompatible with the inclusive Christianity which the Abbey existed to promote. Colenso was later invited to preach in the Abbey but declined because he did not wish to cause further controversy.

Stanley's understanding of the Abbey's vocation caused some other uncomfortable moments. The pulpit was opened to a wide variety of preachers but the fact that it had been occupied by liberal scholars such as Benjamin Jowett and F. D. Maurice was sufficient to cause the leading High Churchmen, Pusey, Liddon and Keble, to decline invitations. When in 1864 Frederick Temple, the future Archbishop of Canterbury but then the headmaster of Rugby School, was invited to preach, the chapter entered a formal protest because he had contributed (an innocuous piece on education) to a controversial book, *Essays and Reviews*. Stanley replied:

> You are acting entirely according to your sense of duty in doing as you do. I am acting from the same sense of duty in insisting on his name. You may sign the protest; but there is one thing you cannot do, and that is, make me quarrel with you for so doing.

Since Free Church preachers and laymen were not allowed by law to occupy the pulpit, they gave addresses and lectures from the floor of the nave. Considerable controversy attended Stanley's invitation to the translators of the Revised Version of the Bible, whose number included some Free Church scholars and a Unitarian, to receive holy communion in the Abbey at the end of their labours.

The celebration in 1865 of the 800th anniversary of the Abbey's dedication consisted of no more than a special service with a decanal sermon on 28 December and was modest indeed when compared with the year-long programme of activities that marked the 900th anniversary in 1965. Thereafter on Holy Innocents' Day – the actual day of the dedication – Stanley held a special service for children, followed by tea in the deanery, and on Christmas Day 1866 the Abbey was crowded for a commemoration of the 800th anniversary of William the Conqueror's crowning. Courses of weekday sermons and lectures were also well attended and the Abbey was packed on Maundy Thursday 1871 for a performance of Bach's *St Matthew Passion* in the context of evensong, and with two addresses by the dean. Even this proved to be controversial but it was repeated in the following and some subsequent years, and copied by several cathedrals.

As a preacher, Stanley was never other than eloquent. He was allowed to preach at statutory services only at Christmas, Easter and Whitsun – a rule designed to free the dean for long absences, rather than exclude him from the pulpit – but for reasons of age and infirmity members of the chapter were often unable to preach and he gladly took their places. The popular Sunday evening service started by his predecessor at the suggestion of the Bishop of London, also gave him many preaching opportunities, as did the courses of sermons which he arranged for some weekdays. His volumes of published sermons indicate that he was at his best on special occasions. For the rest, he preached too often to be consistently outstanding and many of his sermons were used more than once – updated with complex insertions which even he sometimes found confusing when the time of delivery arrived. Most congregations found his face, voice and manner more memorable than his words and this contributed greatly to his influence.

At his first chapter meeting, which left him feeling exceedingly gloomy, the sub-dean, Lord John Thynne, who had been a canon since 1831, acquainted him with two urgent problems related to the Abbey's finances and its relations with Westminster School. In spite of the pillaging of its treasures and confiscation of much of its property at the suppression of the Benedictine monastery in 1540 and during the Commonwealth, the Abbey was left with considerable and increasingly valuable land-holdings in London, as well as estates in various other parts of the country. Those in London included the whole of what is now Victoria Street, the Hyde Park Estate, Covent Garden and parts of the City of London. The dean and canons, who often held other appointments – the dean was also Bishop of Rochester during the period – were very rich men, as their fine houses clearly indicated.

By the time of Stanley's installation, however, it was clear that the Abbey's exemption from the reforms of the episcopal and capitular estates initiated in the 1830s could not be upheld for much longer and in 1869 all its land-holdings in London and all its country estates, apart from a few in Herefordshire and Worcestershire, were by Act of Parliament transferred to the Ecclesiastical Commissioners. In return, the Commissioners transferred some small estates in those counties to the dean and chapter, and it was estimated that together these would yield an annual income of £20,000. A capital sum of £20,000 was also set aside for the repair and improvement of the Abbey's fabric. Unfortunately, a prolonged period of agricultural distress in the 1870s and '80s led to the non-payment of rents and inevitably to very serious problems for the dean and chapter. A more financially astute dean would have foreseen this possibility and, doubtless with royal backing, struck a much better deal with the Commissioners – one that would not have left the Abbey so vulnerable to agriculture's changing fortunes. But this was not Stanley's way and his only regret seemed to be that the loss of most of the estates deprived the Abbey of a valuable link with the outside world.

A similar lack of toughness attended his dealings with Westminster School which had been the direct responsibility of the dean and chapter since its foundation under Queen Elizabeth's Charter in 1560. By the time of Stanley's arrival at the Abbey the school was, in common with all the other English public schools, in urgent need of major reform and under the 1868 Public Schools Act its management was transferred to a newly established governing body on which the dean and chapter's influence was limited by the presence only of the dean, as chairman, and two canons. This in itself created no great problem for the Abbey but the future ownership of the buildings in the limited space of its precincts proved to be a matter of bitter dispute, the effects of which were still being felt a century later. Stanley allowed himself to be outwitted by the educational reformers and the loss of Ashburnham House in particular proved to be a heavy blow since this traditional dwelling of the sub-dean was one of London's finest residences.

The depletion of the Abbey's finances coincided with the discovery of major problems relating to the state of the fabric and these Stanley was unable to solve. His love of the building did not extend as far as enthusiasm for fundraising and all the administrative chores that his successors were unable to avoid when restoration programmes were initiated. In 1869 the surveyor, Sir George Gilbert Scott, reported that the north transept front was in a dangerous condition, but he was responsible for many other buildings and his health was failing, so he carried out only limited restoration of the north porch. During Stanley's time, however, the chapter house was completely restored and a new high altar and reredos installed. Meanwhile other parts of the building, including the cloisters, were showing signs of serious decay and in the year following Scott's death in 1878 his successor, John Loughborough Pearson, carried out a complete survey which indicated that £49,000 was needed for a major restoration of the entire fabric, excluding any work that proved to be necessary on the precincts. In the year following the reception of this report the balance in the chapter's accounts amounted to no more than £358. It was left to Stanley's successors, with the aid of grants from the Ecclesiastical Commissioners, to ensure that Pearson's work was carried out. Unfortunately the Chilmark stone chosen for the purpose could not withstand London's polluted air and lasted less than 100 years.

Arthur Penrhyn Stanley was born in 1815 and named after the victor of Waterloo. His father was at the time rector of Alderley in Cheshire – this being the family living – and later became a notable, reforming Bishop of Norwich. Young Stanley was sent to Rugby School in 1824, just a year after Dr Arnold had embarked on his epoch-making headmastership. No good at mathematics or sports, he nonetheless won many other prizes, but the abiding influence on him was that of the liberal Arnold himself. Stanley later described him as 'the lodestar of my life' and once wondered if his hero worship of the great man might not have gone too far. He was shattered by Arnold's sudden death in 1841 and, although still in his twenties, completed a biography of his mentor which proved to be his best book.

A Balliol scholarship took him to Oxford where he found the university in turmoil over the Tractarian activity and the growing demand for institutional reform in the wake of the 1832 Reform Bill. He heard Newman preach and was for a time attracted by his message, but in the end the influence of Arnold was stronger and, although he took a first in classics and won the Ireland scholarship, his hoped-for Fellowship of Balliol was denied him because of his liberal theological views. Curiously as it would seem today, he was as an undergraduate consulted by the Prime Minister's secretary over the controversial proposal to appoint the liberal R. D. Hampton to the Regius Chair of Divinity.

Instead of Balliol, he secured a Fellowship at University College, which he likened to being appointed to the bishopric of Sodor and Man, rather than to the Archbishopric of Canterbury. At first he was unhappy there, but he became a brilliant tutor and was much involved in the campaign for university reform. This led to his appointment as secretary of a Royal Commission to enquire into Oxford's affairs and he was said to have written most of its report. The divisive religious debates of the 1830s and '40s greatly troubled him and he hesitated before proceeding to ordination in 1859 because of the requirement that the clergy should assent *ex animo* to the *Book of Common Prayer* and therefore to the condemnatory clauses in the Athanasian Creed. In the end he relented and thereafter campaigned vigorously for the revision of the form of consent, which was eventually achieved after much controversy in 1872.

In 1849 Stanley declined the offer of the deanery of Carlisle on the grounds that the cathedral statutes required the dean to reside there for eight months of the year. This was far too long to be away from Oxford. A. C. Tait, who later became a notable Bishop of London and Archbishop of Canterbury, went instead and in the space of one month suffered the trauma of losing five of his seven children as a result of a scarlet fever epidemic. Stanley accepted a canonry of

Canterbury in 1851 and although there for only five years made a considerable impact. The place of Canterbury in the life of Church and nation appealed to his historical imagination and within three years he had written *Memorials of Canterbury* which, like its Westminster successor, told the story of the cathedral in the light of its tombs and monuments. His scholarly reconstruction of the events surrounding the murder of Archbishop Thomas à Becket proved to be of lasting value. His preaching attracted large congregations and he wrote several other books, including commentaries on 1 and 2 Corinthians which attracted some criticism from J. B. Lightfoot. His house became a centre of warm hospitality and, by now a well-known national figure, he entertained guests from all parts of England. The Prince Consort made him one of his chaplains in 1854 and the Queen wished him to become a bishop, but the Prime Minister, Palmerston, objected to this on account of his liberal religious opinions.

Stanley's appointment as Regius Professor of Ecclesiastical History at Oxford in 1856 was by no means unexpected but was not universally welcomed. He received only one letter of congratulation from Oxford residents, and that from Benjamin Jowett. Pusey said that he viewed his appointment with 'sorrow and fear'. But soon his lectures were crowded with enthusiastic undergraduates who were attracted by his vibrant personality and genuine gift for friendship which extended beyond the lecture halls. He resumed his campaign for university reform and amid the continuing religious controversy was the leading proponent of freedom and tolerance. He was unhappy with the highly controversial volume *Essays and Reviews* because he thought some of the writers had been too negative, but he defended fiercely their freedom to write as they did.

Towards the end of his schooldays at Rugby Stanley was taken by his parents on an extended tour of the Pyrenees and this created in him an appetite for travel that remained until almost the end of his life. Few years passed without his going, often for several weeks, to various parts of Europe, the Middle East and America. The purpose always was to study people, places and antiquities – he had little appreciation of natural beauty – and his travels were recounted in several books. In 1862 he was asked by Queen Victoria to accompany the Prince of Wales, the future King Edward VII, on a tour of Egypt and the Holy Land. This was a success except that General Robert Bruce, who was also in the party, contracted an illness from which he died soon after his return to London. The tour and its unfortunate consequences brought Stanley into much closer association with the Court and in particular with Lady Augusta Bruce, the sister of the General, who was a daughter of the Earl of Elgin and a lady-in-waiting to the Duchess of Kent. Before long they were in love.

Meanwhile, Stanley was offered and accepted the deanery of Westminster and it was announced soon afterwards that he and Lady Augusta would be married in the Abbey shortly before his installation as dean. In the event, the death of the bride's father required a quiet wedding which took place two days before Christmas in 1863, the installation following on 9 January. It proved to be a supremely happy marriage. She continued with her duties at Court, but was left with ample time to create a secure and ever hospitable home in the deanery. She went with him on his annual tours and in 1874 they were in St Petersburg representing the Queen at the marriage of the Duke of Edinburgh and a daughter of the Russian Tsar. Stanley took part in the service. The death of Lady Augusta two years later was a cruel blow from which he never really recovered, though he soon resumed the ceaseless activity and was in great demand as a preacher and speaker throughout the country. In 1881 he gave in the Abbey a summer course of Saturday evensong sermons on the Beatitudes and on 9 July, feeling unwell, went straight from the pulpit to his bed. Erysipelas was diagnosed and, lacking the antibiotics discovered in the following century, he died nine days later. A few hours before his death he sent a message of respect to the Queen and soon afterwards said:

> As far as I understood what the duties of my office were supposed to be, in spite of every incompetence, I am yet humbly trustful that I have sustained before the mind of the nation the extraordinary value of the Abbey as a religious, national and liberal institution.

His death came as a great shock throughout Britain and also in America, and was felt by many as a personal loss. On the day of the funeral there were crowds in the streets outside the Abbey and many of the shops and pubs of Westminster were closed for the duration of the service.

8

The Saint
Richard Church, St Paul's

Richard Church, who was at St Paul's from 1871 to 1890, is believed by many to have been the greatest of the Victorian deans, though this might well be challenged by the admirers of Arthur Penrhyn Stanley who was at Westminster Abbey at the same time. What is hardly open to question, however, is that no one before or since has entered the decanal office with greater reluctance than Church. After 15 years as a Fellow of Oriel College, Oxford, he had married and become rector of Whatley – a Somerset parish of 200 souls. There he was idyllically happy. He was a superb pastor and preacher, he loved the countryside, and had ample time to pursue his studies and write learned books.

Then came a letter from the Prime Minister, W. E. Gladstone, asking him to move to the city of London, where there was not a blade of grass to be seen, to live in a fortress-like deanery, and to be responsible not only for Wren's magnificent masterpiece, but also to stir the cathedral into life after long years of slumber during which corruption had become endemic. Church's immediate response was to refuse, but Gladstone pressed him to reconsider and enlisted the support of Henry Parry Liddon, a close friend of Church who had himself recently become a canon of St Paul's. This worked, but Church's letter to an American friend, Asa Gray, written just eight days before his installation as dean, needs to be quoted at length:

> I wish that I could be reconciled to what is to be. But I am not; and I cannot expect to be. I have made a great mistake, the mistake of not knowing how to say no to warm and pressing instances from people whom I respected, when my own judgement was really quite clear the other way. This comes on me more and more strongly every day . . . . I have made a great mistake in exchanging this peaceful life where I could work calmly and at my leisure, for that tangle

and whirlpool of ecclesiastical politics, in which so few people see their way, or are strong enough to meet temptations which are subtler and keener, and of a worse order than those of politics .... The place – one of hard business administration, organization, management of a troublesome and powerful staff, of representation and speech-making, of reform of old and strong abuses – is not fit for me, nor I for it. What I could do, I shall have neither time nor strength for longer; what I shall have to do, I have neither aptitude nor experience for. It used to be a place of literary leisure; and so it was under Milman. But times are changed. What is required now is that St Paul's should wake up from its long slumber, and show what use it is of, and how it can justify its existence as the great central church of London.

He went on to say that he doubted if he would stay there for a year. The change would be too great and his health might well break up.

A visit to Liddon, made soon after Gladstone's offer had arrived, left him in no doubt as to what was urgently needed at St Paul's. First, a bargain was to be made with the Ecclesiastical Commissioners about the future of the cathedral's finances. A recent Act of Parliament now permitted the surrender to the Commissioners of cathedral estates in return for a commuted annual payment and it was necessary to extract from them whatever was required for a reformed St Paul's. Second, the architectural restoration started under the late dean, Milman, must be continued at a cost of £250,000 – something over £5 million in today's money. Third, to fight and reduce to order a refractory and difficult staff of singing men and others, strong in their charters and inherited abuses. Liddon pointed out that the dean would not be expected to achieve this single-handed – the chapter would play its part – but there was no doubt the responsibility would fall on him.

The choice of a shy scholar from a tiny Somerset parish for this Herculean task was passing strange, yet Gladstone and all Church's friends believed that St Paul's was absolutely the right place for him. A. P. Stanley, who had left Oxford eight years earlier to become Dean of Westminster, sent him a note of welcome: 'If together we cannot do something for London, may the malison of St Peter and St Paul fall upon us.'

That the appointment turned out to be a brilliant success was undoubtedly due to the calibre and character of the chapter which Church was called to lead and the credit for this must go to Gladstone who chose the canons. Robert Gregory, who had arrived three years earlier and stayed long enough to succeed to the deanery, was the treasurer, and a superb financer and administrator. He had already started negotiations with the Ecclesiastical Commissioners and convinced them that the money needed by St Paul's would be well spent. He relieved Church of virtually all the administrative burden of an institution undergoing a major reform. Liddon, one of the Victorian era's great scholars and outstanding preachers, was an important figure in London life and attracted thousands of people to hear his sermons. He was also Dean Ireland's Professor of Exegesis at Oxford until 1882, but spent most of his time at St Paul's. Joseph Barber Lightfoot was the leading New Testament and Patristic scholar of his day. He, too, held a chair – at Cambridge – and, like Liddon, gave much to the cathedral as a preacher and as a general member of the community. When he left to become Bishop of Durham in 1879 he was succeeded by William Stubbs, the greatest British historian of his time and also an Oxford professor. Later the chapter was strengthened again by the appointment of Henry Scott Holland, theologian, social reformer and another outstanding preacher.

Even more important than their great gifts was their readiness to work harmoniously as a chapter. In the words of Scott Holland:

> It was not as is so usual in cathedral bodies, an odd assortment of stray goods, a collection of contradictory specimens, each of which has been specifically selected in order to neutralize the others.

The distinction and wide interests of the canons undoubtedly made them less likely to stand on their dignity and fight their colleagues over matters which were bound to seem to them of minor importance. But the key factor was the character of the dean. Church was quite without those personal traits that enable a man to dominate a community, and he lacked managerial skills, as these are now commonly understood. Humility was one of his chief hallmarks and his slight figure was scarcely noticed as he flitted in and out of the cathedral. When he knelt on the floor of his stall, he became invisible. Neither was he a Liddon or a Scott Holland in the pulpit. He spoke in a monotone and without gesture, and he once confessed that often when he sat at his desk trying to prepare a sermon he was so destitute of ideas that he felt 'like a hen contemplating a chalk egg'. He rarely appeared at public gatherings or on a platform. Yet there was something about his preaching – an elegance and a profundity – that many found fascinating and irresistible. Among these was that most exacting of critics,

Bishop Hensley Henson, who said that he had never heard a more impressive teacher, and in a birthday letter to his Durham chaplain in 1935, accompanying a present of several volumes of Church's works, recalled that, during his undergraduate days in Oxford, he had heard Church preach in the university church. 'He had the unearthly refinement of a scholar saint, and when he kindled with his theme his thin features glowed with enthusiasm and he looked a prophet.'

More than this, he was revered and utterly trusted by his chapter colleagues. He combined holiness, wisdom and a certain moral power that made them always ready to submit to his judgement. And not only his chapter colleagues: Gladstone constantly consulted him on political matters, as well as on church affairs, and as the years passed an ever-increasing stream of people from all walks of life found their way to the St Paul's deanery to seek his opinion. 'What does the dean say?' was the question on the lips of the perplexed. Such was Church's influence and power that, when A. C. Tait died in 1883, Gladstone wanted him to become Archbishop of Canterbury, but this time he refused to be persuaded.

Richard William Church was born in Lisbon in 1815. His father, who came from Cork, had moved there to further his business interests but in 1816 retired to Somerset. Two years later, however, ill health caused him to move to Florence – a city which exercised a formative influence on young Richard and where he always felt at home. His stay there ended with the sudden death of his father in 1826 and he was then sent to an evangelical school at Redlands, near Bristol. This evangelical choice, which took him later to Wadham College, Oxford, where the tutors were known to be of this persuasion, owed something to the fact that his grandparents on both sides were Quakers.

He was, however, soon exposed to other Oxford influences. Charles Marriott, a Fellow of Oriel and one of the founders of the Oxford Movement, called on him and became his mentor and lifelong friend. He introduced him to John Keble, John Henry Newman and others who were seeking to renew the Church of England's Catholic tradition. These, too, became close friends and thus Church was drawn into the new, highly controversial movement. Another important influence came through his widowed mother's re-marriage. One of Church's new step-sisters married George Moberly, who was at that time a Fellow and tutor of Balliol and later became headmaster of Winchester College, then Bishop of Salisbury. He saw to it that the young Wadham undergraduate found his way around the rest of Oxford.

After taking a first in classics, Church stayed on and had a few pupils. He now started attending St Mary's where Newman was the vicar and making a deep impression with his sermons. Church became a disciple. In 1838 he was elected a Fellow of Oriel, which brought him into even closer contact with Newman, and in the following year was ordained deacon, in company with A. P. Stanley, in St Mary's. He also attended lectures on anatomy and other scientific subjects. The Oxford Movement was now moving beyond its early stages and making its presence felt through a series of tracts, some of which were highly controversial. Starting as no more than four-page leaflets these developed into learned monographs and the publication in 1841 of Tract 90, in which Newman argued that the Church of England's Thirty-Nine Articles of Religion needed to be interpreted in ways generally agreeable to the decrees of the Roman Catholic Council of Trent, caused a violent explosion. Newman was already having doubts about the Church of England's claims, so the Bishop of Oxford imposed silence on him. In 1843 he resigned from St Mary's and two years later was received into the Church of Rome. Throughout this stormy period Church stood by him, and Newman described their friendship as 'close and intimate'. In 1845, when the university Convocation sought to censure Tract 90, Church and his fellow proctor used their power of veto to make this impossible and, with feelings in Oxford running high, over 500 members of the university sent an address of thanks to the two courageous proctors. Newman's secession was, however, a heavy blow and led to a breach in their friendship which lasted for 20 years.

Church felt obliged to resign from his college tutorship, since the Provost of Oriel was one of the Tractarians' fiercest opponents, and his offer was accepted. He remained as a Fellow, however, and having become treasurer of the college found himself lumbered with much extra work following the introduction of income tax. The year of his election to a Fellowship saw the publication of his translation of *The Catechetical Lectures of St Cyril of Jerusalem*, with a preface by Newman, but college duties and involvement in the Oxford Movement precluded any more substantial writing during his time at Oriel. In 1846 he and a few friends started *The Guardian* – a weekly newspaper which promoted Tractarian principles and provided comment on political and social, as well as theological issues. This survived until 1951 and in its early years Church was the reviews editor and a regular contributor of editorials and articles.

At the time of his resignation from the college tutorship the Provost

indicated that if he required a testimonial in order to be able to pro-
ceed to the priesthood this would be unlikely to be forthcoming. Some
years later, however, at Christmas 1852 when 'Church of Oriel' was
one of the most admired figures in Oxford, he was ordained priest, so
that he could become rector of Whatley – a rural parish twelve miles
from Wells and three from Frome – and minister to 200 poor peasants.
The parish had not had a resident rector for many years and both the
church and the rectory were in disrepair. Six months after his institution Church married, but he was lonely for a time until he settled into
the work of a parish priest and began to earn a reputation which led
Henson to number him with George Herbert and John Keble as the
supreme exemplars of the Church of England's pastoral ministry. He
also found plenty of time for study and writing and, besides his work
for *The Guardian*, edited the *First Book of Hooker's Ecclesiastical
Polity* (1868) and wrote a biography of *St Anselm* (1870). Two
volumes of his *Village Sermons* were published towards the end of his
life and are still worth reading. He was among the opponents of
Essays and Reviews – a collection of what now seem moderately
liberal essays by seven writers, published in 1860 – but the review in
The Guardian was much more temperate in its criticism than most of
the other reviews and pronouncements.

In 1869 Church was offered one of the Crown canonries of
Worcester Cathedral but he declined, ostensibly on the grounds
that his recent public support of Gladstone might lead some to
conclude that the offer was a reward. The truth was that he had not
the slightest desire to leave Whatley. Gladstone was not, however,
so easily deterred and two years later despatched the St Paul's bomb-
shell.

During his first year in the deanery, Church was, as anticipated by
him, very miserable. The cathedral itself was a place of gloom: Queen
Victoria described it as 'dirty, dark and undevotional'. Milman had
embarked upon an ambitious scheme of cleaning and decorating
the distempered walls which led to the insertion of mosaics in two
spandrels of the dome and some gilding of the roof. But the funds for
this ran out. Most of the building remained unused, the daily services
being held in the choir and until recently behind the huge organ screen,
the erection of which had been vehemently opposed by Wren. Everything was carried out on the smallest possible scale, and as slowly as
may be imagined. Crowds would sometimes attend when a great
preacher was announced or a national hero was due for burial, and,
after pressure from Bishop Tait, Milman had instituted Sunday

evening services under the dome at certain times of the year. Otherwise the cathedral was virtually redundant.

Church tackled the situation by declaring that the building, like any parish church, must be used from end to end. People must be made to feel that it was a place of prayer and praise, with the Eucharist as the central act of worship. The new, High Church dean was nailing his colours to the mast, but with the full agreement of the chapter. And he would not wear vestments. The worship must be open to all, with no suggestion of payment or of reserved seats. Neither must there be any 'shaking of the money bags'. Art and music at its very best must assist the offering of dignified worship. The cathedral must be open to the diocese and all its organizations made welcome. The shy scholar from rural Somerset was in fact a revolutionary.

The carrying out of his revolution took many years to accomplish and during the early days hard decisions had to be made and tough, painful confrontations with vergers, vicars choral and other entrenched interests overcome. In his later years Church could hardly bear to refer to these or have them mentioned, but throughout the period of conflict he was always strongly supported by the Bishop of London. It is not easy to discover precisely who was responsible for the many changes in the life of St Paul's that took place during Church's reign. In general he did not himself tend to formulate proposals or frame policies. The canons were the initiators and implementers – Liddon in liturgical and devotional matters, Gregory everything to do with finance and administration – but they knew that only the highest standards in their respective fields would meet with Church's approval, only the best would be acceptable. Later Scott Holland, who also was a very active member of the chapter, wrote:

> We at the cathedral went about our work with the consciousness that the dignity of a great name was behind us – a name which did not merely win the admiration and love of those who knew him, but which had a hold on the imagination of the large world outside.

Gregory negotiated successfully with the Ecclesiastical Commissioners and in exchange for the remainder of the dean and chapter's estates (the most substantial part had been surrendered earlier) secured an annual payment of £18,000, plus a capital sum of £10,000 for the maintenance of the cathedral and other buildings. The number of minor canons was reduced from twelve to six and these were forbidden to hold city livings to which they had by rotation been allocated since 1855. Instead they were required to undertake pastoral and educational work in the city from their cathedral base and this some of them did with conspicuous success. Special services for warehousemen and clerks, held every day, attracted very large numbers and the minor canons gave the addresses and provided the follow-up pastoral work. Their removal into houses in Amen Court brought to St Paul's much more of the atmosphere of a cathedral close.

The worship was taken in hand and the music required immediate attention since Church found the standard extremely low. A year after his arrival the organist, John Goss, was persuaded to retire with the honorary title of organist of St Paul's and the compensation of a knighthood. In his place came John Stainer who brought the music to a high professional level and also composed a great deal of choral work – of a varied standard. The number of choristers was raised from eight to 40 and the Ecclesiastical Commissioners' £10,000 grant was used to build a choir school to enable them to become boarders and receive a better all-round education. The vicars choral, whose number was increased from ten to 18, proved to be much more difficult to deal with. Most of them held freeholds which, irrespective of their musical competence, made it impossible for them to be dismissed or retired. One, whose voice had gone in 1859, was represented by a deputy until his death in 1901. Rehearsals were, however, made compulsory and extra payments encouraged the men to sing oratorios at various times of the year. For the Festival of the Sons of the Clergy, always an important St Paul's occasion, the choir was augmented by an orchestra. A daily 8 a.m. Eucharist was started in 1881.

The high quality of the preaching attracted increasingly large congregations. During Lent 1852 sermons were preached every day of the week at midday and these also attracted huge crowds. At certain times of the year there were sermons at evensong on Wednesdays and Fridays and addresses after a late evening service on Tuesdays and Thursdays. One result of this was that some people began to attend the cathedral regularly and treat it as their parish church. Pastoral care of these was provided by the minor canons and altogether it was apparent that St Paul's had at last awoken from its long slumber and was now justifying its existence as the great central church of London.

The one area in which only limited progress proved possible involved the restoration of the building. In the year following Church's appointment a service of thanksgiving was held for the recovery of the Prince of Wales from typhoid fever. This was followed by a thanksgiving appeal, to which the Queen contributed £1,000 and which raised £56,000. Canon Gregory thereupon went to the South of France and Italy to study Byzantine decoration. On his return the cathedral architect produced an extravagant scheme for refacing the whole interior of the cathedral with a veneer of polished marble in various colours. In spite of advice to the contrary from various experts, the dean and chapter adopted the scheme, but after it had been tried out on a section of the apse it was agreed that the result was unattractive, so it was dropped. Attention turned instead to increasing the ring of four bells to twelve, one of which, the 17-ton Great St Paul bell, took three days of strenuous handling by the Royal Engineers to reach its place. The completion of the mosaic work in the interior of the building started by Milman, had to await the death of Church and his succession by Gregory who, although aged 72, was still full of vigour and gave the interior of St Paul's the Byzantine appearance which it has now had for over a century. It involved him in great and sometimes bitter controversy.

Throughout this long period of reform and renewal Church was occupied not only with much personal counselling but also with substantial research and writing. *The Beginning of the Middle Ages* (1877) was followed by biographies of Spenser (1879) and Bacon (1884). A collection of his essays and articles appeared in five volumes in 1888 and a magnificent *History of the Oxford Movement*, which was completed shortly before his death and published posthumously, remains the standard work on the subject today. His final years were, however, marked by increasing ill health and greatly saddened by the deaths of a 33-year-old son, John Henry Newman and other close friends. Canon Liddon died suddenly in 1890 and Scott Holland recorded:

> No one who was present in St Paul's on the occasion of Dr Liddon's funeral could have been unmoved the wasted, fragile figure of the dean, or have listened, without a sense of its pathos and significance, to his broken and scarcely audible voice as it was heard for the last time in the cathedral of which he had been for so long the head, in the recital of the sentences of committal to the grave.

In November of that year Church went to Dover to escape from London's suffocating air, and took with him his favourite authors – Homer, Lucretius, Dante (in whose works he was steeped), Wordsworth and Matthew Arnold. But more than Dover's fresh air was required and on 10 December he died. St Paul's was crowded for the funeral and he was buried at his beloved Whatley in a spot in the churchyard he had chosen some years earlier. He left instructions that no memorial was to be erected, and his grave is marked by a simple stone on which is inscribed six lines from *Dies Irae*.

9

The Innovator
Edward White Benson, Truro

Edward White Benson is remembered as the creator of Wellington College, the pioneering Bishop of Truro and, most of all, as a late-Victorian Archbishop of Canterbury. But he was also a notable cathedral man who wrote a significant book on the role of the cathedral, took Lincoln by storm when he became its cathedral's canon chancellor, and having started the building of Truro Cathedral combined the offices of bishop and dean. He was essentially a dynamic innovator and his biographer son, A. C. Benson, believed that acceptance of the Archbishopric of Canterbury was the greatest mistake his father ever made. He was by no means the best of the nineteenth-century Primates, but his life and that of his family is endlessly fascinating.

Benson's interest in cathedrals began when he was busy making Wellington one of England's leading public schools and, as an examining chaplain to the Bishop of Lincoln, was one of Lincoln's many prebendaries. It owed more, however, to what became a lifelong interest in Cyprian, a third-century Bishop of Carthage whose views had a formative influence on the Church's understanding of the role of the bishop.

Cyprian had a high doctrine of episcopacy, balanced by the belief that the bishop must be close to his clergy and consult them before making decisions about all important matters in his diocese, including the choice of candidates for ordination and the re-admission of the lapsed to communion. Benson noted that this conciliar approach eventually found expression in the cathedral community – the bishop's church where the clergy were available for consultation and also to share the bishop's mission in the surrounding territory. He believed that the recovery of this model was essential to the renewal of the Church's life in his own day. His ideas appeared first in an article in the *Quarterly Review*, then in an essay contributed to a symposium on cathedral reform edited by Dean Howson of Chester. These were brought together, augmented by material relating to his proposals for Truro, and published in 1878 as *The Cathedral: Its necessary place in the life and work of the Church*.

The greater part of the small book is taken up with a historical survey demonstrating the long association between the bishop and a community of other clergy: 'It is not possible to point to any episcopal chair which is not at one seen surrounded by its "Senatus", its "presbytery", "council" or "cardinals".' He deeply regretted the loss of this corporate leadership during the Middle Ages and the failure to restore it at the Reformation. Welcoming the revival of the Convocations of Canterbury and York during the second half of the nineteenth century he argued that the conciliar restoration would not be complete until the cathedral chapter had returned to their true role, standing with the Bishop 'like a bridegroom at the side of his bride'.

There were also many other things for them to be doing, of which the first and most important was clergy training. Pointing out that 100 years earlier the country clergy were often learned men, and the town clergy of above average education, he complained that not a tenth of the candidates for ordination in even the most attractive dioceses could be said to pass the necessary examinations satisfactorily. Since the universities could no longer provide all the required training, theological colleges must be established at the major cathedrals, with the canons constituting the teaching staff.

The cathedrals should also create a staff of 'free preachers', based again on a primitive model and continued at Canterbury by Cranmer's foundation of six preachers. These would be drawn from the most able of the parochial clergy, augmented by some others from outside, and headed by a canon missioner. Their task would be to conduct missions in the parishes, to help the parish clergy in other ways – not least in the cathedral's own city, where relations with the parishes were often strained or non-existent, and where there were professional people whom the Church was neglecting. The involvement of the Church in the ministry of healing was something else that needed to be revived: 'Is it a hopeless vision to dream that there may one day exist a cathedral corps of hospital chaplains, a diocesan staff of trained nurses, deaconesses, Sisters?' Benson asked. All of which would require radical change in the way cathedrals were now organized. 'Well-earned repose has a value of its own', he declared, 'but for the present we want work out of these institutions, not repose . . . . "Precedent" that potent cathedral spectre, though when faced, it rarely proves to be 50 years old, must no more rule cathedrals than it rules any useful institution.'

With these ideas and opinions in the public domain it was hardly surprising that in 1872 his friend Bishop Christopher Wordsworth of Lincoln should invite him to leave Wellington to become canon chancellor of his cathedral. In the letter making the offer Wordsworth said that certain conditions were attached: 'I could not offer the vacant chancellorship to anyone who could not engage to devote himself entirely to the study of theology, and to the training of theological students to the sacred ministry of the Church; and to the work of Christian education, especially in the City of Lincoln, according to the Statutes.' He added in a postscript, 'I believe that in the Consecration of the Holy Eucharist your use at Wellington differs from ours at Lincoln: but I am sure you would follow, in such matters as this, the advice of St Ambrose, and, "do at Rome what they do at Rome".'

Benson immediately consulted his friends, Lightfoot and Westcott, who thought he should go, and in a very lengthy letter of acceptance he took the opportunity to instruct Wordsworth about certain other educational aspects of the chancellor's duties prescribed by the statutes. As for taking on other responsibilities, either inside or outside Lincoln, this would never enter his mind but he would prefer to be bound by the required oath of obedience to the cathedral statutes than by an additional, and unnecessary, promise. As for the Wellington 'use' he did not know what the bishop was alluding to, since he always stood at the north side of the altar and would have thought himself a law-breaker had he stood in front.

The move to Lincoln necessitated a substantial reduction in income – from £2,000 to £1,000 a year – but he had counted the cost and was resolved to live simply in the beautiful chantry, employing only maids. He had always dreamt that one day he might be a canon and, although his stay at Lincoln was for less than four years, his impact was tremendous. Never before had there been such a dynamic member of the chapter. The highest priority was the foundation of a theological college in which he had the strong support of the bishop. It began with a handful of students in a couple of rooms in the close. A rich MP friend agreed to endow temporarily one of the prebendal stalls, so that a theological tutor might be appointed, and Benson himself undertook much of the teaching. One of the earlier students, who later became a dean in America, recorded his impressions:

How vividly one recalls the Chancellor. His quick strong nervous steps as he enters the lecture-room, the prayer usually concluding with the Lord's Prayer in Greek, the students reciting it with him: and the strong brilliant intellect glowing and lighting up a wondrously beautiful face, pouring forth stores of learning: Old and New Testaments alike had new and unlooked for meaning and depths. His dignity, his kindness, his look which always brought the best things in you to the surface, his humour, his rippling laughter – the whole atmosphere of the lecture-room can never be forgotten.

Thus began Scholae Cancellarii which was destined to become one of the Church of England's leading theological colleges, attracting scholars of the first rank to its teaching staff and training men who became prominent bishops and deans. It was characteristic of Benson, the classicist whose writings were always littered with Latin and Greek, that it should have been given a Latin name and it was merciful that he did not live to see this changed to the prosaic Bishop's Hostel. Besides his college teaching, he gave courses of lectures in the chapter house on the Bible and Church history and provided weekly Bible classes for 'mechanics'. Large congregations assembled for his Sunday afternoon sermons in the cathedral.

The greatest local impact, however, was made by the night schools held in the lower part of the city. These had been suggested by one of the bishop's daughters and under Benson's enthusiastic leadership they attracted over 400 working-class men and boys to study a wide variety of subjects. He established a surprisingly close relationship with them, being entirely at ease in their company and winning both their admiration and affection. He believed that he had a vocation to teach the poor. University extension lectures were organized for those who needed stronger fare. Neither was the diocese neglected. A society of clergy for evangelistic work in the parishes was formed and he, himself, led an intensive and hugely supported mission to the city of Lincoln. It was fortunate that he could manage on only five hours of night-time sleep, though he often refreshed himself with a brief nap at other times.

There was no possibility of a man of Benson's gifts and energy remaining for long in a provincial cathedral canonry, important though this work might be. In 1875 it was indicated to him that if he would stand for the vacant Hulsean Professorship at Cambridge he would certainly be elected. It was expected that he might combine this with his Lincoln post, J. B. Lightfoot having done this successfully with his St Paul's canonry, but Benson knew that Lincoln required his

whole attention, so he declined. A year later he was approached infor-
mally by Lord Salisbury, at that time Secretary of State for India, as to
his willingness to accept the bishopric of Calcutta. Bishop Wordsworth, the intermediary, told Benson that he believed this place to be
next in importance in the English Church to the Throne of Canterbury
and feared that he ought to go, 'though it will be almost like losing a
hand to part with you'. After much thought and prayer he replied to
Wordsworth, pointing out that if he and his wife went to Calcutta it
would be necessary to leave behind their six children, aged between
sixteen and four:

> Whatever other charge is offered, these six souls have been com-
> mitted to me – and after praying for light I cannot see how to leave
> them in danger of darkness. I must therefore, and without question,
> and only now wondering that such an offer should in God's pro-
> vidence have come to me so placed, say that I should not be able to
> entertain the offer of the bishopric of Calcutta.

Within a matter of months, and on a day when he had told his wife
that he had never been so happy in his life, came a letter from the
Prime Minister, Lord Beaconsfield, offering him the newly constituted
bishopric of Truro. It was thought that Benson would be offered the
bishopric of Rochester, which was also vacant, but his pioneering
spirit was needed for sorely neglected and Methodist-infested Cornwall and, after some initial hesitation, he accepted the challenge. On 1
May 1887 he was enthroned by the Bishop of Exeter in St Mary's
Church, Truro, which had been designated as the cathedral of the new
diocese. An eighteenth-century Gothic building of no great merit apart
from a fine Perpendicular south aisle, this was far removed from the
glory of Lincoln, and Benson immediately secured the appointment of
a committee to consider the kind of building that would further the
Church's mission in Cornwall and at the same time be appropriate for
the first new cathedral to be built in England since the Reformation. It
was agreed that the south aisle of St Mary's be incorporated into its
design.

Meanwhile there was a cathedral community to be founded and it
was to this that Benson devoted his address at the diocesan conference
convened soon after his enthronement. After a brief history of the
development of cathedrals and the roles of their officers, he noted that
he was empowered to appoint 24 honorary canons and to define their
duties. He proposed therefore to follow the model of Lincoln's

statutes, providing titles for the canonical stalls and appointing a sub-
dean, a precentor, a chancellor and a treasurer. Since there was no
money available, these would have to be honorary offices, and the
appointment of a dean would have to await the securing of an endowment. The existing archdeacon would rank above all the other ecclesiastics in the diocese, apart from himself; the chancellor would start a
theological college, and a missioner, attached to the cathedral, would
recruit other clergy and lay readers to spearhead evangelistic work in
the diocese. The rector of St Mary's would always be the sub-dean.

A year later he reported that ten honorary canons had been
appointed, instituted and installed. The senior among them was now
the treasurer, another was chief missioner in the diocese, while
another was the chancellor. A theological college and hostel already
had 18 students, a second clerical vicar was leading the services, and a
second archdeacon had not only been appointed but also held his
primary visitation. The county, under the Lord Lieutenant, had undertaken to raise the money for a new cathedral and it was intended to
start building a choir and transept as soon as sufficient funds became
available. This was not bad going for the first year of a new diocese
and cathedral and, while acknowledging the acute financial problems
they were facing, Benson concluded, 'We acknowledge with a thankful
heart the sympathy universally expressed towards those good works.'

John Loughborough Pearson, one of the most distinguished of the
Victorian architects, won the competition for the design of a cathedral
which, it was decreed, must be in the Gothic style. The foundation
stone was laid on 20 May 1880 by the Prince of Wales in his capacity
as Duke of Cornwall. Forms of daily prayer were compiled for use
with the workmen at the beginning and ending of their labours,
though this was later replaced by a weekly service. Demolition of the
old church began a few months later and a temporary wooden structure accommodating 400 people was erected at a cost of £430 to serve
as the cathedral until the first stage of the new building was completed.
This, consisting of the choir, transepts, two bays of the nave and the St
Mary's aisle was consecrated in 1887, some four years after Benson's
departure for Canterbury, so the wooden building had to serve for the
remainder of his time in Truro.

It was a very long way from ideal and tended to be too hot in
summer and too cold in winter, but Benson was determined that the
quality of its worship and the character of its capitular life should in
no way be inferior to that of the great, historic cathedrals. He tried to
be present at at least one service every Sunday and the honorary

canons took turns in preaching, had a voice in the chapter, and joined the residentiary canons to form a bishop's council. A 17-year-old organist, George Robertson Sinclair, was appointed to lay the foundation of the new cathedral's choral tradition. He was inevitably very much under Benson's authority – 'I was a sort of prefect', he said, 'with the bishop as headmaster' – but he built up a great reputation and, following his move to Hereford in 1889 came to be regarded as one of the outstanding organists of the late nineteenth century. At Hereford he became a close friend of Edward Elgar who dedicated one of his *Enigma Variations* to him.

Before this, however, Benson, with Sinclair's assistance, had broken more new ground by devising a Christmas service of nine lessons and carols, consisting of Bible readings tracing the path of human redemption from the creation to the incarnation, interspersed with carols and hymns. A chorister read the first lesson and other members of the cathedral community, in order of seniority, read the rest. The service was held at 10 p.m. on Christmas Eve in order to get men out of Truro's pubs. All of which was some way removed from the splendour of King's College, Cambridge, where Eric Milner-White adopted and refined the service in the 1920s and, through broadcasting, provided the rest of the world with the characteristic sounds of an English Christmas. But it began in a hut in Cornwall with Benson, as ever, demanding the highest standards and in a setting not inappropriate for the celebration of a child who was born in a stable.

In his book on the role of the cathedral Benson declared himself to be strongly opposed to the suggestion, then being made in certain quarters, that the position of bishop and dean should be combined. He believed that the bishop should be closely involved in the life of his cathedral but not responsible for its day-to-day running. At Truro, however, the lack of a decanal endowment gave him no choice (it was not until 1960 that the necessary money was found) and in the early stages of his episcopate he quite enjoyed the joint responsibility. But it was not long before the demands of establishing a new diocese in a long-neglected territory were too great for him to give sufficient attention to the life of the cathedral, and, although he was involved in all significant decision-making, he was content for the sub-dean to manage the rest.

Benson proved to be an ideal pioneering Bishop of Truro. Cornwall's history and unusual traditions appealed to the romantic and artistic side of him and he loved visiting the remote villages, which had not seen a bishop for centuries. Some of the clergy were very odd indeed, too many of them were living in debilitating poverty, and a high proportion were depressed by the lack of response to their ministries and the complete absence of pastoral care. The dynamic, caring Benson knew how to handle this and, on a number of occasions, when he sensed that a priest was in need of a holiday, sent him away for a month and moved into the parish himself. The church was then packed with people who came from far and wide to hear him preach. By this time he had also become a High Churchman and, while always getting on well with the Methodists, he was able to foster a Catholic type of church life that was distinctive and impossible to confuse with anything else on offer.

The diocesan conferences became famous for Benson's statesman-like addresses and business-like despatch of the agenda and he established ruri-decanal conferences at which clergy and laity together could discuss local church opportunities and problems. A high school for girls was established in Truro, his own daughters being among the first pupils, the maintenance of church schools was secured and extensive Sunday School work was developed throughout the diocese. Of special significance was the Guild for the Advancement of Holy Living which already existed in a small way before he arrived in Truro but which, under his leadership, became a very strong diocesan organization, with branches in many parishes. There was good reason for the description of him as a 'humming top'.

Such pioneering work cried out for further development and consolidation, but in 1883, when Benson had been at Truro for a mere six years and was aged only 53, a handwritten letter came from the Prime Minister, W. E. Gladstone, offering him the Archbishopric of Canterbury. There was nothing political about this, for Benson was a Tory, though Gladstone, the Liberal, was always keen to appoint the most able men, irrespective of their politics.

Soon after his enthronement at Canterbury Benson wrote in his journal, 'The Church of England has to be built up again from the very bottom. It is the lower and lower-middle classes who must be won.' This represented quite a lot of people but in 1891 he felt able to say, 'It is well known that throughout the country the number of those who attend church has largely increased and is still increasing.' In the absence of statistics it is impossible to judge the accuracy of this assessment but Benson obviously felt that the Church was growing. By the end of his reign, however, there were signs that the mini-revival had peaked and that the Church's growth had not kept pace with the rise in population. The working class remained alienated from church life and even if Benson had known how to tackle this problem, which is doubtful, he was far too constrained by the demands of his almost powerless office to do much about it.

Neither was he able to make a significant impact on national life through the House of Lords where, unlike his predecessor, A. C. Tait, he never felt entirely at home. A minor but lasting achievement was the wide acceptance of his suggestion that parish churches should display a list of their former rectors and vicars, partly for interest sake but mainly to demonstrate the continuity of the Church of England's life since records began in the eleventh century. The lists began to appear in Norfolk churches in the early 1880s.

St Cyprian remained his model when he moved to Canterbury and he included laymen among his advisers. This led to the establishing in 1886 of a House of Laymen to sit with the clerical Convocations, but only in a consultative capacity. For better or worse, the way was now paved for the inauguration of Synodical Government a century later. Meanwhile Benson's attempt, with Bishop Stubbs of Oxford, to amalgamate the two Convocations and the two Houses of Laymen into a single assembly failed, though the laying of the foundation stone of Church House, Westminster, in 1891 pointed to the shape of things to come.

His finest hour, however, came in 1890 with the making of what came to be known as the Lincoln judgement. Edward King, the saintly Bishop of Lincoln, had been accused by the ultra-Protestant Church Association of allowing a number of High Church practices. King was arraigned before various secular courts and eventually before the Judicial Committee of the Privy Council, which, having failed to agree, remitted the matter to the Archbishop. Benson sat in his library at Lambeth with a number of assessors and pronounced in King's favour. The judgement, which was a masterpiece of erudition, was endorsed by the Privy Council and not only permitted a degree of liturgical freedom but also asserted the Church's jurisdiction over certain aspects of its worship and discipline. R. W. Church, the revered High Church dean of St Paul's, said, 'It is the most courageous thing that has come out from Lambeth for the last 200 years.'

Edward White Benson was born in 1829 in Birmingham where his father was a white lead manufacturer. At King Edward's School he had Brooke Foss Westcott and Joseph Barber Lightfoot, both of whom became famed scholar-Bishops of Durham, as fellow pupils, but in the year when he became 14 his father died and the family business failed. A consequence of this was poverty and when young

Edward left school friends of his late father offered him openings in business. These he declined choosing instead to go to Trinity College, Cambridge, financed by a scholarship, support from relations and eventually by the generosity of the college bursar who seems to have taken a shine to him. After he had been at college for only a year both his mother and his eldest sister, Harriet, died of typhus fever, but Benson pressed on and rewarded his sponsors by securing high firsts in mathematics and classics and winning the Chancellor's Gold Medal.

He then became a master at Rugby School, was ordained and elected a Fellow of Trinity College, though he never went into residence. His teaching duties at Rugby were relatively light, but he took his position seriously and before he was ordained appeared in the chapel on Sundays clad, by his own account, in, 'light pearl grey trousers, a blue frock coat, collars which rose to the middle of the cheek, and an expansive silk tie tied in a hand knot and very much fluffed out at the ends with a wonderful ornamentation of birds like toucans or bit baskets filled with flowers, a pair of lilac gloves'. A silk Bachelor's gown and cap completed the vision. While he was at Rugby Frederick Temple, who was to succeed him as Archbishop of Canterbury, became headmaster and it was Temple who recommended him for the Mastership of the about to be born Wellington College.

Following the death of the Iron Duke in 1852 a collection was taken throughout the country to finance a national memorial. The Prince Consort presided over the enterprise and it was decided to found a new public school for the education of the sons of impecunious army officer widows. Benson was not yet 30 when he took charge of this enterprise which was officially opened, with 80 pupils, by Queen Victoria in January 1859. Even before he arrived he had got the trustees to agree that the school should not be confined by the original concept and be allowed to expand beyond the needs of poor military families. And so it did. By the time Benson left for Lincoln in 1872 Wellington College was a leading public school created by a man of genius endowed also with an amazing capacity for hard work and an obsession with detail. None of which made for popularity with either the teaching staff or the boys and, A. C. Benson wrote candidly, 'As a schoolmaster my father was, I suppose, one of the sternest and severest disciplinarians that ever ruled a school: he could inspire devoted admiration – it was admiration even more than love – but he could and largely did rule through fear.' A former pupil said, 'It was an awful sight to see the headmaster fold his gown round him and cane a liar before the school.' Yet after his final service in the college chapel the whole of the cloister was crowded with boys who cheered and put out their hands to be shaken. His face was streaming with tears – 'Goodbye, my dear, dear fellows', he said falteringly – and as he went out into the dusk there was a cry 'God bless you, Sir'.

The truth is that Benson was a manic depressive. Throughout his life intense creative activity was punctuated by bouts of melancholy and depression. As he grew older these black periods became less frequent but they never went away and inevitably affected his marriage and family life. This is a story in itself and has provided the subject for three fascinating biographical studies as well as four volumes of family memoirs. David Newsome, the biographer of A. C. Benson, suggested: 'It is possible that no family in history has written so prolifically about itself.'

The beginning can only be described as bizarre. While still at Cambridge Benson went to Clifton to stay with his widowed cousin, Mary Sidgwick, who had been left with four children. The youngest, who was named after her, was at that time aged 11. Recording the visit in his diary, Benson, who was then 23, wrote:

> As I have always been very fond of her [Mary] and she of me with the love of a little sister, and as I have heard of her fondness for me commented on by many persons, and have been told that I was the only person at whose departure she ever cried, as a child, and how diligent she has always been in reading books which I have mentioned to her, and in learning pieces of poetry which I have admired, it is not strange that I, who from the circumstances of my family am not likely to marry for years to come, and who find in myself a growing distaste for forming friendships (fit to be so called) among new acquaintances and who am fond indeed (if not too fond) of little endearments, and who knows also my weakness for falling suddenly in love, in the common sense of the word, and have already gone too far more than once in these things and have there-fore reason to fear that I might on some occasion be led [the meaning now becomes unclear] . . . it is not strange that I should have thought first of the possibility that some day dear little Minnie might become my wife.

In the same year that Benson took up his appointment at Rugby Mrs Sidgwick moved there in order to be near two of her sons who were pupils at the school and he took the opportunity to invite Minnie to accompany him on some of his regular horse rides. Soon he felt free to confess his feelings:

Let me try to recall the circumstances: the armchair in which I sat, how she sat as usual on my knee, a little fair girl of twelve with her earnest look, and how I said that I wanted to speak to her of something serious, and then got quietly to the thing, and asked her if she thought it would ever come to pass that we should be married. Instantly, without a word, a rush of tears fell down her cheeks, and I really for the moment was afraid. I told her she was often in my thoughts, and that I believed that I should never love anyone so much as I should love her if she grew up as it seemed likely. But that I thought her too young to make any promise, only I wished to say so much to her, and if she felt the same, she might promise years hence but not now. She made no attempt to promise, and said nothing silly or childish, but affected me very much by quietly laying the ends of my handkerchief together and tying them in a knot and quietly putting them into my hand.

Like her brother, Henry, who became a famous philosopher, Minnie was highly intelligent but when on 23 June 1859 she, aged 18, and Benson, aged 30, were married it seems that she knew nothing of the physical side of marriage. What appears to have been a horrendous honeymoon in Switzerland followed and when they returned it was to take up residence in the Master's Lodge at Wellington.

Minnie was never other than utterly devoted to him, and he to her. Outwardly it was a wonderfully successful marriage and at Wellington, Lincoln, Truro and Lambeth she did all, and more, than was expected of her. But it is doubtful if she ever really loved him and later she had a much closer relationship with two women, including Lucy Tait, the daughter of Benson's predecessor at Lambeth, who called her Ben, and shared her bed.

Nonetheless, she bore Benson six children. The eldest, Martin, a brilliant scholar of Winchester College died when only 17, and his father never fully got over this. Nellie, the elder of the two daughters, died in her twenties; the other, Maggie, was an archaeologist and wrote a book *Venture of Rational Faith*, but she inherited her father's depressive tendency and for the last seven years of her life was insane. Arthur, a gifted and prolific writer, wrote his father's two-volume biography and kept a diary which ran to over four million words. He became Master of Magdalene College, Cambridge, but suffered long periods of disabling melancholy. Fred, a very successful novelist, wrote over 100 books and spent much of his life on the island of Capri. Hugh, the youngest, was ordained by his father and became a monk at

Mirfield, but two years later converted to Roman Catholicism, was made a monsignor and died aged 43. None of them married.

Benson, who overworked throughout his life, was warned by a heart specialist in the early part of 1896 that unless he took a long rest and went on a diet he could not expect to live longer than two years. He found both impossible and in October that year undertook a heavy programme of engagements in Ireland. On his return he went to Hawarden to spend the weekend with Mr Gladstone and, having been with Minnie to the 8 a.m. holy communion in Hawarden church, returned after breakfast to mattins. During the Confession he suffered a major heart attack and died almost immediately. He was 67 and shortly before his death completed his monumental study of St Cyprian, remarking that everything else in his life had been but interruptions of this task.

10

The Parish Priest
William Butler, Lincoln

William Butler's tenure of the deanery of Lincoln (1885–96) was but a post-postscript to his life as one of the nineteenth century's outstanding parish priests. The market town of Wantage, in Berkshire, where he was the vicar from 1847 to 1880, was the scene of his remarkable parish ministry and no less remarkable foundation of a women's religious order which became one of the largest and most active in the Anglican Communion. He was a deeply committed High Churchman of the Tractarian school and a close friend of John Keble, but was opposed to the later Ritualists and anything that seemed likely to take the Church of England in the direction of Roman Catholicism.

William John Butler was born in the St Marylebone district of London in 1818. His father was a partner in a firm of merchants and bankers who, after some financial ups and downs, provided him with what proved to be a helpful private income. He was a Queen's Scholar at Westminster School in the 1830s and read classics at Trinity College, Cambridge where he failed to achieve honours because of his lack of aptitude for mathematics – an essential requirement of the time.

In 1841 he was ordained by Bishop Charles Sumner of Winchester to a curacy at Dogmersfield in North Hampshire. He was there for only two years but these influenced him greatly, since the scholarly rector was a friend of John Keble and John Henry (later Cardinal) Newman who often visited the parish. He also met Henry Edward (later Cardinal) Manning and Charles Marriott, both Tractarians, and espoused their cause. In 1843 he became curate of Puttenham, near Guildford, and had sole charge of the parish, in the absence of the rector. Again, his stay was brief but long enough for him to marry Emma Barnett, his second cousin, whose uncle was a canon of Windsor and who in due course presented him to the vicarage at Wantage. She also strongly supported his ministry, not least through her administrative and financial skills.

In 1844 Butler became the first vicar of the newly formed parish of Wareside in east Hertfordshire. The village had a population of only 700, but £1,800 had been expended on the building of a church to seat 400. Unfortunately nothing was left over for the erection of a parsonage so the young priest and his wife occupied a house in neighbouring Amwell. It turned out to be a challenging assignment. The largely peasant people had little knowledge of the Bible or the Christian faith and since Butler's first Sunday in the parish coincided with the Feast of the Circumcision he had some difficulty in explaining the significance of the observance. He later estimated that the congregation did not understand one in twenty of the lessons read at services and wondered why the lectionary should be used. Their failure to understand the Christian year became evident on his first Christmas Day when there were fewer in the church than on normal Sundays and those who came were in their working clothes. On Sunday mornings the congregation was comprised mainly of men – the women being at home cooking the dinner – and this led to Butler publishing a volume of *Sermons for Working Men*, the contents of which had sometimes been discussed with Keble.

It was perhaps his two years' experience at Wareside that lay behind his constant assertion that parish ministry required prayer, grind and love. Certainly these characterized his years at Wantage and were carried into his subsequent cathedral work. When his wife's uncle appointed him to Wantage in 1847 he became the first resident vicar for over 150 years. It was a fairly rich living and the patrons, the dean and canons of Windsor, had normally appointed one of their own number who employed a curate to undertake the ministry. Butler's predecessor was the Dean of Windsor who had left both the church and the parish badly neglected.

Butler's arrival came shortly after the great reforming Bishop Samuel Wilberforce had taken over the diocese of Oxford and, although Wilberforce was not as High Church as Butler, the two men got on very well and provided mutual encouragement. Market towns such as Wantage were at that time regarded as difficult places for the Church. Larger than villages, they lacked gentry and were less open to social control. Wantage's declining ropeworks had been succeeded by an iron foundry which attracted workers from further afield whose number included many who, according to the new vicar, were heathen or apathetic.

He was, however, undaunted, for he belonged to a new breed of clergymen who felt called to compete in energy and zeal with the rampant evangelicals. It was, he said, his duty to 'prepare 3,282 souls for eternity'. Butler was an austere man, driven by a sense of divine calling. His strong personality combined with enormous energy and commitment to 'Church principles' made him a formidable character who could more easily evoke fear than love. But those who came to know him, and over his 32 years at Wantage there was ample opportunity for this, discovered a deeply caring pastor whom they would admire, love and never forget.

This was specially true of his curates. There were usually two, sometimes three, of these – whose payment made considerable inroads into his own stipend – and they included some who were to become leaders among the next generation of High Churchmen – A. H. Mackonochie, V. S. S. Coles, W. C. E. Newbolt and H. P. Liddon. Liddon, the great preacher, whose sermons were to fill St Paul's, spoke for them all when he said, 'I owe all the best I know to Butler'. Wantage became a model parish in a period when the Church of England was undergoing a much-needed renewal. Its influence in the South of England was not less than that of Walter Hook at Leeds, and a detailed account of the vibrant church life is contained in Butler's parish journals now lodged in the Berkshire Record Office.

Central to Butler's ministry were the communicant classes which he started in 1848 and continued until he moved to Worcester in 1880. They were held during the week before the first Sunday of the month and before the great festivals. They included Confirmation candidates and post-Confirmation communicants and were a means of continuing instruction, based on the contents of the *Book of Common Prayer*. By the end of his ministry there were twelve such classes with a total membership of over 300. This work was accorded the highest priority. It was, he said, 'part of the campaign against evil'. Absentees were immediately visited.

The schools of the parish were visited daily and opened with prayer, and new schools were built as the number of pupils increased. When he arrived at Wantage there was a dame school for 36 children in the churchyard; when he left there were 750 in church-controlled schools. He was specially good at training young teachers and every day after breakfast held a girl pupil teachers class in his study and at 12.45 p.m. on Saturdays the staff of all the schools came to the study to report on their week's work. His standards were high and he would not tolerate what he called sloppiness, but the teachers developed a great affection for him and many of them kept in touch with him for the rest of his life.

During his first four years in the parish Butler was careful not to change any of the existing services, few as these were, and be content to add to their number. Thus he instituted a weekly celebration of the holy communion at 8 a.m. on Sundays, except on the first Sunday of the month when it was customary to have a celebration after the morning service. This he regarded as 'a very serious step' and sought the bishop's permission for it. He also started a choral mattins but abandoned this when some objections were raised. Daily services fared better and were attended by some of the older people. In 1849 he celebrated the holy communion at 4.45 a.m. on New Year's Day and Ascension Day, but the time was deemed too late for labourers going to work and when next year it was brought forward to 4 a.m. there were over 300 communicants on both days. The early years also saw the building of a small church in the nearby hamlet of Charlton, a new vicarage, a chapel for the local workhouse and a girls' school.

But there was a setback in 1852 when Butler convened a vestry meeting to consider the restoration of the interior of the parish church, which was in a sad state and unworthy of the offering of divine worship. This provided an opportunity for Dissenters and others in the town to voice their opposition to the new vicar's approach. Responding in large number to the call of the town crier they accused him of popery and by a large majority rejected his proposals. There followed a period of some difficulty but he bided his time and the scheme went forward in 1855 without opposition. There were 1,000 people in church, and over 100 robed clergy when the bishop came for the dedication. Butler's services were in fact quite austere: he wore no vestments apart from a surplice and stole, there were no candles, the daily services were sung in plainsong, and whenever he heard Confessions it was in the vicarage and never in the church.

Butler was a powerful, but hardly a popular, preacher inasmuch as he believed it to be his primary task to denounce evil and sin, rather than offer what he regarded as cheap comfort. He was in the pulpit every Sunday, gave ten-minute addresses after evensong on Tuesdays and Fridays, and biblical meditations twice a week in afternoons during Lent. None of which prevented his spending three and a half to four hours every day visiting homes in the parish. The purpose was 'to win souls for Christ' but he recognized the importance of talking about general subjects, sometimes for several years, before broaching religious matters. 'There is', he said, 'nothing more refreshing to one who has the slightest love for souls than an afternoon thus spent.' Sometimes this would extend to the early evening in order to meet the men.

Involvement in the life of the town included an assault on the sources of typhoid and the securing of an adequate water supply and drainage system. He bought a row of cottages that were unfit for human habitation, had them pulled down and replaced with new ones. Other parishioners with money were encouraged to do the same. A Penny Bank was started to encourage saving and every Saturday evening the vicar was present to express his approval. He went to the annual camp of the Berkshire Volunteers of which he was the regimental chaplain. The Parish Journal at the end of 1876 summarized Butler's policy:

> Our work then lies before us: steady persistent visiting, gaining a thorough knowledge of our people, and bringing them to know us, our motives and ends; earnest thought-out sermons and instructions in Church of every variety; inculcation of Christian duties, especially of private prayer and holy communion; watchfulness over our children to see that they are taught why they are (1) Christians, (2) Churchmen; trying by all legitimate means to win Dissenters and the careless, of whom, alas we have very many among us; preparing bright attractive services; readiness at all times and at all costs to devote and sacrifice our time, our means, and all that we have for the sake of those to whom we are sent. Nothing short of all this will be strong enough to resist the atmosphere of evil and indifferentism, of ignorance and perverseness. May God grant to us all the strength and grace we need.

Butler needed strength and grace for something more. The early Tractarians had discussed the possibility of forming Sisterhoods, after the manner of the Roman Catholic religious orders, and in 1845 Dr Pusey established a small Sisterhood in Park Village, Regents Park. On going to Wantage two years later Butler had the idea of a Sisterhood that would assist in female education, visit the sick and poor and eventually train other Sisters to go out, two by two, to teach the poor in nearby villages. The following year saw two significant developments: with the encouragement of the Bishop of Exeter, Miss Lydia Seddon founded a Sisterhood to work among the poor in Plymouth; and Archdeacon Manning sent Miss Elizabeth Lockhart to found one at Wantage. This was with Butler's enthusiastic approval and two cottages were provided to house two Sisters and two assistants. Two more cottages housed a girls' school in which the Sisters would teach.

Before long, however, Miss Lockhart, who was greatly influenced by Manning, felt drawn to abandon education work in order to establish a penitentiary in which Sisters could minister to 'fallen women'. Butler was sorry to lose their involvement in education but approved the new project and found another house for the Penitentiary, it being understood that the Sisters would be under Manning's direction. When Manning left the Church of England to become a Roman Catholic, Miss Lockhart and one of the Sisters followed him, leaving a small nucleus which came under Butler's influence and began to grow. In 1856 the Sisterhood moved into a newly built St Mary's Home and the original cottages were retained for the teaching staff of the girls' school. Five Sisters moved into the parish to form a School Sisterhood particularly concerned with education, but they had hardly settled in when the Superior and another Sister became Roman Catholics; a third died later. But Butler persevered with his vision and gave endless time to the struggling community. This continued after he had left Wantage and by the time of his death the Community of St Mary the Virgin was involved in 34 works in various parts of England and some in India – 13 with schools, nine in penitentiary work, eight in parishes and the rest in mission work. The Community also had 700 external Sisters or associates.

Not surprisingly, Bishop Wilberforce sought to use Butler's great educational expertise in the Oxford diocese. He made him a school inspector, which took him far and wide, imposing his high standards on every aspect of a school's life. He also got him deeply involved in the foundation of Cuddesdon Theological College, of which one of the Wantage curates, H. P. Liddon, became the vice-principal. Wilberforce, himself, conducted missions at various centres in the diocese and Butler was among the small group of talented priests who were asked to share in these enterprises. It was, however, left to Wilberforce's successor to make him an honorary canon of Christ Church. More pleasing to Butler was his election by his fellow clergy to the Convocation of Canterbury where his short speeches often enlivened a debate.

In 1865 Butler's life was disturbed, though his ministry at Wantage was not interrupted, by the possibility of appointment to the bishopric of Natal in South Africa. This became vacant as a result of the Archbishop of Cape Town's deposition of Bishop Colenso on the grounds of heresy. The ensuring furore dominated the church scene in England for over a year and Colenso, refusing to accept his Archbishop's jurisdiction in the matter, clung to the title and stipend of the see. Butler was in no way keen to exchange his beloved Wantage for such a hotbed of controversy but he was persuaded that it was his duty to go if elected. This, in due course, he was, but with seven clergy dissentients and there followed several months of suspense. The decision was settled for Butler when, in 1867, his name appeared at the head of a declaration on the Eucharist signed by a number of High Churchmen. Archbishop Longley of Canterbury took fright and recommended him to withdraw from Natal, which he did with mixed feelings as he had by this time reconciled himself to going. Wantage was delighted.

Three years later, while on holiday in North Germany, he was moved by the sight at Cologne of the sick and wounded victims of the Franco-Prussian War. He immediately offered to help and was sent to minister at Red Cross hospitals in France and Germany. This occupied him for several weeks until the serious illness of his senior curate required him to return to Wantage. In 1872 he became a casualty of a different sort when he was thrown out of his pony carriage in Wantage and suffered a serious spinal injury. This kept him on his back for six months but he made a good recovery and returned to carry the heavy load of the parish and the Sisterhood. By 1880, however, it was evident that the strain was telling and the Prime Minister came to the rescue by offering him one of the Crown canonries of Worcester Cathedral. Having ascertained that he could continue to use the east-ward position at the holy communion and be free to continue his work as Warden of the Wantage Sisterhood he accepted.

Nonetheless, there was no possibility of Butler treating Worcester as some sort of retirement post. Prayer, grind and love remained his formula for priestly ministry and he immediately threw himself into the life of the cathedral and the city. Communicant classes were started for the cathedral's workmen and the servants of the houses in the close, and he made a point of getting to know everyone on the staff. His appearances in the pulpit greatly strengthened the preaching and during Lent he gave two addresses every week in the lady chapel. The vigour of his style made a considerable impact and he was in demand for sermons in other parts of the diocese and further afield. During Lent 1883 he preached in five different cathedrals.

What he offered was nothing if not orthodox in its theology, though his emphasis on the divine character of the Church and the centrality of the Eucharist was news to many of his congregations. His assaults on Dissenters also enlivened any who might have been tempted to slumber. A suggestion during the early days of the Salvation Army that an attempt to divert the new movement into orthodox channels was rejected by him on the grounds that, 'their fundamental principles are opposed to Church doctrine; their fierce and dangerous enthusiasm could never be made to harmonize with our system and any attempt to accomplish this must fail'.

Butler's politics were no less conservative and, although the founder of what became an important women's religious order and a notable teacher of women, he had strong views about the place of women in society. In March 1884 he wrote from Worcester to Canon Liddon, now installed at St Paul's:

It is to my mind by far and beyond all comparison, the saddest feature of this generation, that women are claiming, and are encouraged to claim, a position which is not intended for them; and that they do not perceive the inevitable consequence, that while they can never emulate men in men's work, and can at best be poor imitators, they will lose that most grand power and influence which are really and by God's providence their own.

Here he was expressing the commonly held view of the churchmen of his time and Liddon did not disagree with him. He advised against knitting on Sundays.

Education continued to be a major concern. He led a move to found a school for the cathedral choristers and also promoted the establishing of a school for upper class girls, based on Church principles and with a first headmistress chosen by himself. Soon he was a well-known figure in the city, but he was often back in Wantage, advising the Sisters and conducting their retreats. And he retained the chaplaincy of the Berkshire Volunteers.

Butler's High Tory views did not stand in the way of a second preferment at the hands of Liberal Mr Gladstone. In 1885, aged 67, he became Dean of Lincoln and, again, he accepted on the understanding that he could maintain his connection with the Wantage Sisterhood. At first he was, like many another dean, uncertain how to move since the job was so ill-defined. And he soon discovered that his power was severely limited – confined, more or less, to the vetoing of proposed change. There was, however, no shortage of work for a dean of Butler's disposition and energy, and his influence became all pervasive.

There being only one celebration of the holy communion on Sunday, he provided another at 8 a.m. Later, he boldly re-arranged the main pattern of the cathedral's Sunday worship having endured during his early years a combination of mattins, anthem, litany, sermon and holy communion which sometime extended over two and a half hours. Mattins was shortened, the litany was transferred to 4 p.m., when it was sung with an anthem and a hymn, and evensong provided the fare for a new Sunday evening service, at which he preached once a month. This was initially strongly opposed but he persevered and eventually it was accepted as a better arrangement. The prebendaries, of whom Lincoln had a considerable number ('as common as cats', someone said) were invited to join a rota for celebrating holy communion at 8 a.m. on Thursday, the dean always being present, unless away. Holy communion with a short address was celebrated on saints days at 7 a.m. When objections were raised to holy communion on Good Friday he pointed out that this was primitive practice and prescribed by the *Book of Common Prayer*.

When he arrived at Lincoln Butler found the cathedral sanctuary poorly furnished – only one altar cloth, two brass candlesticks, but the candles were never lit, and the space very cramped. This he transformed with the aid of gifts and arrived for breakfast on his seventieth birthday to announce that he had just helped the workmen lift the new altar stone to its place. The workmen were among those he prepared for Confirmation.

He got on with everyone in both the cathedral and the city, offering warm hospitality at the deanery and interesting himself in every aspect of civic life. The austere side of his character would, however, permit him to dine out only infrequently. Relations between the cathedral and the city corporation were said to be better than ever before, he played a leading part in the foundation of the Lincoln School of Science and Art, and was often in the grammar school and the school attended by the choristers. He befriended the city curates and told the diocesan clergy that he was ready to assist them whenever they needed a hand on Sundays. Although he remained strongly opposed to the Dissenters' beliefs and ways, he enjoyed very cordial relations with them at the personal level and said that they flourished because the Church of England's clergy had neglected their duties. He was always impatient of the idleness and discontent of many of the clergy and when asked if it was permissible for a clergyman to smoke he replied, as to many other questions raised with him, 'Mr Keble never did it'.

Wantage continued to claim and refresh him – 'There is no place which I love to be in so much as my old parish' – but he began to sense that the end of his life was approaching. In 1891 he suffered another accident when he was knocked down by a cab outside Charing Cross Station and had his arm broken – 'take that man's number' was his immediate reaction to an offer of help – but he soon recovered and in

October 1883 when his wife became very ill it seemed that she might die first. On New Year's Day 1894 the choristers were invited to supper at the deanery and although Butler was his usual cheerful self, he was obviously unwell and during the next few days was confined to his room with influenza, which turned to pneumonia. He died on Sunday 14 January and his wife died a week later. The cathedral was crowded for the funeral and a contributor to his biography published three years later wrote: 'He was so entirely unlike the conventional dean'.

11

The Preacher
Frederick William Farrar, Canterbury

When in 1895 Frederick William Farrar received a letter from the Prime Minister, Lord Rosebery, offering him the deanery of Canterbury he was disappointed – and with good reason. He had been a distinguished master of Marlborough College, and for the last 20 years an outstanding rector of St Margaret's Westminster. Among England's middle class his was a household name. On their bookshelves was a work of schoolboy fiction *Eric, Or Little by Little*, the phenomenal circulation of which made it the Harry Potter of the age. Alongside the family Bible was a *Life of Christ* with gilt-edged pages, often leather bound, which also enjoyed huge sales and was probably more widely read. During the latter part of the nineteenth century no one wrote more books, of unrivalled success, than Farrar, or attracted larger congregations when preaching. Moreover he was a great parish priest in a Westminster which was still overpopulated and for the most part desperately poor. Farrar was one of the Victorian age's leading lights and should have been a bishop. The deanery of Canterbury was too little, and came too late.

The explanation of this extraordinary neglect of a great talent can be traced from his late teens when, lacking the financial resources to go to either Oxford or Cambridge, he became a student of classics and theology at King's College London. This brought him under the influence of Professor Frederick Denison Maurice whose challenge to the then traditional doctrine of eternal punishment for unrepentant sinners was soon to lead to his expulsion from the College. Farrar imbibed the teaching of the man who later came to be regarded as the nineteenth century's most original theologian and the doctrinal objections to eternal punishment were reinforced by an emotional element in Farrar's make-up which would not permit him to believe that anyone could be damned for all eternity. Later expressions of this belief in public school chapels went unnoticed but not long after his arrival at

Westminster a course of five sermons on the subject in Westminster Abbey caused a sensation. He was in fact doing no more than voicing the views of many of the theologically educated of the time, but the evangelicals did not like it, neither did the Tractarians represented by Dr Pusey and Canon Liddon. Farrar's concern with the subject was partly pastoral and partly evangelistic as this extract from one of the sermons clearly indicates:

> '*Comfort* ye, comfort ye my people, saith our God.' Son, or brother, or friend, or father dies; we have all lost them; it may be that they were not holy; not even religious; perhaps not even moral men; and it may be that, after living the common life of man, they died suddenly with no space for repentance; and if a state of sin be not a state of grace, then certainly by all rules of theology they had not repented, they were not saved. And yet, when you stood – O father, O brother – heavy hearted by their open grave; when you drank in the sweet words of calm and hope which our church utters over their poor remains; when you laid the white flowers on the coffin; when you heard the dull rattle of 'earth to earth, ashes to ashes, dust to dust'; – you, who if you knew their sins and their feelings, knew also all that was good, and sweet and amiable, and true within them – *dared* you, *did* you, even in the inmost sessions of thought, consign them as you ought logically to do, as you ought if you are sincere in that creed to do, to the unending anguish of that hell which you teach? Or does your heart, your conscience, your sense of justice, your love of Christ, your faith in God, your belief in him of whom you sing every Sunday that his mercy is everlasting, *rise* in revolt against your nominal profession then?

This offers also an example of Farrar's eloquence, and of the florid, rhetorical, exuberant and highly personal character of all his preaching. Attached to a controversial subject it could be explosive and the publication of his sermons as *Eternal Hope* did nothing to calm the debate. By the time of his death in 1903 it had run to 18 editions. Among the readers of the first edition was Queen Victoria and when, soon after its appearance, Dean Stanley died and it was suggested that Farrar should succeed him at the Abbey she confided to her friend, the Dean of Windsor: 'The Queen admires Canon Farrar, and likes him personally, but thinks he is too vehement and violent in his expressions. . . . The Queen *owns* she *would not* like to see him in our dear friend's place.' This was sufficient to deny him not only the deanery of

Westminster but also appointment to the episcopal bench, and the offer of the deanery of Canterbury when he was 64 was no more than a consolation prize.

Nonetheless, he was, after the initial disappointment, pleased to have been accorded some recognition and threw himself into the work at Canterbury. In the sermon at his installation he declared, 'What the Abbey is for the history of the English nation, that this Cathedral is for the history of the English Church' and after recounting something of its history and the famous people associated with Canterbury, he exhorted the cathedral community to maintain the highest standards of worship. Then, curiously as it may seem, he addressed the choristers:

> Never whisper together; never stare about you to right or left as you enter this holy place; never enter in a straggling or irregular manner. Let no wandering thoughts taint with worldliness or sin the prayers and praise which will be so blessed if you learn to offer them with a pure heart fervently.

He proved to be a very good friend of the choristers, taking great interest in their progress and assisting them in their next schools and beyond. Fearful that constant attendance at the cathedral's services would dull their spiritual sensitivity, he conducted a Sunday afternoon Bible class for them and took great pains over his preparation for this.

His recent predecessors had done something about the restoration of the cathedral's seriously decayed fabric but they had appealed for help only within the county of Kent, which was too poor to give much. Farrar, with his high view of Canterbury's significance, decided to appeal wider for £20,000 (over £400,000 in today's money) for urgent structural work and, without the expertise of modern fundraising methods, undertook the task himself. He wrote innumerable personal letters to prominent people and to his many friends. He also travelled the length and breadth of the country to speak about Canterbury's needs and within three years had raised over £19,000. This proved to be sufficient to put the building in good shape.

Farrar was assiduous in his attendance at the daily services and instituted a Sunday evening sermon which he usually preached himself. As in London, he attracted huge congregations and this, together with the holding of many other popular services, led to some friction with the city clergy who, not without reason, regarded him as a competitor. No famous preacher could, however, have been more generous in his acceptance of invitations to preach elsewhere – in tiny rural parishes and struggling urban churches as well as in the universities and other cathedrals. Close relations were established between the cathedral and the diocese. Church and secular organizations were encouraged to attend the cathedral on special occasions and the chapter house and the library were in constant use for meetings of one sort and another. In 1902 the honorary canons felt moved to suggest that collections for the cathedral fabric should be taken in all the parish churches of the diocese. In the cathedral itself Farrar revived a custom which had fallen into desuetude and had taken the dean and chapter down the nave after evensong on Christmas Day in order to shake hands with members of the congregation. Its revival was much appreciated and a boy wrote to his mother, 'Please God I shall be with you on Christmas Day and shake the dear dean's hand again'. Farrar was on terms of friendship with the Mayor and Corporation of Canterbury and there was hardly an organization or good cause in the city with which he was not involved. On hearing of his death, a citizen exclaimed, 'Canterbury has lost its best friend'.

This friendship also found expression in the offering of hospitality at the deanery. He and his wife kept open house and at the frequent dinner parties and 'at homes' distinguished visitors from London were mixed with local people and often sixth-formers from the King's School, whose company he always enjoyed. The move from Westminster Abbey to Canterbury had involved some financial sacrifice, since canons of Westminster were still relatively highly paid, and in a letter to Archbishop Frederick Temple in 1898 Farrar said, 'In the good old days all the canons of Canterbury had carriages; now none of them have, and even the dean cannot afford to keep a gig.' By these times, however, his children were no longer a drain on his financial resources and his literary earnings were considerable. The family felt that the final Canterbury years were probably the happiest period of his life and his relations with the chapter were always warm and quite without the difficulties experienced by Dean Alford. This was partly because the awkward canons had moved on and been replaced by more sympathetic characters. More important than this, perhaps, was something in the character of the dean. Farrar was a highly sensitive man who needed to be approved and loved. He could not bear opposition which he always took in painful, personal terms. So much so that one of his canons confessed at the time of his death that the chapter had often agreed with his proposals because they could not bear to hurt one whom they so greatly admired.

Farrar's Canterbury years were, however, but a brief episode in a remarkable ministry of extraordinary influence exercised first as a schoolmaster, then at St Margaret's, Westminster. He was born in 1831 in Bombay, where his father was a Church Missionary Society chaplain. At an early age he was sent to King William's College in the Isle of Man – a school of evangelical fervour but limited academic achievement. Young Frederick became head of the school and won most of the prizes and, by the time he was due to leave, his father had returned to England to become curate in charge of a church in Clerkenwell. It was from there that the 16-year-old started as a day student at King's College, London, from where, having secured a first in classics and theology, he went on a scholarship to Trinity College, Cambridge. His entire education was paid for by scholarships and cost his impecunious parents nothing. At Cambridge he eschewed all forms of sport, worked hard and was near the top of the list of those who obtained firsts in both the classical and the mathematics tripos. He also won several prizes, including the Chancellor's Medal for English Verse for a characteristically Victorian and unmemorable poem.

Even before his results had been announced he was appointed an assistant master at Marlborough College. There he proved to be a brilliant teacher of the sixth form and, being more humane than most of the schoolmasters of that time, was much loved by the boys. He was ordained in Salisbury Cathedral on Christmas Day 1853 and, at next to no notice, prevailed upon to preach in the local workhouse on the afternoon of that day. He described his sermon as 'a dead failure'. His stay at Marlborough was short, for in 1855 he was enticed to Harrow as an assistant master, later becoming a house master. During the next 15 years his achievements in the school and beyond it were astonishing. He was elected to a Fellowship of Trinity College, Cambridge, in 1856 and two years later, when aged only 27, published *Eric, Or Little by Little*, the fictionalized school story that made his name echo throughout the English-speaking world. It ran to 36 impressions during his lifetime, was reprinted for some years after his death – most recently in 2003, though by this time it was interesting only as a period piece.

A period piece it most certainly was. Published just a year after the appearance of *Tom Brown's Schooldays*, it did not claim to be true to life. It was, however, partly autobiographical in that Roslyn School, attended by Eric, was clearly based on King William's College. Highly idealized, it was the story of the battle for Eric's soul and combined emotion and morality in a heady brew which Victorians found irresistible. Little by little Eric's innocency was lost as he succumbed to temptation in a world where every detail of life was seen as important in the light of eternity. One day a master passed by without returning Eric's salute. 'What a surly devil that is', remarked Eric to a fellow pupil, 'did you see how he purposely cut me?' 'Oh Eric', came the reply, 'that's the first time I ever heard you swear.' 'Eric blushed', the author tells us, 'and that night knelt at his bedside and prayed as he had not done for many a day. And here let those scoff who deny the sinfulness of little sins.' In the background there is thinly veiled homosexuality and after a boy had said something indecent in the dormitory Eric felt challenged – 'Now Eric, now or never! Life and death, ruin and salvation, corruption and purity, are perhaps in the balance together, and the scale of your destiny may hang on a single word of yours. Speak out boy!'

Eric's failures and the surprisingly frequent appearance of the Grim Reaper in the school make the story a real tear-jerker and not least at the ending when Eric flees from the school in disgrace, following a false accusation of theft against him, and learns of the death of his little brother, Vernon, after falling over a cliff, and the imminent demise of his mother in India who cannot cope with the news of death and disgrace. There is only one course open to Eric – he must die, too.

'Oh, I have killed her, I have killed my mother!' said Eric, in a hollow voice, when he came to himself. 'Oh God, forgive me, forgive me!' They gathered round him: they soothed and comforted and prayed for him; but his soul refused comfort, and all his strength appeared to have been broken down at once like a feeble reed. At last a momentary energy returned; his eyes were lifted to the gleaming heaven where a few stars had already begun to shine and a bright look illuminated his countenance. They listened deeply – 'Yes, mother', he murmured in broken tones, 'forgiven now for Christ's dear sake. Oh thou merciful God! Yes, there they are and we shall meet again. Verny – oh, happy, happy at last – too happy!' The sounds died away and his head fell back; for a transient moment more the smile and brightness played over the fair features like a lambent flame. It passed away, and Eric was with those he dearliest loved, in the land where there is no more curse.

There could be no clearer evidence of the vast cultural change that had taken place in England since the mid-nineteenth century than the existence of this book and its huge readership, though even at the time of its publication there were literary critics who complained that it was well over the top. Encouraged by its success, however, Farrar immediately penned another volume, *Julian's Home: A Tale of College Life*, based on his experience at Trinity College, Cambridge, and two years later *St Winifred's or the World of School* (which owed something to the life at Marlborough and Harrow). Again the high moral purpose of the author was apparent and, although neither book created quite the same stir as *Eric*, the first had 18 impressions and the second 26.

Fiction was, however, only a sideline. Farrar was something of a polymath and an *Essay on the Origin of Language* (1860) followed by *Chapters on Language* (1865) so impressed Charles Darwin, because of its evolutionary approach, that he nominated him for the Fellowship of the Royal Society. Lifelong friendships with Darwin, T. H. Huxley and other leading scientists followed. Farrar taught classics brilliantly and, becoming impatient with the old Greek Primer, produced two replacements which were soon accepted as standard textbooks. At the same time he grew increasingly concerned about the limitations of an exclusively classical education in the modern world and gave expression to this in a lecture to the Royal Institution in 1867. A Royal Commission had recently reached the same conclusion but Farrar's handling of its findings brought much greater publicity and as a result a committee, on which he served, was set up to make provisions for a revised curriculum that would include the sciences, modern languages, geography, music and drawing. Gradually the new curriculum was adopted by all the public schools.

As at Marlborough, Farrar's kindness and evident concern for the welfare of the boys made him much loved but he could be stern and sometimes scathing – 'How many centuries have elapsed since your boots were last cleaned?' he would ask. 'Your ignorance is so profound that it ossifies the very powers of scorn' was another of his long-remembered criticisms. He also exercised very great influence through his sermons in the college chapel, many of which were subsequently published, and, although classics was his main subject, he introduced his pupils to the delights of English literature, of which he had an encyclopaedic knowledge. And he even found time to marry 19-year-old Lucy Mary Cardew who bore him five sons and five daughters and provided just the kind of sympathetic, yet stimulating, family life he needed.

During the final year at Harrow he embarked on the major literary task of his career *The Life of Christ*, having first spent four months in

Palestine to master the geography and imbibe the atmosphere of the setting of the Gospels. His 1870 Hulsean Lectures on *The Witness of History to Christ* had also done some necessary spadework. He completed the project in four years, which included his move to be Master of Marlborough College in 1871, and when it appeared in 1874 it was a runaway success. Twelve impressions were needed during the first year and by the time of his death 30 impressions had been sold. It was translated into every European language, Russian and Japanese, and a pirated edition sold widely in America. Unfortunately, he had undertaken to write the book for a fee, rather than for royalties, and the publisher, who had conceived the project, was by a long way the chief beneficiary.

The character of the work may be judged by the fact that it is over three times longer than the Gospels themselves. Creating a continuous narrative from the dislocated Gospel material, it consists of a paraphrase, a commentary and a good deal of hortatory material. It makes no attempt to deal with the critical problems that were being voiced at the time of its writing, though Farrar shows his awareness of them, neither does it doubt the possibility of finding the historical Jesus. Its length is not unrelated to its author's purple prose. He doesn't use one word when half a dozen will do. All that acknowledged, it is impossible to withhold admiration for a very remarkable achievement. Had it represented the life work of a full-time scholar it would have won applause; that it was accomplished in four years by a very industrious schoolmaster beggars belief. Intended primarily for the layman, but also for the parish clergyman – there is a wealth of engraved illustrations – it displays immense erudition and even today offers invaluable insights into the ministry and message of its subject. The temptation to dismiss it as unscholarly popularization of Christianity's foundation texts must be tempered by the knowledge that at the time of its publication it was warmly approved by J. B. Lightfoot and B. F. Westcott – two of England's greatest New Testament scholars.

The *Life* proved to be the first in a sequence of studies of Christian origins. It was followed by *The Life and Work of St Paul, Darkness and Dawn: A Tale of the Days of Nero* and *Lives of the Fathers: Church History in Biography* – all of which had many impressions. Over the course of his ministry Farrar published no fewer than 75 books, of which 61 appeared in American editions, and the last of which *The Life of Lives: Further Studies in the Life of Christ* was completed in 1900 shortly before a final, cruel illness robbed him of the power to write.

His Mastership of Marlborough College was fairly brief (1871–6) but nonetheless notable. G. G. Bradley, who later became Dean of Westminster in preference to Farrar, had left the school in good order but scarlet fever had taken its toll of numbers and renewal was needed. The new Master's fame soon took care of this. He had the drainage improved, got the governing body to buy the freehold of the land on which the college stood, built two new houses, appointed a science master, and decorated the chapel. Within the chapel his sermons were eagerly awaited and long remembered – most of all the one he gave shortly before the college was due to play at Lord's its chief cricket rival, Rugby. The subject was 'Moral Collapses' – a Farrar favourite – and after a pause at the close he added, 'And a defeat in cricket may be due to a collapse – to a moral collapse'. Marlborough won.

Soon after his arrival at the College Farrar was appointed as a chaplain to the Queen – an unusual honour for a schoolmaster – and throughout his time there it was widely anticipated that before long he would be claimed for high office in the Church. In 1875 he was offered the Crown living of Halifax – an important, well-paid post and a parish which was expected, wrongly, to become the centre of a new bishopric. After much thought and consultation he declined, and in the following year accepted the Rectory of St Margaret's, Westminster, which was annexed to a canonry of the next-door Abbey. At the time of his appointment the life of St Margaret's was at a low ebb. There had been talk of demolishing the church to allow a new underground railway to pass beneath the site. Its historic role as the parish church of the House of Commons had fallen into desuetude and, although it was still attended by a handful of influential people, it was quite out of touch with the 20,000 and more poor people who lived in the surrounding tenements. The fabric of the church was in a neglected state and Farrar was horrified by the gloomy Georgian furnishings which obscured the elegant beauty of the early sixteenth-century interior.

He tackled this with characteristic vigour and, having raised £30,000 for the purpose, had the huge galleries and the box pews removed, a false apse taken down, ugly memorials transferred to a room in the tower and the walls stripped of plaster. Stained-glass windows were installed to commemorate events and people associated with St Margaret's. The transformation was astonishing, and acknowledged to be for the better, though the despatching of a beautiful two-decker pulpit to a church in Kent was a great and unnecessary loss, and not all of the stained glass was worth having. Before long Farrar's sermons, delivered in a rich voice from a new, rather mean, stone pulpit, were attracting congregations of 1,000 and more, with every inch of standing space occupied. On the Sunday of a national church attendance census the congregations at St Margaret's were larger than at either the Abbey or St Paul's and if Farrar was preaching in the Abbey on Sunday evenings a notice 'Abbey Full' directed the overflow to St Margaret's.

On the last Sunday of 1876 the Prime Minister, Disraeli, who was responsible for Farrar's appointment, caught up with Dean Stanley while walking down Whitehall. His mind was full of matters related to the fact that Queen Victoria was about to be proclaimed Empress of India but he expressed a wish to go to the Abbey to hear Farrar preach. Stanley explained that it would be too late to find him a seat but the two men went into the Abbey unrecognized and climbed on to the pedestal of a monument to catch a glimpse of the preacher. Farrar was in the midst of an eloquent passage about the length of eternity and the ageing Prime Minister could not hear very well but as they came away told Stanley, 'I would not have missed the sight for anything. . . . Fifty years ago there would not have been 50 persons there.' The sermons, which were fully scripted but delivered as if extempore, occupied Farrar for four to five hours' preparation every week, and either in Westminster or elsewhere, for he was in great demand, he gave about 120 every year. Herbert Hensley Henson, who was Farrar's successor but one at St Margaret's, offered in his journal a characteristically pungent verdict:

> Farrar was at once the most popular and the most criticized of Anglican preachers. A persistent but unmerited suspicion of doctrinal unsoundness alienated the most orthodox churchmen. The exuberance of his rhetoric offended fastidious hearers. But the multitude of churchgoers devoured his books, and crowded to his sermons. It would perhaps be true to say that his wide learning and genuine intellectual power were obscured, rather than commended, by the Asiatic richness of his literary style, and the purple rhetoric of his preaching.

It was nonetheless of the greatest benefit to the Church of England that there should have been at Westminster for a short overlapping period A. P. Stanley and F. W. Farrar – the leading exponents of religious tolerance and theological liberty. Farrar's impact in America, made during a four months' preaching tour in 1885, was tremendous and,

wonder of wonders, he found time to deliver in Oxford in the following year a course of Bampton Lectures on *The History of Interpreta-
tion*.

Neither was the pastoral work in the parish neglected. The bulk of
this was carried out by a team of five curates who reported to him
every week on their activities in the back streets and handed over to
him any pastoral problems that called for his personal attention. A
team of 50 lay visitors augmented the work of the curates and a
mission church was erected to accommodate those of the poor who
could not find room in St Margaret's or would not in any case have
felt at home there. Farrar's experience of working in the more disorderly parts of the parish drove him into active membership of the
Temperance movement – a cause which he espoused for the remainder
of his life. Normally less disorderly was the House of Commons which
was encouraged to make greater use of what had been its parish
church since 1614. Special services were held at the beginning of
Parliamentary years and on national occasions, the Speaker was allocated a special pew at the front of the nave and behind him on Sunday
mornings many pews were occupied by Members and officials of the
House.

In 1890 Farrar became the first rector of St Margaret's to be
appointed Speaker's Chaplain and during the next five years conducted the daily prayers and was a highly valued pastor and friend to
many in an unusual community. There was in fact hardly anyone of
influence in the capital whom he did not know. Besides his long-
standing friendships with the leading scientists of the day, his literary
gifts gave him an acknowledged place among the artists and friendship
with poets such as Wordsworth and Browning, and now he knew all
the politicians. But no amount of influence could secure for him the
bishopric for which he pined. It may be argued that desire for a place
on the episcopal bench is not a sign of spiritual health, though the confession of a calling to the priesthood has never been despised, and
when Farrar and his friends and admirers saw men with only a small
fraction of his gifts raised to high office they were entitled to wonder if
the best interests of the Church were being served by the neglect of his
claim.

The final years at Canterbury were, however, by no means wasted,
though they ended prematurely and sadly. In 1899, when he was 68,
something akin to muscular dystrophy robbed him of the use of his
right hand, so that he could no longer write. Gradually it spread to his
left hand, then to his neck, causing his head to droop. His mental

faculties were unimpaired and he could dictate a sermon to a secretary, though he needed a King's School pupil to turn the pages for him in the pulpit. In the end he had to be carried into the cathedral services and at the enthronement of Randall Davidson, one of his Harrow pupils, as Archbishop of Canterbury in 1903 he was present but too feeble to take any part in the service. He died later that year, and those who witnessed his courageous and uncomplaining acceptance of suffering found it to be an even more powerful witness to the Christian faith than any of his books and sermons had been. Among his grandsons was Viscount Montgomery of Alamein – a hero of the 1939–45 war – whose father had been a curate at St Margaret's, Westminster, and married one of Farrar's daughters.

12

The Rosarian
Samuel Reynolds Hole, Rochester

The popularity of the rose in English gardens owes a great deal to Samuel Reynolds Hole, who was Dean of Rochester from 1887 until his death in 1904. During the early years of the nineteenth century roses were not widely cultivated and were generally confined to the shrub and climbing varieties. But as the century advanced the bush tea rose became attractive for smaller gardens and increased skill in hybridization led to the creation of many new and beautiful species. Before he became a dean, Hole was for 37 years both vicar and squire of the small Nottinghamshire parish of Caunton and in the spacious garden of his manor house planted 1,027 roses in 434 varieties.

In 1858 he organized at a cost of £200 the first National Rose Show in London and was largely responsible for the founding of the National Rose Society, which still awards a Dean Hole Medal. Later in the century he was President of a National Rose Conference held in Chiswick. Most influential, however, was his *A Book about Roses* which was full of hints for ordinary gardeners about the growing and showing of roses. Published in 1869, this was reprinted 11 times in six months and was still in print in 1896 when a revised edition was called for.

Until the publication of this book Hole was little known outside Nottinghamshire and the small world of rose-growing specialists. But thereafter he was in great demand for judging at rose shows all over the country and also as a preacher and conductor of missions. At one point he was receiving over 400 speaking and preaching invitations a week and towards the end of his life he claimed to have preached in more than 500 different churches and virtually all the cathedrals – 50 times in St Paul's. Missions in Hull, Reading, Northampton, Norwich, Nottingham, East London and many other industrial towns lasted a week or more, and several days of lectures in Truro seems to have caused something of a sensation. In a most effusive thank-you letter afterwards, the bishop – Edward White Benson – professed his love of Hole and added that many ladies were deeply disappointed that they had lacked opportunity to shake his hand. Church attendance in the area increased dramatically.

Standing over six foot three inches tall, Hole had a commanding presence and a loud, raucous voice that enabled him to be heard with ease in the largest buildings and the open air. He laid no claim to intellectual gifts and there was an artless simplicity about his understanding of the Christian faith and the meaning of life. A great raconteur, he never failed to discern a moral lesson in any incident or experience and his warm, friendly manner, combined with a larger than life personality, made him specially popular at gatherings of working men. They were even prepared to sing, to a tune specially composed by Sir John Stainer, his hymn 'Sons of Labour', which found a place for a time in *Hymns Ancient and Modern* and begins:

> Sons of Labour, dear to Jesus,
>   To your homes and work again;
> Go with brave hearts back to duty,
>   Face the peril, bear the pain.
> Be your dwellings mean and lowly,
>   Yet remember by your bed,
> That the Son of God most Holy
>   Had not where to lay his head.

Hole's own duties took him frequently to the Trent Bridge cricket ground at Nottingham where he was on terms of friendship with most of the county players and where he learned a lesson which he felt impelled to share with a meeting of mechanics:

> Cricket is the first of all games: auxiliary to the noblest and most sacred purposes of life, to morality and to religion, helpful to temperance, manliness, self-command, obedience, endurance and unity.

Football was less to his liking, though he once preached to 1,400 members of football clubs in St Mary's Church, Nottingham, and presented prizes and cups at a large gathering of sportsmen on the Notts County football ground. A lecture 'The Vulgar Tongue', repeated many times during the 1870s and '80s on behalf of charities, consisted of a lengthy analysis, in alphabetical order, of misused words and rustic words peculiar to Nottinghamshire. Read today, this lecture seems unbearably tedious, but at the time of its delivery it was apparently much enjoyed.

Appointment to the deanery of Rochester came in 1887 when he was 68, but still full of energy, and during the next 17 years he achieved a great deal. On hearing the news of his appointment from the Prime Minister, Lord Salisbury, Archbishop Benson, now a dear friend, wrote, 'You will care for the Church and you will care for the souls of men. And we shall have no pettiness. *Deo Gratias.*' It is not apparent whether Benson, in this opaque message, was urging the new dean to avoid pettiness or simply rejoicing in his belief that with Hole there would be no pettiness. Certainly there could be no doubt as to his concern for the souls of men and, besides his immediate cathedral responsibilities, he threw himself into mission work among Rochester's sailors, soldiers and dockyard workers. Popular preaching services, with himself in the pulpit, were arranged in the cathedral and he soon began to make an impact on the Medway towns. 'When Dean Hole continued his series of discourses upon the Career of the Prodigal Son', *The Chatham and Rochester News* reported on 4 August 1888, 'the Nave of Rochester Cathedral was again crowded to its limits on Sunday evening – fully 1,000 persons being present.'

Yet, although he was by now a well-known national figure, he always steered well clear of controversy and the contentious issues of the day. His outlook was essentially conservative and on one of the few occasions when he wrote to *The Times* it was to express the hope that the historic formularies of the Church would not be replaced by 'the views of German commentators, the scribes and disputers of the twentieth century, magazines and encyclopaedias'. He also took the opportunity to deplore the fact that at fashionable London weddings there was a growing reluctance to use the blunt language of the Prayer Book marriage service, and a desire for what called 'a short sentimental address'.

In the cathedral pulpit and elsewhere his own sermons were marked by fervour and an earnest desire to convince the congregation of the basic simplicity of the Christian faith. They were not to fancy that it was something remote from them, or strained or difficult. His use only of notes dated from an occasion during his early years at Caunton when his practice of reading his sermons was disturbed by an early failure of the light one Sunday afternoon. Completing the sermon in the semi-darkness without the aid of the script proved to be easier than he had ever imagined and thereafter he relied only on a few notes – to the great benefit of his style, it was said. He used to tell how the curate of a neighbouring parish had been moved in the same direction when his landlady's puppy chewed part of his sermon shortly before mattins.

Fundraising for the restoration of the cathedral was urgently necessary but by no means easy and occupied a lot of Hole's time. Nonetheless, he managed to get the west front and the crypt restored, the choir screen decorated and vestries built. Then towards the end of his life came out of the blue a gift of £5,000. He asked the donor if part of this might be used for the repair of the organ which was in a sad state of decay and the response was a further 500 guineas, conditional upon 1,000 guineas being raised by public subscription. This was, Hole said, 'one of the most memorable and happy days of my life'. The initial gift could now be used for remedial work on the tower and small, blunt spire – a fourteenth-century structure which had been deformed by a botched rebuilding in the mid-nineteenth century. Additional funds for this were provided by the Freemasons, Hole being the Grand Chaplain of the Grand Lodge of England. Unfortunately he did not live long enough to see the work completed, but from the deanery garden, in which he had planted 135 varieties of rose, he saw during the final weeks of his life the re-built tower rising.

Reynolds Hole (he was always known by his second Christian name) was born in 1819 in Ardwick, near Manchester, his father pursuing at that time his successful business interests. Before long, however, the family returned to their ancestral home at Caunton, six miles from Newark, where back in 1537 the vicar was Hugh Hole. Young Reynolds was brought up in a manor known throughout Nottinghamshire as 'a house of sport', such was the preoccupation of its residents with fox-hunting, partridge-shooting and fishing. The future dean's interest in gardening started when he was only 13 and a full generation before it became a popular pursuit in England. It was in the friable Nottinghamshire clay of the large manor garden that his roses would one day flourish. Meanwhile he attended a small prep school, from which he moved to Newark Grammar School. His chief recollection of his schooldays was a celebratory day off following the election of the young W. E. Gladstone for the Newark parliamentary constituency.

Naturally, he was with his family in the squire's pew at Caunton church every Sunday and he lived long enough to experience and to play a small part in the remarkable transformation of the Church of England's life that took place during the second half of the nineteenth century. He left a graphic account of church life at Caunton during the late 1830s. The vicar was an absentee and the curate, who lived five miles away, came every Sunday to conduct a dreary service. This consisted mainly of a duet between the parson and the parish clerk, relieved only when an aged bricklayer gave a note on his bassoon, 'sounding like an elephant in distress', for the hymn. The altar consisted of a rickety deal table covered by a patched and faded green baize cloth, and on this the curate placed his overcoat, hat and riding whip. The font, which was never used for baptism, was filled with coffin ropes, brimstone matches and candle ends. Sparrows twittered and bats floated beneath the rotten timbers of the roof, while beetles, moths and flies made themselves at home below. 'There were cushions for the rich and bare benches for the poor', reported Hole, 'and the darkest and most dismal building of the parish was that called the House of God.' It was locked during the week.

His own Confirmation at Newark was somewhat livelier though hardly less deplorable. It was conducted by the Archbishop of York, Vernon Harcourt, who chanced to be passing through the town when travelling to London. Hole recalled that he was a tall, aristocratic-looking man who wore a wig. The infrequency of a Confirmation brought crowds of candidates from the surrounding villages, but with little or no preparation. There was much irreverence and levity both inside and outside Newark parish church and Hole considered it to be more like a fair than the administration of a Christian sacrament. In due course he went to Brasenose College, Oxford with, he hoped, a real prospect of securing a first. And for the first two terms he worked hard, but then came the fateful day when he spotted a fellow under-graduate crossing the quad, clad in 'a black velvet coat and scarlet cap, a bird's eye blue tie, buff keyseymere waistcoat, buckskin breeches and pale brown gloves'. The temptation was too great: he immediately went off to buy a horse and sent home for his hunting pink. And that was the end of his academic ambitions. He did, however, leave the chase on Sundays to hear Newman, Keble and Pusey preach and, although he never openly identified himself with the Tractarian Movement, he emerged from Oxford as a reforming High Churchman.

The Bishop of Lincoln's modest academic requirements were met without too much difficulty and in 1844 he was ordained to the curacy of his home parish with an above average stipend of £100 per annum. For the first time in over a century Caunton had a resident priest. The death in 1850 of the absentee vicar opened the way for Hole's succession to the benefice and on the death of his father he also became the squire. For the next 37 years he was the epitome of the sporting 'squarson', but also a diligent parish priest. A weekly celebration of holy communion was started, there were two sermons every Sunday, and daily services were announced by the ringing of the church bell. After the building of a school he recruited six boys to form a choir, which sang Venite and a hymn at the daily mattins, then he accompanied them back to school for a period of teaching. A gallery was erected to accommodate the Sunday choir and the church band, which was eventually replaced by an organ – a move that Hole came to regret. Children's services were conducted with the assistance of posters and other visual aids and, following the example of Parson Hawker of Morwenstowe, the Harvest Festival was instituted. Hole insisted, however, that the church service of thanksgiving should not replace the traditional Harvest Home at which the labourers received their roast beef and plum pudding, had a glass of good beer, smoked their pipes and sang songs – 'all within the limits of becoming mirth'. His tolerance did not, however, extend as far as the Primitive Methodists whom he described as 'bumptious, self righteous, and bitter enemies of the church'. A Methodist preacher caught poaching was admonished. 'You may encroach my spiritual, but I won't have you on my earthly ground.'

The church in Caunton came alive and flourished without any impediment to its vicar's many other interests inside and outside the parish. These included membership of the Royal Sherwood Archers and the chaplaincy of the local Yeomanry. His reputation as a gardener brought friendships with leading horticulturalists in France and Italy and an invitation to edit the 1851 *Gardeners' Annual*. This and a close friendship with John Leech, a notable early Victorian illustrator, took him into London's literary circle where friendships were established with W. M. Thackeray, Edward Lear, and the painter Millais. He was elected to the Garrick Club and for many years was a member of the exclusive *Punch* table, though his wit was not quite sharp enough to merit more than occasional contributions to the magazine's columns. *The Six of Spades* (1872) – a general book about gardening, based on an imaginary club of six gardeners – was an immediate success and remained in print for the remainder of the century. *Hints to Preachers* (1880) included specimens of his own sermons and addresses.

Like many other Victorian churchmen, Hole was deeply concerned about what he described as 'the three evils of our time' – drinking, betting and horse racing. But he was unusual in his advocacy of

moderation, rather than total abstention, and shocked a Church
Congress in 1890 by warning, 'I am not sanguine of grand results from
a cannonade against raffles and bazaars.'

Hole's admiration for his bishop, Christopher Wordsworth, knew
no bounds and he was proud of his appointment as one of Archbishop
Benson's honorary chaplains. His association with these two prelates,
and his membership of the English Church Union and the Con-
fraternity of the Blessed Sacrament, occasioned a little local difficulty,
however, when in 1886 he sought election as a Proctor in Convocation
for the newly created diocese of Southwell, in which Caunton
was now located. At a crowded election meeting in Nottingham his
opponents accused him of being a Ritualist and a Romanizer, but he
could have never been anything other than a most loyal Church of
England priest and demonstrated his commitment to the *via media* by
denouncing Papal supremacy and announcing that he had never
accepted an invitation to preach in a church where holy communion
was celebrated in the evening. He was elected by 200 votes to 136.

Appointment to the modest deanery of Rochester was a fitting conclusion to his picturesque ministry and was welcomed by the *Church
Times* which predicted that the new dean would stir Rochester out of
its lethargy by the brilliance of his oratory. The official stipend of
£2,000 per annum was never achieved during Hole's time owing to the
decline in agricultural rents, so literary earnings were important for
his solvency and for the sustaining of the generous hospitality for
which he was famed. A volume of memories, well laced with moral
opinion on a variety of subjects, makes heavy reading today, but was
quickly reprinted and helped to pay the bills. So also did *Our Garden*
published in 1899. An avid letter writer – a volume of his letters was
published after his death – he never forsook his quill pen.

As a dean, Hole retained the style of the parish priest which he had
been for so long, and won the admiration of the Bishop of Rochester,
Anthony Thorold, who had his own exacting pastoral standards.
There were, however, conflicts with a member of the chapter, Canon
Cheyne, who adopted the new methods of biblical criticism and in a
cathedral sermon in 1891 created a local stir by suggesting that the
David and Goliath story was a myth. Hole complained about this to
the bishop (now Randall Davidson) and when Cheyne made his
defence he described the dean as 'an old man, frank, impulsive and
injudicious who was brought up from a country rectory, where he
never absorbed any new facts or ideas in theology'. Yet until the end
of his life Hole was a popular national figure and on his eighty-fourth

birthday, not long before his death, he received over 100 letters, post-cards and telegrams, including one from the cabmen at London's Waterloo station.

13

The Scholar
Joseph Armitage Robinson, Westminster

A Spy cartoon of Joseph Armitage Robinson, published during his time as Dean of Westminster (1902–11), was captioned 'An Erudite Dean', and the accuracy of this was confirmed by a member of his chapter, Herbert Hensley Henson, who later described him as 'a walking arsenal of sacred erudition'. During his 18 years as a Fellow of Christ's College, Cambridge, for the last six of which he was also the Norris Hulse Professor of Divinity, he was an associate of Lightfoot, Westcott and Hort – the three greatest names in English New Testament scholarship – and became an international authority on Christian origins.

With obsessive zeal, and sometimes the manner of a recluse, he spent long hours on the study of ancient manuscripts, publishing the fruits of his work in learned journals and books such as *A Collation of the Athos Codex of the Shepherd of Hermas* and *The Gospel According to Peter* and *The Apocalypse of Peter* – both dating from the second century. At Westminster the dean's verger, who was also his man-servant at the deanery, reported that every night at 10 o'clock he took to the dean's study all that was required for making several cups of tea and a large supply of cigarettes:

> The dean would then place what books he wanted on the floor in front of the fire, for he had the habit of crawling about his study from one book to the other. He rarely retired until well after midnight, and often I heard him going to his room at 5 a.m. and sometimes later. He smoked at least 50 cigarettes in the night. He would remain in bed until about 11 most mornings. I had to place his clothes in proper order for putting on and I am sure if I had made a mistake by putting his gaiters on top of the pile he would have put them on first. I had to take care that he had money in his pockets.

Erudition and eccentricity were accompanied by an arresting appearance. Henson described him as 'Tall, spare, a countenance of striking dignity, a slow and impressive manner of speaking and an air of almost monastic remoteness. He looked a successor of the medieval Abbots and was a magnificent figurehead.'

What more could be required in a dean? Just one thing: the ability to work with other people, and this Robinson conspicuously lacked. Like many other gifted human beings, his personality was lop-sided and he was the archetypal loner. Such personalities are by no means uncommon in capitular bodies but Robinson's autocratic style exercised in the company of distinguished Westminster canons like Henson was never going to make for peace. Men of this sort were not prepared to act as decanal ciphers and abandon the authority and responsibilities with which they believed themselves to have been entrusted by the Church.

Their chief complaint was that they were not sufficiently consulted over a wide range of matters relating to the Abbey's life, particularly over the matter of appointments. Even when he sought their advice, he rarely followed it and seemed hostile to his intellectual equals. Robinson, for his part, believed the Dean of Westminster to have been entrusted with much greater authority than that held by cathedral deans, and his belief was supported by the Royal Charter granted to the Abbey by Queen Elizabeth in 1560. While reserving to herself and her successors the right of appointing future deans and prebendaries, the dean was empowered to make all appointments to 'inferior' offices, and also given powers of discipline and dismissal. A draft book of statutes went further: 'Let there be one Dean, the Governor of the whole College even as the mind is in the body. To his authority all the others are to be obedient.' This, it might be thought, left no room for argument, but Henson and his fellow canons found plenty. They pointed out that the statutes were no more than a draft document, almost certainly compiled by William Bill, the first dean, and never signed by the Queen. This, it appears, was no oversight on her part, since she failed to sign statutes for Peterborough and Canterbury Cathedrals in spite of the pleading of the bishop and the Archbishop.

In the absence of undisputed authority the power of the Dean of Westminster must therefore (argued the canons) rest on custom. On 24 July 1905 it was resolved in Chapter that Canons Henson and Beeching should prepare a statement showing how, in practice, relations between the dean and the chapter had been conducted since the sixteenth century. In spite of the magnitude of this undertaking the historical statement was presented to a special chapter meeting in December of that year, together with two essays by the dean. Predictably, the evidence was inconclusive. No fewer than nine deans had also been Bishops of Rochester and not troubled themselves overmuch with the affairs of the Abbey. Until the nineteenth-century reforms the prebendaries had often been absentee pluralists, appearing in the Abbey only to fulfil their periods of residence and to ensure that they received their due share of the capitular revenues. The concept of the dean and chapter working corporately to determine how the Collegiate Church might respond to the demands and opportunities of a changing world was entirely new and for this the past customs provided little assistance. The canons also argued that, if the dean had as much power as he claimed for his office, this left the chapter with no worthwhile function.

So the strife continued unabated and unedifyingly for another five years. In 1908 Henson, Beeching and Duckworth, the sub-dean, appealed to the King to settle the matter 'in order to end friction'. The King asked the Lord Chancellor to act for him and in 1911 it was announced that the statutes had no legal authority and that the College was governed by custom and by the authority of royal letters (which had been issued from time to time), but that where the custom was not clear or continuous the statutes had weight of evidence of what the ancient custom presumably was. The Lord Chancellor also decreed that the dean ought to be treated as the Ordinary which gave him control of interments, the erection of monuments, and the use of the Abbey for purposes other than statutory services.

This was favourable to Robinson, but by now he had had enough and, although the coronation of King George V in which he was heavily involved was only a few months away, he seized the opportunity to move to the tranquillity of the deanery of Wells, where he married and lived happily ever after. But most, if not all, of the unhappiness of his Westminster years would have been avoided had he understood the meaning of compromise and been prepared to collaborate with his colleagues.

He was born, the fourth of 13 children, in 1858 at Keynsham near Bath, where his Irish father was the vicar. Movement to a poor parish in Everton led to young Armitage's enrolment at Liverpool College where the headmaster, George Butler, was the husband of Josephine Butler, the pioneering social worker now commemorated in the Church of England's calendar. He went as a scholar to Christ's College, Cambridge, carried all before him and ended as fourth

Classic and second Chancellor's Medallist. Ordination and election to a Fellowship of the College followed. By this time Lightfoot had left Cambridge to become Bishop of Durham and he invited Robinson to work for a time in a Sunderland parish before becoming his domestic chaplain at Auckland Castle. There he shared in Lightfoot's research into the Apostolic Fathers and also assisted in the training for ordination of the small group of Oxford and Cambridge men who resided in the Castle.

He returned to Cambridge in 1884 as Dean of Christ's College and for the next 15 years devoted himself to academic work, serving for a short time as a curate at Great St Mary's, the university church, and from 1885 to 1892 as vicar of All Saints' Church, Cambridge. This proved to be incompatible with his literary work and travels abroad for research and when the congregation failed to meet its financial obligations he resigned. In the following year he became the Norris Hulse Professor and the year after that was appointed a prebendary of Wells Cathedral which opened his eyes to the attractions of life in a beautiful cathedral close.

First, however, he must serve his time in London and in 1899 he was appointed rector of St Margaret's, Westminster, and to the annexed canonry of the Abbey. This was not a sensible move since he succeeded F. W. Farrar – one of London's most popular preachers who had won international fame with his schoolboy fiction *Eric, Or Little by Little* and his best-seller *Life of Christ*. Moreover there was a parish of 20,000 and half a dozen curates to manage. All of which he had been warned against by his Cambridge colleagues who saw clearly that the work of a scholar of Robinson's type was certain to be ended. By great good fortune, however, another of the Westminster canonries fell vacant in 1900 and Robinson was appointed to this, leaving St Margaret's to be filled with distinction by Hensley Henson. By this time he had fallen in love with the Abbey and its history and thus virtually abandoned his New Testament and Patristic studies, for which he had an international reputation, in favour of research into the Westminster archives. An important series of books on the early history of the Abbey resulted and in the process of writing these Robinson became an expert medievalist.

More immediately useful, however, was his knowledge of the history of the coronation rite, since 65 years had elapsed between the coronations of Queen Victoria and King Edward VII in 1902. Although the rite used for the Queen had been a considerable improvement on those used for her two predecessors, the ceremonial had been inept and reports of the occasion indicated that further revision and rehearsals were needed. Neither of which was within the capacity of the dean, G. G. Bradley, who was old and infirm and almost blind. Robinson did much of the preparation of the service, which in the event had to be curtailed by 90 minutes because the King had recently undergone an operation for appendicitis. The sub-dean stood in for the dean who never left his stall and resigned soon afterwards. Robinson happily accepted the offer of the succession, though once again his friends were puzzled and concerned.

There was a good deal of work awaiting him, since the final years of Bradley's reign had been lethargic rather than dynamic and the Abbey's financial situation was still precarious. And in spite of the considerable difficulties that attended Robinson's occupancy of the deanery his contribution to the development of the Royal Peculiar's life was as notable as his research into its history. Under the influence of Charles Gore, who was for a short time a fellow canon of Robinson, the Abbey had become more High Church and this continued moderately under the new regime. Altar candles were lit and celebrants at the Eucharist, now held more frequently, took the eastward position. A special sequence of liturgical colours – white for Advent and red for Easter – dating from the thirteenth century was restored, and remained in use until the 1980s. The introduction of red cassocks for the clergy and the choir, as well as for royal chaplains, was commanded by the King who was intent on making the Court more colourful.

Robinson had great flair for the ordering of special services to mark national events and other community commemorations, and a sensitivity to language which found expression in the compilation of prayers. His translation of a prayer from the early seventh century Leonine Sacramentary remains widely used:

> Remember, O Lord, what thou has wrought in us, and not what we deserve; and, as thou hast called us to thy service, make us worthy of our calling; through Jesus Christ our Lord.

And a special prayer for use in Westminster Abbey expresses an understanding of its role which continues to have meaning for those who worship there today:

> O everlasting God, with whom a thousand years are but as one day, and in whose Name are treasured here the memorials of many

generations: Grant to those who labour in this place such measures of thy grace and wisdom, that they may neglect no part of their manifold inheritance, but so guard and use it to thy glory and the enlargement of thy Church, that the consecration of all human powers may set forward thy purpose of gathering up into one all things in Christ, through whom to thee be glory now and evermore.

The number of these memorials, which had increased greatly during the eighteenth and nineteenth centuries, was however a matter of concern to him and, Dean Stanley's proposal for a special new building to serve as a national Valhalla having been rejected, Robinson's proposal that the undercroft beneath the former monks' dormitory should be used for this purpose. But the Prime Minister, A. J. Balfour, would not agree and the undercroft eventually became a museum. Robinson also had a scheme for rebuilding the former monks' refectory and turning it into King Edward VII's chapel which would become the burial place for kings and queens. Again, this came to nothing. A scheme for stained glass portraying kings and abbots in the windows on the north side of the nave was, however, successfully completed, though not until after he had left for Wells.

The custom of the Sovereign in person distributing the Royal Maundy was revived by King George V and until then it was carried out by the Lord High Almoner – an office to which Robinson was appointed in 1906. This was one of the few occasions on which he wore a cope and his presence was almost regal, but it was characteristic of him to run the whole thing himself – ordering the Maundy money from the Mint, selecting the recipients and even auditing the accounts.

It is only fair to record that not all the canons found their dean difficult to deal with. Samuel Barnett, who joined the chapter in 1906 after many years of social work in London's East End formed an early impression that he was 'scholarly, kindly and under the impulse of duty'. After attending his first chapter meeting, which he described as 'very uneventful', he added, 'I thought the dean really ill and felt very tender towards him as a bit of fine china among rather coarse pots'. Barnett had yet to experience Robinson's sometimes violent temper or the disappointment of having his ideas rejected by him. The suggestion that special services should be arranged for trade unions, co-operatives, teachers' associations, settlement workers and club members did not find favour with the dean; neither did the admittedly revolutionary proposal that part of the chapter clerk's office should be turned into a shop, selling pictures and other mementoes of the Abbey as well as Christian literature. The idea that women graduates attending the annual London University service should be permitted to wear their academicals was, said Barnett, 'pain and grief to the dean'. The recently completed Revised Version of the Bible was rejected on the grounds that it was based on an imperfect text.

Robinson always took his teaching responsibilities seriously and, although not a crowd-pulling preacher, his sermons, delivered in a simple, stately style were always worth hearing for their wide learning and intellectual acuteness. He also gave courses of lectures in the Abbey during Advent and Lent and one of these, published as *Some Thoughts on the Incarnation*, enabled the young William Temple to articulate his beliefs about the virgin birth and the resurrection in a way that overcame earlier objections to his ordination. On Wednesdays the captain of the Queen's scholars and four other Westminster School boys were invited to tea at the deanery when Robinson talked to them about the origins of the Abbey. He was always ready to lecture on junior clergy courses, supported deaconesses and, after the example of Bishop Lightfoot, took into the deanery young graduates who were preparing for ordination, their number including future deans of Chichester and Wells, future Bishops of Southwark and Melbourne, Tubby Clayton, the founder of TocH and F. A. Simpson, a notably eccentric Fellow of Trinity College, Cambridge. Other residents included some who achieved distinction in secular professions.

Many visitors were also welcomed to the deanery, though he would himself visit only the Lord Chancellor and the Speaker of the House of Commons, preferring to find his social life at the Athenaeum and at the British Academy, of which he was for many years an active member of the council. His Westminster years were, however, dogged by poor health, which was hardly surprising in view of his life style, and by sight problems. Thus, after nine stressful years and in spite of the nearness of King George V's coronation, the opportunity to move to Wells was irresistible and his decision almost certainly a wise one.

The historic 40-room deanery at Wells delighted him and he had no difficulty in managing the chapter. None of the canons, all of whom were over 70, was spoiling for a fight, neither were they over-anxious to become actively involved in the running of the cathedral. The sub-dean and master of the fabric was 85 when Robinson arrived and had already spent 57 years at Wells. They stood in awe of the distinguished scholar who had suddenly, and most unexpectedly, appeared among them, and Robinson, as aloof as ever, was determined to keep them at arm's length. They were not difficult to outwit and one of his often-used ploys was to assume their consent at chapter meetings, without troubling to take a vote or even seeking an opinion. Celebrating the holy communion early on his first Sunday as dean, he announced that he could not see to read and commanded the verger to light the candles. Thus was restored at Wells the ancient tradition of lighted candles on the altar.

As at Westminster, he showed no great aptitude for administration or finance and whenever the Ecclesiastical Commissioners sent delegations to Wells to sort out matters that were causing concern he tended to disregard their advice and, on at least one occasion, refused to see them. He was, however, skilled at raising money for his own pet projects – usually the conservation or the embellishment of the cathedral – and this he kept firmly under his own personal control. The fabric required a considerable amount of attention, since a major restoration carried out in the 1840s after centuries of neglect had left the interior of the building looking somewhat forlorn. All the memorials had been removed to the cloisters, but the money ran out before the surface of the walls could be renewed. Further work on the towers and the west front was also required and Robinson, being Robinson, could not tackle any of this without at the same time digging deeply into the history of the building and the mode of its construction.

His major concern, however, was with the conservation and re-ordering of the beautiful fourteenth-century glass. The location of misplaced pieces and the return of the portraits and scenes to something close to their original form provided him with an endlessly fascinating occupation and in the process he became an expert on medieval glass. His discovery of the sockets which had once held a medieval rood in the central arch of the nave encouraged him to commission a twentieth-century replacement and when the bishop was unwilling to dedicate this Robinson recruited the Archbishop of Canterbury, a frequent visitor to the deanery, to take his place.

During his years at Cambridge and Westminster one of Robinson's sisters kept house for him and she moved with him to Wells. It seemed unlikely that so obsessive a personality and so eccentric a character would ever consider the possibility of entering into the delights and demands of marriage, but in 1915, when he was 57, he astonished his friends by marrying Amy Faithful, the personal secretary of Archbishop Davidson. Thanks to her love for him and her heroic tolerance this proved to be a most happy and sustaining liaison. He remained unpredictable and demanding, and it was difficult to keep servants for long. Her patience was often sorely tested, but she stood firm and provided both a secure, trouble-free home life for him, and a welcoming reception for his many visitors. Those who bored him, which was not difficult, were however quickly despatched from the study and invited to select an off-print from one of his latest articles, kept for this purpose near the front door.

These articles, published in learned journals, numbered well over 100 during his 22 years at Wells. Virtually all of them were on historical subjects and he became as fascinated with the early history of Wessex as he had been with that of Westminster Abbey. He was an active member of the Somerset Archaeological Society and often went on digs, his particular interest being the Saxon period. Besides articles, there were volumes on *The Times of St Dunstan*, *The Saxon Bishops of Wells* and an important collection of his *Somerset Historical Essays*. Only very rarely did he return to the field in which his scholarly reputation had been cultivated, but he contributed to an important symposium on *The Early History of the Church and Ministry* and translated, with an introduction, a work on preaching by St Irenaeus.

Robinson's unrivalled knowledge of Christian origins led to an invitation to share in unofficial meetings of a small group of Anglican and Roman Catholic scholars, held between 1921 and 1925 and later known as the Malines Conversations. Under the presidency of the Belgian Archbishop of Malines, Cardinal Mercier, these made considerable progress towards agreement on matters such at the Eucharist, Episcopacy and Papal Primacy, with Robinson making significant contributions. But the whole enterprise was viewed with considerable suspicion by the Evangelical wing of the Church of England and the publication of a report in 1928 led to its condemnation by Pope Pius XI. The same year saw the final rejection by Parliament of a revision of the *Book of Common Prayer*. Although he had considerable knowledge of the early liturgies, Robinson was not directly involved in this, partly because he was known to be almost impossible to work with on a committee, and partly because he had little respect for the judgement of those who had been entrusted with the task. He was consulted from time to time on specific points of liturgical history, but he was highly critical of the final proposals, believing that the Prayer Book should be left unchanged and simply augmented by an appendix containing additional material, including alternative eucharistic prayers to meet different situations and needs.

In this, as in his approach to Anglican–Roman Catholic relations, he was half a century ahead of his time.

Robinson's scholarly output continued throughout most of the 1920s but by the time he had reached his seventieth birthday poor health was seriously affecting all his activity. He was a picturesque figure in the close and still regular in his attendance at the cathedral services, but appointment as KCVO in 1932, for his services as Dean of Westminster and Lord High Almoner, came too late to mean much to him. He retired in March 1933, having been a dean for 31 years, and died at the beginning of May. His biographer, T. F. Taylor, was of the opinion that Robinson ranked among the most outstanding ever of the deans of Westminster, though he added 'of great gifts and wayward husbandry', and others believed that these gifts would have been better employed had he remained in Cambridge and been one of the most influential of New Testament scholars. But Robinson himself did not underrate the importance of the work of a cathedral dean and in response to a request from Archbishop Randall Davidson in 1917 for 'information on the history of deans and your view of their use' remarked: 'You might appoint men deans whom you could not make bishops, for example Henson, Hastings Rashdall and myself. The post is also one which in these busy times gives a man leisure to think. Further, if you choose your deans wisely, you could find them an effective permanent opposition to the episcopate, not individual bishops, but critics of and checks on general episcopal policy.'

This was probably not the answer for which Davidson was hoping but it is certain that Robinson was a great adornment of the two deaneries he occupied, and that the life and witness of the Church of England would have been immeasurably the poorer had not the office of dean provided him with the opportunity to pursue relentlessly the truth as he discerned it. One of his nephews was John A. T. Robinson, Bishop of Woolwich, Dean of Trinity College, Cambridge and author of *Honest to God*.

14

The Reformer
Frank Bennett, Chester

Frank Selwyn Macauley Bennett was astonished when he was offered
the deanery of Chester in 1920. He had just completed ten years as
rector of Hawarden in North Wales and the whole of his previous
ministry had been spent in the diocese of Chester, first as bishop's
chaplain, then as the notable vicar of parishes in Stockport and the city
of Chester. He later confessed that until he became a dean, 'I do not
think it ever struck me that I had anything in particular to do with the
Cathedral or the cathedral with me. I regarded it, probably quite
wrongly, as a place where leisured people received largish salaries and
I looked upon deans as the fortunate occupants of an office in the
Church of England that could easily be dispensed with altogether.'

During the next 17 years he transformed the life of Chester
Cathedral and, by demonstrating what a cathedral might become,
exerted an enormous influence on cathedral life throughout the
country. He is one of the two most important cathedral figures of the
twentieth century, the other being Bill Williams of Coventry, and his
78-page book *The Nature of a Cathedral* (1925) is remarkable for its
combination of vision and concrete ideas.

Although he knew next to nothing about cathedrals before his
appointment to Chester, Bennett learned fast, particularly from
Walter Frere, the historian Bishop and Dean of Truro, who introduced
him to the earliest medieval concept of the cathedral as the place where
the bishop lived with his domestic and diocesan clergy. This greatly
influenced Bennett's understanding of the role of a cathedral, which,
he said, should be, 'The Bishop's and his Family's great House of
Prayer and not the special property of a small corporation'. He went
on to describe as 'outrageous' the fact that, 'the said small corporation
charges those to whom the cathedral really belongs sixpence or a
shilling for going round what is their own or, more monstrous still,
excludes them from it altogether on Sundays between services I

do not believe that a cathedral can even begin to do its proper work until it has replaced visitors' fees with pilgrims' offerings.'

The doors at Chester were opened from early morning until dusk every day of the year. Entrance fees were abolished and the salaries of the vergers were increased by 50 per cent to compensate them for the loss of tips. They were no longer, 'to act as a policeman or showman but should help those who come to feel and to profit by the religious impression of the place'. A leaflet extending a welcome, in religious terms, was handed to visitors. The boxes for voluntary offerings increased receipts fourfold and these went up every year. Bennett believed that the explanation for this lay in the fact that the building had been made, 'religiously interesting'. Beautifully printed and framed notices explaining the purpose of various parts of the cathedral and its furnishings were displayed, while the side chapels were allocated to a number of organizations in the diocese – the Cheshire Regiment, the Mothers' Union, the Scouts and Guides, and so on – and these were encouraged to provide photographs and literature about their work. A children's corner was also established.

When Bennett arrived at Chester he was faced immediately with the need to raise a large sum, £25,000, for urgent repairs to the cathedral's fabric. This accomplished, he was then able to use the greatly increased annual income to pay for the rebuilding of the ruined monastic refectory and the provision of a kitchen. He emphasized that this was not to be regarded as a general teashop but rather as an encouragement to parishes and other organizations to come to the cathedral for 'some religious purpose'. And come they did, in very large numbers. Parish groups concluded their visits with a short service, often conducted by their own clergy who were told that they had as much right as the dean and chapter to officiate in 'their own cathedral'. Choirs were expected to sing a few hymns and invite other pilgrims to join in. Those attending diocesan meetings were encouraged to begin with prayer in the cathedral and to have lunch or tea afterwards in the refectory.

A nave altar was installed as a focus for the worship at the ever-increasing number of crowded services attended by diocesan and other organizations, and also as a statement to all who entered the building by the west door of what the cathedral was all about. Red sanctuary lamps hung before all the altars and, although incense was not used ceremonially in the cathedral's services, it was burned frequently in the building to increase a sense of the numinous. The fixed pews were replaced by chairs for the sake of flexibility and spaciousness. On Bank Holidays and other 'Great Days of Opportunity', when very large numbers came, short services consisting of two hymns, an address and prayer, were held at frequent intervals; guided tours were abandoned in favour of 20–30 trained volunteers stationed in different parts of the building and ready to answer questions and offer explanation.

At the centre of all this was the dean himself. An engagingly dynamic personality, with an immensely pastoral heart, Bennett understood the human psyche (he had written a small book on *A Saint in the Making* and another which he described as an essay towards a biology of the world to come) and regarded the inside of the cathedral as his main sphere of work: 'The dean should live in his cathedral, and this should have priority before his other interests, however excellent and congenial. It is his life's work. No man could desire a larger opportunity.' This opportunity was to mingle with people, listen to what they had to say, offer comfort and consolation where necessary, and use the building as a means of commending the Christian faith. Clad in his cassock – it was thought unwise for a dignitary to appear before pilgrims in gaiters – he spent long hours in the cathedral and made a considerable impact on those who encountered him. Provision was also made for the hearing of Confessions at regular, advertised times.

News of this, aided by the publication of his book and a flair for publicity, soon reached the other cathedrals and, although Bennett's ideas were a very long way ahead of those of most of his fellow deans, he recorded in another little book *On Cathedrals in the Meantime* published in 1928 that only a few cathedrals now charged fees. The time was ripe for reform and Bennett served on a Cathedrals Commission which met from 1924 to 1927 and made a number of proposals regarding the size, duties and payment of chapters. Not all of these were bold enough for his liking and he was particularly dubious about the suggestion of a permanent Commission to assist the cathedrals in legal and other related matters. He said this would only be useful if the prophetic mind predominated in its membership.

His two books expressed in vivid language and imagery his own prophetic outlook. 'The present form of government in most cathedrals', he wrote, 'is about as awkward a machine as the perverse wit of man could well have devised.' In particular, the bishop had less of right in his cathedral than he had in any other church in his diocese, and a system that required canons to be present only when in residence, for three months of the year, made friction not only possible but actually probable.

Bennett's starting point, and it was a theme to which he constantly returned, was that the true unit of the Church must always be the diocese, led by the bishop. The cathedral must, therefore, be not only, 'the Bishop's and his Family's great House of Prayer', but also, 'The Diocesan Town Hall'. The bishop should always live close by – near enough to use one of the cathedral's chapels, rather than a domestic chapel, for his own spiritual life and ministry. Also near at hand must be a chapter house, refectory, common room, diocesan offices, consistory court, and simple bedroom accommodation for 20–30 people – to be used for recitals, conferences and the housing of ordinands.

Not all of this was achieved at Chester though the bishop was drawn more fully into the cathedral's life. He celebrated holy communion on Sunday and Thursday at 8 a.m., and preached once or twice a month. The increased number of special services brought him into the cathedral on many other occasions and, as a keen supporter of the dean's policy, he took care over appointments to canonries to ensure that the chapter were co-operative. The diocesan office was moved to a house near the cloister and the refectory thrived, but the building of bedrooms remained a dream.

Bennett's concept of a cathedral as comprising more than a church led him to declare of the cathedrals needed for newly created dioceses, several of which were founded during his time: 'The rule should be – an old parish church should never never never be chosen for this purpose. Rarely has it around it sufficient free ground for the erection of other essential buildings. A cathedral is not merely a parish church on a huge scale.' He urged the designation of a parish church as a pro-cathedral until such time as a suitable site and sufficient resources had been found for the erection of a new great church and its ancillary buildings – 'think spaciously and plan spaciously from the start. There is no need to achieve quickly.'

He believed the appointment to new cathedrals of a provost, who would exercise the rights and responsibilities of the former rector or vicar of the former parish church, was bound to create problems, not least an excessive workload. All had better be deans. He was, however, strongly opposed to the idea of the bishop being also the dean, promoted for a short time by E. W. Benson at Truro. Initially he thought it desirable for cathedrals to have a large parish, but he later changed his mind about this: the cathedral should be diocesan, not local, and members of its congregation should be urged to do some active service in the parish where they lived. Sunday evening nave services, becoming common at the time, were, he believed, undesirable since they hampered the work of the other city churches and attracted large congregations of people who had no responsibilities for Christian witness in their own locality.

Naturally, Bennett devoted much thought to the composition of chapters and the roles of their members. At that time it was common for two or more canons to be engaged mainly in diocesan duties and seen only during their three months of residence. This he regarded as entirely unsatisfactory and, since no cathedral could make sensible use of four full-time canons, he recommended that chapters should be reduced to a dean and two full-time canons, with one of the arch-deacons co-opted to serve on a cathedral executive committee. One of the canons should, after the tradition of the old foundation cathedrals, hold the office of precentor and sacrist, and the other that of treasurer and librarian. The precentor need not be a singer, though he should have a wide knowledge of church music and, in collaboration with the dean, oversee all aspects of the worship. Bennett was himself meticulous in his concern for every detail of the services. The treasurer would have special responsibility for financial matters and the cathedral's valuables and, as librarian, not only supervise a reference library but also a good lending library which he should exhort the diocesan clergy to use. The canons, after the example of the dean, should spend as much time as possible in the cathedral and there should be at least one priest in the cathedral all day and every day. 'A canonry', he declared, 'cannot really be like a college fellowship. The primary duty of deans and canons is to have leisure for people.' What is more when they become infirm they should retire, since an active ministry is essential to the cathedral's wellbeing.

Besides the chapter there should be at least two minor canons. At first Bennett prescribed four (he had three at Chester) but he came to accept that two might suffice, since the dean or one of the residentiary canons should be capable of singing the few parts of a service allocated to a priest. The minor canons should be young priests, appointed for a maximum of six years, and given assistance with their studies. Their liturgical responsibilities would leave them with plenty of time to teach in the choir school or engage in pastoral work in and beyond the cathedral.

Something entirely new was Bennett's suggestion that the money saved by the suspension of the residentiary canonries should be used to pay six or eight pensioner canons. These would usually, but not always, be recruited from the diocesan clergy and, in return for housing and a supplement to their modest pensions, they would attend the daily services, unless otherwise let or hindered, and be available for occasional duty in the parishes of the diocese. This was another of his unrealized dreams, for he came to see that it was impracticable. (One, at least, of the problems arising from such an arrangement is now to be seen at the Duomo in Florence where all the canons are retired priests, some of whom are too infirm to climb the steps to the altar.) Neither was he able to persuade the bishop to suppress the two residentiary canonries occupied by diocesan officers.

More encouraging to Bennett was the outcome of his proposal that honorary canons should all be present or past rural deans and priests who were known to say mattins at evensong daily in their own parish churches. Rural deans should not be elected to the clergy. Pleading for a more dynamic role for the greater chapter, he said, 'I doubt whether we shall cut much ice with greater chapters unless we face and settle the question whether an honorary canonry should be regarded as a reward for long service in the diocese well done, or as an office to which are to be called by the bishop his most effective men. You cannot have it both ways.' He thought that the greater chapter should consist of the dean, the archdeacons, the two whole-time residentiary canons, the honorary canons, the six or eight pensioner canons and the cathedral organist. They would provide the bishop with a permanent council that would be summoned to the chapter house from time to time to discuss and offer advice on diocesan as well as cathedral affairs. Whenever a new bishop was required the greater chapter would submit three names to the Crown for choice or alternatively choose from three names submitted to them by the Crown. None of which should be allowed to hinder the recovery of a Diocesan Synod of clergy or compete with a Synod re-established.

The primary duty of the clergy resident in the precincts was, said Bennett, daily attendance at worship to offer prayer for and on behalf of the bishop and the diocese. Occasional attendance was not acceptable. There must always be two or three members of the chapter present at the statutory services and they, combined with the minor canons and the pensioner canons, would provide a significant worshipping community whether or not the choir be present. He believed that the role of the choir was to assist the clergy in the offering of worship rather than the then current practice of the choir accepting the main responsibility, with the clerical presence confined to the residentiary canon and the minor canon on duty.

Bennett believed that daily choral mattins, then normal in cathedrals with a choral foundation, should be abandoned. He confessed that he himself found it tedious and thought it undesirable that young choristers should have to submit to two choral services every day. Choral evensong was a different matter, provided that the music was well chosen, with popular items when large congregations assembled on Saturdays. The daily services at Chester became – 7.30 a.m. mattins (said), 7.50 a.m. Eucharist (said, but on Wednesdays and Fridays sung by the choir at 9.15 a.m.), 5 p.m. evensong (sung). Bennett would have liked Sext to be said at midday and the day to close with Compline, after which the chapter would say Goodnight to each other, but it is not clear that this was ever achieved.

Bennett was one of the earliest pioneers of what became the parish communion and, a quarter of a century before the Parish and the People movement, argued powerfully for what he called a people's communion, accompanied by organ and singing, and celebrated on Sunday at an hour which made the keeping of the traditional fast not difficult. This would, he said, give tired folk a little longer to lie in bed and busy people a free morning after a service that ended at about ten o'clock. The crowded Sunday programme of services and Sunday Schools, common in most parishes, served only to, 'fairly wear the godly out and frighten the not very godly clean away'. So Chester had its people's communion at 9 a.m. and this soon became the best-attended Sunday service.

Although Bennett was unable to achieve all that he desired, what he did achieve was, in the context of its time, extraordinary – and accomplished with remarkable speed. A mere four years after his appointment to Chester a *Times* journalist reported:

> No traveller can enter Chester Cathedral today without feeling at once that it is different from other cathedrals. There seem to be a great many people in it; and they are all moving about, or sitting quiet, or unpretentiously on their knees, just as if they were very much at home there. If he is used to the ways of English cathedrals, he may even feel a little ill at ease when he can find no notices forbidding him to do this or that, no locked gates, and not a single official demanding 6d. He begins by wondering whether he has had the bad luck to be an intruder upon a specially invited party, and whether he ought not apologetically to slip out. A very little perseverance will show him that he, too, has been specially invited, and that all day and every day throughout the year the whole cathedral is open and free and his.

In his *The Church of England 1900–1965* (1966) Roger Lloyd, himself a canon of Winchester for 29 years, described Bennett as a genius, and it seems that a cathedral was needed for his genius to flower. Born in Somerset in 1866, he went from Sherborne School to Keble College, Oxford, and, having been drawn to holy orders, embarked on what he believed would be a lifelong and deeply satisfying ministry as a parish priest. And this, in a sense, is what he never ceased to be. E. W. Benson at Truro and R. W. Church at St Paul's had demonstrated in the nineteenth century that cathedrals could be made useful; it was left to Frank Bennett in the 1920s to show that they could be made lovable.

15

The Gloomy Philosopher
William Ralph Inge, St Paul's

When, in 1911, the Prime Minister, H. H. Asquith, wrote to William Ralph Inge, at that time Lady Margaret Professor of Divinity at Cambridge, offering him the deanery of St Paul's, he explained that he wished to 'restore the tradition of scholarship and culture associated with the deanery in the past'. He could not have chosen better, for Inge, having overcome his reluctance to embark upon an ecclesiastical career, became one of the Church of England's most distinguished and most famous deans.

This had little if anything to do with his achievements in St Paul's, where he remained for 23 years, but had everything to do with his huge intellectual gifts, a compulsive urge to lecture, preach and write books, and unusual skill as a journalist which gave him celebrity status and a vast audience for his views. This fame could not, however, be separated from his position as Dean of St Paul's which, during his time, was still regarded as a post of considerable eminence in London society and in the life of the nation as a whole. He mixed with the leading politicians, the heads of all the professions, the most prominent writers and artists, and, naturally, the bankers on his own doorstep. These greatly valued his breadth of outlook and originality of thought, and they much enjoyed his biting wit, provided it was not directed at themselves. George Bernard Shaw, who was not normally an admirer of clergymen, described him as, 'Our great dean, our most extraordinary writer and in some respects our most extraordinary man'.

Inge loved St Paul's as a building and as a focus of the nation's religious life, but he did not care for much of what took place within its walls. This he recorded in his diary at the end of his first Sunday as dean –

May 28. Spent nearly the whole day in church 8–9; 10.30–1.15; 3.15–4.45; 7–8.30. I have never before had work to do which wounded my conscience, but these services seem to me a criminal waste of time. I have held different views at different times about the character and value of the Creator of the Universe, but never at any time have I thought it at all probable that he is the kind of person who enjoys being serenaded. However, I believe I can, without giving offence, pursue my theological studies in my stall. But for this, I really could not reconcile it with my conscience to spend about 20 hours a week in so futile a manner. – June 7. I am getting more and more depressed by the intolerable boredom and waste of time of the services. I find it won't do to read books – the congregation would not notice, but the choir, who are more important, would. The noise gets on my nerves and interferes with consecutive thought – I am conscious of growing irritation and dislike of the cathedral.

Part of Inge's problem was that he was quite unmusical. The singing of the cathedral choir seemed to him to be no more than 'howling and caterwauling'. Acknowledging that 'music has charms to soothe the savage breast', he went on to explain, 'It has the opposite effect on me who am not a savage . . . . If I believed that I shall listen through all eternity to the seraphim blowing their loud uplifted trumpets, it would almost deter me from the practice of virtue . . . . They turned the Nicene Creed into an anthem; before the end I had ceased to believe anything.' It was not, however, simply his aversion to music. His religion, expressive of his personality, was individualistic. As a Christian Platonist, he saw heaven as the primary sphere of God's unceasing activity and mysticism as the means by which the individual might, during his days on earth, experience something of the heavenly life. Corporate worship had, for him, little to offer in this direction and when a young priest asked him if he was interested in liturgy, he replied testily, 'No; neither am I interested in postage stamps.' Nonetheless, having discovered that it was, with an effort, possible to read during choral services, he became a diligent attender who was present more frequently than any of the canons, and when away from St Paul's much enjoyed the simplicity of the worship offered in village churches.

Preaching was different. Inge was undeniably one of the great preachers of his day and people flocked to hear him, whether in the pulpit at St Paul's or, as so often, in other cathedrals, and in parish churches up and down the country. Yet he had none of the gifts of the born orator. His sermons were carefully prepared utterances in which he expressed in uncompromisingly intellectual terms his own personal beliefs and his understanding, from a religious point of view, of the significance of the important moral and social issues of the time. There was little concession to the individual members of his congregations. A visitor to St Paul's noted that in the pulpit the dean seemed glued to his manuscript and hardly aware of the presence of the congregation, though they were aware of the verbal shrapnel flying all around. Unlike his lectures, few of the sermons have survived in print but these are of a style and quality that would enable them to be preached, with profit, to an educated congregation nearly a century after their first delivery.

Inge's entry to the deanery was not without problems. His predecessor, Robert Gregory, a reformer who had been at St Paul's as a canon, then as dean, for 43 years, retired aged 92 on the understanding that he could continue to occupy the deanery for the remainder of his life. There being no other house available in Amen Court, where the cathedral clergy live, Inge was driven to rent a large house in Bedford Square, a mile away. And while he was preparing to move in Gregory died, so the removal van went to the deanery instead.

In common with every other dean, before and since, Inge inherited a chapter which had been appointed at various times and for various reasons, but never with a view to its members working together as a team. Soon after his arrival he discussed with the Archdeacon of London, who was also a canon, one or two things he hoped to do at St Paul's, but was immediately assured that 'As long as Canons Alexander and Simpson are both here you are not going to be allowed to do anything'. Someone else advised him that the Dean of St Paul's was 'like a mouse watched by four cats'. The cathedral's statutes accorded considerable responsibility to the canon in residence, who during his period on duty had much of the authority normally vested in a dean. This dated from the days – until 1849 – when the deanery was held by a diocesan bishop who needed the St Paul's income to augment his bishopric pay, and who was only too pleased for the canons to assume responsibility for the cathedral during his long absences.

The arrangement also suited Inge, up to a point, since he was not really interested in the cathedral's administration and often left chapter meetings soon after they had started. On one occasion the canons were determined that he should stay until an important vote had been taken on a particular matter, and when he rose from his chair to go one of them tried to bar his way to the door. But Inge pushed him aside and got away. The one subject in which he was interested was the dean and chapter's patronage of its numerous livings. He tried to get liberal clergymen appointed to some of these, but was often thwarted by the canons, some of whom were Tractarian High Churchmen. Not all, however. In 1917 Canon Simpson absented himself from the chapter for 18 months after authorization had been given for prayers for the dead – these being mainly the soldiers killed in France and Flanders. A King's Counsel was consulted and advised that it might be possible to remove the absentee on the grounds of neglect of duties, but Inge was against this, pointing out that Simpson had recently lost his wife and, adding in his diary, 'I like him'.

Inge's relations with his colleagues were correct and on the whole reasonably cordial. There were inevitable disagreements and when in 1928 Simpson again became unhappy Inge managed to get him appointed Dean of Peterborough – this being the first change in the composition of the chapter since his own arrival in 1911. He was not consulted about Simpson's successor who soon complained about backbiting in Amen Court and had to be persuaded to stay by the Archbishop of Canterbury. Some other changes followed and thereafter Inge found life at the cathedral more congenial, but a year after his retirement he wrote in his diary, 'I am not sure that this has not been the happiest year I ever spent . . . . I am afraid that I did not realize how great the relief would be to be free of Alexander and the minor canons.'

The minor canons of St Paul's, six in number, formed a college founded by Royal Charter in 1394. After the Reformation they continued to draw stipends from estates allocated to the college, their office was freehold, and there was a warden or custos, a senior and a junior cardinal. In 1855 it was decided by Order in Council that certain city benefices should be offered in rotation to appropriately qualified minor canons. In 1878 enough money had accrued from the estates to enable houses to be built for them in the cathedral precincts. All of which survived until the end of the 1914–18 war, by which time the increase in the cost of living required the suspension of one minor canonry to enable the rest to be paid more. Questions also began to be asked about the need for so many clergymen to conduct the cathedral's services. A revision of the constitution and statutes in 1936 annulled the legal status of the college, while allowing the retention of its names and offices, providing £500 a year and a free house for up to five minor canons, forbidding the holding of a benefice and requiring retirement at the age of 55 on a pension provided by the chapter. The office of sub-dean was abolished.

None of this was achieved without a battle involving the minor canons, the dean and chapter, and the Ecclesiastical Commissioners, who had initiated the reforms. Inge, unsurprisingly, found the conflict exceedingly tedious. He also disliked some proposals for liturgical and ceremonial reform made by the minor canons in 1930 shortly before the re-opening of the major part of the cathedral, which had been closed for five years for extensive restoration. He recorded in his diary a difficult Chapter meeting on 3 January, 'The minor canons have sent us a long series of resolutions about the cathedral services, the cumulative effect of which would be to change the type of service which has always been maintained at St Paul's to one of a definite catholic character.' Later that year he caused great offence when in an *Evening Standard* article he deplored the penchant of junior clergy for dressing up in church. The minor canons felt he was referring to them and asked for an apology, but none was forthcoming.

Canon Sidney Alexander, who arrived at St Paul's shortly before Inge, and stayed for 39 years, was an awkward man but had a flair for fundraising. He master-minded three major fabric appeals and not only raised over £400,000 but ensured that it was wisely spent on work essential to the stability of the great building. Inevitably this led to the accumulation of power and relations between him and Inge were often difficult. In 1915 Alexander and the cathedral surveyor organized the St Paul's Watch – volunteers trained to deal with any fires caused by enemy bombing – and, although it was not required to go into action during that war, its revival at the beginning of the 1939–45 war played a vital part in the protection of the building during the German air attacks on London.

Meanwhile Inge was busy writing books, lecturing and preaching. He was involved in many London intellectual societies and organizations, helped to found a Religious Thought Society, became a Fellow of the British Academy, was a Trustee of the National Portrait Gallery and, along with John Masefield and Max Beerbohn, was elected to the academic committee of the Royal Society of Literature. Several evenings in most weeks he dined with the great and the good and, always in difficulty over remembering faces, confessed in his diary that he had failed to recognize three duchesses. He was in fact a shy man, without small talk, and rather deaf. The success of his social life owed everything to the skills of his charming wife, Kitty, to whom he was most happily married for over 44 years. Asquith noted in his diary for 10 November 1925 –

We have had to lunch the Dean of St Paul's and his wife. He is a strange, isolated figure, with all the culture in the world, and a curiously developed gift for expression, but with kinks and twists both intellectual and temperamental. Still, he is one of the few ecclesiastics in these days who is really interesting.

Inge and his wife also gave frequent dinner parties at the deanery, though he believed that a clergyman ought not to entertain on the same scale as his lay friends, and he disapproved of the banquets held in the deanery at Westminster and in the home of the rector of St Margaret's, Westminster. In any event it became increasingly difficult to obtain servants, whom Inge believed to be essential to the life of an intellectual and a writer, and towards the end of his time at St Paul's it was possible to employ only maidservants. This did not, however, affect the choice of guests –

January 21, 1928:
When we have preachers to stay, we usually have dinners to meet them. On this day we entertained Canon Creed from Cambridge and Canon Hannay (George Birmingham, the novelist). We had to meet them Lady Cromer, Lord Haldane, Sir Lawrence and Lady Jones, Miss Haldane, Colonel and Mrs. Carruthers (Violet Markham), Sir Herbert and Lady Cohen.

This entry from his published diary (1949) is not untypical of a multitude of guest lists at one social occasion or another and suggests a snob, but it reflects the kind of life that was normal for a dean of St Paul's in his time and the diary is a much abbreviated version of several volumes of a journal which has yet to see the light of day.

Inge's encounter with Lord Beaverbrook, the Press Baron, proved to be of special significance. Following the huge publishing success of his first volumes of *Outspoken Essays* (1919) Beaverbrook invited him to contribute a weekly column to the London *Evening Standard* which then had a circulation of over 400,000. Inge had previously written some articles for the *Sunday Express* and, although he did not like the *Standard*, he accepted Beaverbrook's invitation because it gave him a large regular audience and was very well paid. He earned his fee (£40 a contribution) with a series of brilliantly written pieces mainly on topical issues which extended from 1921 to 1924 and were resumed for another three years in 1927. He was often highly controversial and frequently enraged his readers, but he never wrote a platitude and filled a column that few readers would miss. During the interval between his *Evening Standard* stints, he wrote a weekly, then a monthly, column for the *Morning Post* and was in constant demand for articles for other newspapers and magazines. In one four-year period in the 1920s he accumulated £20,000 from his writings, and such was his fame that his utterances and activities were constantly on the news pages. When he went on a preaching and lecturing tour of the United States in 1925 reporters followed his every step from the moment he disembarked at New York.

Most of his many books were attended by similar success and although his two major works *Christian Mysticism* (1899) and *The Philosophy of Plotinus* (two volumes 1918) could hardly be classified as best-sellers they were widely read and became very influential. Both broke new ground. Inge saw mysticism as an intense element in all true religion and he believed that this element was being seriously neglected: 'The testimony of the saints and mystics has far greater evidential value than is usually supposed. They testify to what most wish to know – that the eternal things, which are not seen, are real.' Inge's survey of the mystics of former ages aroused interest in long-forgotten figures such as Julian of Norwich. But, although he wrote much on the subject, he confessed that he had himself made only limited progress towards the eternal and experienced no more than 'rare and fitful flashes of light which have seemed to come from some higher source than my own personality'. He added later, 'Sometimes God gives himself to us as absent.'

Inge's interest in mysticism fitted in well with his study of the writings of Plotinus – a little-known Egyptian Neo-Platonic philosopher who lived in the third century. Plotinus, a pagan, proposed a cosmology consisting of a triad of beings, of which the third, the World Soul, had created all material things and orders the universe. Individuals, who have become separated from the World Soul, can attain unity with the Divine by means of contemplation and various ascetical practices. Inge, following St Augustine of Hippo, recognized that this mystical philosophy needed to be supplemented, and some of its values corrected, by New Testament Christianity, but he had no doubts that the combination of the two provided the only solution of present-day problems. He also found Plotinus 'a wise and inspiring spiritual guide' and towards the end of his life he wrote 'I have lived with him for nearly 30 years and I have not sought him in vain, in prosperity or adversity.' Inge devoted his 1917 Gifford Lectures to *The Philosophy of Plotinus* and, although wartime conditions allowed him only small audiences in St Andrews, the publication of them in two substantial volumes aroused wide interest, requiring second and third editions during the 1920s. Most of his many other books, on such subjects as *Christian Ethics and Modern Problems* (1930), *England* (1926) and *God and the Astronomers* (1933) were reprinted several times, often selling out within a few days of publication, and it was rare for him not to have a book in the course of writing.

Inge played little part in the government of the Church. He regarded the Convocation of Canterbury and the Church Assembly as unbearably tedious and an expression of the kind of religion that Christ had sought to vanquish. But he was a prominent member of the Modern Churchmen's Union and served as its President from 1924 to 1934. He did not like the word 'modernism' and his views were closer to those of the Liberal Evangelicals of his time than to the more radical opinions being expressed by some German theologians. But he believed that Christian ministers must face the religious and philosophical implications of the advances in natural science and the challenge to Christian ethics posited by scientific humanism. These were subjects on which he often preached and lectured, and he regarded Modernism as representing a long tradition in the Church which stands for 'what is best in the old Greek civilization, its spirit of unfettered enquiry, its long tradition of deep thought, its reverence for knowledge, the robust faith that divine truth is accessible to man'.

It was unfortunate that Inge's tenure of the St Paul's deanery coincided with many years of Arthur Foley Winnington-Ingram's over-long reign as Bishop of London. The two men could hardly have been more different in temperament and outlook. Winnington-Ingram was a kind and generous bishop who saw his role primarily as that of an evangelist, and, although he had a good academic record, he preached simple, and often emotional, sermons. Inge could not cope with him. 'The mental processes of the bishop', he wrote in his diary on 2 October 1911, 'are for a man in his position, of almost childish simplicity.' On 6 January 1918 he recorded – 'A Day of Intercession and Thanksgiving for the War. There were great crowds. The Bishop of London preached a most unchristian sermon, which with a few words changed might have been preached by a court chaplain in Berlin.' Nonetheless, he was happy to partner him at tennis – 'I played tennis with the Bishop of London against Sir Frederick Kenyon and Mr Parker. We beat them, for the bishop, who is 55, darted about the court like a boy.'

William Ralph Inge was born in the village of Crayke, about 12 miles north of York, in 1860. His father, who had been a Fellow of

Worcester College, Oxford, and later became its Provost, was serving a long curacy in the parish, having married the Rector's daughter. Young Ralph was educated intensively at home and was sent to a preparatory school for just three months before taking the Eton Scholarship, gaining second place on the roll. At Eton he was a brilliant classicist and won a special Eton Scholarship to King's College, Cambridge. There he was taught by J. E. C. Welldon, the future Dean of Manchester, then of Durham, and took firsts in both parts of the Classical Tripos as well as winning a number of major university prizes. During his time at King's he was greatly influenced by Brooke Foss Westcott, the New Testament scholar and mystic, who was a professorial Fellow of the college.

He then taught briefly at Harrow and Winchester before embarking on a four-year spell of teaching at Eton. For this he was not suited and had difficulty in keeping order in the classroom, so he secured a Fellowship at King's and, although he did not go into residence in the college, it provided a location for his ordination as a deacon in 1888 by Bishop Edward King of Lincoln, the Visitor. Soon after this he became a Tutorial Fellow in classics at Hertford College, Oxford, where he worked hard and also played a lot of cricket (a lifetime interest) and other games. He delayed his ordination to the priesthood until 1892 because of some doubts concerning what the Church required him to believe. It was during his 16 years at Hertford that his interest changed from classics to the work of the Neo-Platonists and the Mystics, and he read much theology. One of his colleagues was Hastings Rashdall, a distinguished liberal theologian who later became Dean of Carlisle, and a mutual friend asserted, 'Rashdall could not believe that Christianity was true but wished it was, while Inge believed it was true and wished that it was not.'

Another friend, Herbert Hensley Henson, who later became Dean of Durham and eventually Bishop of Durham advised him to give up classics teaching and concentrate instead on theology in the hope of securing appointment to a canonry of Westminster or St Paul's. But Neo-Platonism and Mysticism continued to absorb him and he hoped at that time to become a headmaster or to hold high office in the Church. Shyness and increasing deafness were, however, a problem in his personal relations, and there were signs of a depressive personality which afflicted him until his marriage to Kitty Spooner – a niece of the legendary Warden Spooner. This coincided more or less with his appointment in 1905 as vicar of All Saints, Ennismore Gardens, near London's Knightsbridge. He was there for only two years and had a disturbing start when many in the largely conservative congregation who did not want intellectual sermons forsook the church. These were, however, soon replaced by others, including three High Court judges, who greatly appreciated Inge's preaching. He also managed to build up the church's financial reserves, leaving his wife to visit the poor, and continued to lecture and publish. In 1907, however, he left to become Lady Margaret Professor of Divinity at Cambridge and a Fellow of Jesus College, and during the next four years his lectures attracted very large audiences, so that by the time he went to St Paul's in 1911 he was already a well-known public figure, easily recognized by his thin, pale face, hollow cheeks and spare figure.

Before long he was being known as 'the gloomy dean' – a description that stayed for the remainder of his life. It was pinned on him by the *Daily Mail*, one of whose reporters attended a course of lectures which he gave to the Women's Diocesan Association at Sion College. The reporter, as well as many others in the audience, were startled when he called democracy 'a superstition and a fetish' and the Church of England 'the Church of the honestest and most illogical nation on the face of the earth'. The main thrust of the lectures was that the Church should not co-operate with the Spirit of the Age – a theme to which he would constantly return – and the message was not exactly cheering.

The outbreak of war in 1914, to which he was strongly opposed, greatly depressed him. He saw it as a return to barbarism and forecast the end of democracy, with Britain emerging as a second-rate power. He ceased to keep his diary between 1915 and 1917 and in 1917 stopped reading the newspapers. Suffragettes who came to the cathedral to demonstrate their concerns, and once placed a tin of gunpowder under the bishop's throne, were dismissed as 'hussies' – a description he was later to give to the writer Rebecca West when she reviewed one of his books unfavourably. Inge, the liberal churchman, was deeply conservative in his politics and view of society. Fear that population increase would inevitably lead to the destruction of England's cultural landmarks led him into membership of the Eugenics Society. 'When natural selection is forbidden to operate', he declared, 'rational selection must take its place or we shall have none but a C3 population.' He believed that unemployment could be solved only by reduction of the population, which might be activated by birth control and the despatch of large numbers to the colonies. Capital punishment should be extended to 'all incorrigibly anti-social offenders'.

Inge retired in 1934 to a house – Brightwell Manor – a few miles from Oxford. The final entry in his published diary reads 'I went back into trousers.' He continued to write and remained in demand for lectures and sermons, but the happiness of retirement ended with the outbreak of war in 1939, which once again plunged him into a deep depression. A year earlier he thought Britain should not be dragged into war for the sake of Czechoslovakia – 'a ramshackle republic, not twenty years old'. In June 1940 he believed Britain had definitely lost the war and by 1942 he was advocating peace negotiations with Germany. Personal tragedy struck when one of his sons, Richard, a promising curate in Horsforth, near Leeds, resigned to become an RAF pilot and was killed in action.

An earlier tragedy involving the death of a 12-year-old daughter from diabetes brought national sympathy. St Paul's and the streets outside were crowded for the funeral and Inge's brief memoir of her sold 50,000 copies. He lived on until 1950 when, in his ninety-fourth year, he succumbed to an attack of bronchitis. His wife had died five years earlier. During his closing years he had found great consolation in his re-reading of the classics, and shortly before his death he wrote a 3,000-word article for *The Modern Churchman* in which he assured its readers that 'Liberalism is not dead'. In the address given at the memorial service in St Paul's W. R. Matthews, his successor, said –

> William Ralph Inge was a great man, a unique man. We shall not look upon his like again. It is sad to know that we shall not hear his voice again commenting, in his individual and forceful fashion, on the topics of the day. It is sadder that we shall have no more penetrating discourses on the great themes of Freedom, Love and Truth, the three values and ideals which he always venerated and tried to serve. He is added to the roll of deans who have shed lustre on the office and to the roll of those who have added to the treasures of learning and wisdom in our English tongue.

16

The Headmaster
James Welldon, Durham

Disagreements between dean and bishops are not rare, but the clashes between James Welldon and Herbert Hensley Henson at Durham in the 1920s were in a class of their own. As is often the case, contrasting personality, besides differences of opinion, was the cause of the friction. Henson, a small man, with a razor-sharp mind and a remarkable command of the English language, thrived on controversy. He found himself working for 13 years alongside a dean who stood six foot five inches tall, had a 63-inch waist, weighed over 20 stone and, although credited with a distinguished academic record, tended to favour emotion rather than intellect, in his overlong utterances. Moreover he never ceased to be the tiresome Victorian schoolmaster who dispensed moral advice on every conceivable subject. It was a fatal episcopal/decanal partnership and only rarely tempered by Christian charity.

Thus Henson, attending a meeting at Eton at which the conversation turned to the origin of old sayings, was asked if he had ever seen a 'pig in clover'. 'Not really', came the instant reply, 'but I have seen the Dean of Durham in bed.' Thirty years earlier Henson, at that time a Fellow of All Souls, recorded the impression made on him by Welldon, then headmaster of Harrow, when he preached in the university church in Oxford:

He is tall and stalwart, very ugly, yet withal vigorous and manly. His style is simple, his manner slow and monotonous, his matter scarcely ever original – platitudes put forth with extraordinary appearance of sincerity.

Henson's final verdict, expressed with no less candour in a letter to the Dean of Norwich in 1942, some five years after Welldon's death, was even less flattering:

He never grew up. . . . He united a heavy frame with a blustering manner, which suggested a truly virile personality, and a sentimental sensitivity which would have been hardly pardonable in a schoolgirl. And he was found, in the experience of colleagues, to be radically untrustworthy, not deliberately or consciously, *but because he could never resist the appeal to the gallery*. He would never fail to sacrifice a friend to a cheer!

Welldon's opinion of Henson was never recorded, but he is known to have criticized him from the cathedral pulpit, in his presence – memorably on Remembrance Sunday 1930, after Henson had advocated the cessation of the observance. It was, however, an incident beyond the confines of the cathedral which entered powerfully into Durham's folk memory. The occasion was the annual Miners' Gala Day in July 1925 when, as usual, thousands of miners from the pit villages converged on the city with their banners and bands to attend a mass meeting, addressed by leading politicians, on the racecourse followed by a great service in the cathedral. The previous year Welldon had also been invited to speak on the racecourse on the subject of Temperance – he being one of the leaders of the national Temperance Movement – and in the course of the speech he attacked Henson, who was often called 'the liquor bishop' because he believed freedom to be more important than sobriety.

By 1926, however, the miners had more serious matters on their minds – a crisis over pay and working hours that would lead to a General Strike. Earlier in July Henson had written an article for the London *Evening Standard* in which he defended the coal owners and criticized the miners' leaders. Welldon had also joined the fray with a speech critical of the miners at Bishop Auckland Rotary Club. There was therefore considerable hostility to both bishop and dean on the Gala Day, at which Welldon was due to address a fringe meeting – again on Temperance. When he reached the racecourse, however, he was greeted by an angry crowd. 'Put him in the river', 'Duck him' some cried. Then, as Owen Chadwick described in his biography of Henson, in which he made good use of local newspaper cuttings, Welldon was swept by the crowd out of the enclosure. His top hat flew into the river, he was kicked and struck on the head. But by the time he had been pushed to the river bank the police were on the scene. They hailed a passing river boat, got the dean aboard and took him to safety, accompanied by jeers and boos. Later it was put about that Welldon had been mistaken for Henson, but, given their different sizes, this was highly improbable and Henson suggested that Welldon had got his deserts – 'He has given abundant provocation by his incessant and untimely talking: and his folly in appearing at the demonstration was in all the circumstances gross.' The Labour leader, Emmanuel Shinwell, deplored what had happened but excused the miners on the grounds that they had 'had no other means of curbing the tongue of a dean'.

Although Welldon applied a finely tuned mind to his academic studies and was an outstandingly good public school headmaster, he was an inveterate gasbag who never refused an invitation to address a popular meeting on any subject of common interest. During his time as Dean of Manchester (1906–18) he spoke in factory canteens at lunchtime and sometimes out of doors. He believed that a dean 'should be outspoken in telling people of their faults, such as drinking and gambling, provided only he does not use violent or abusive language – that is what they expect'. But an elderly lady on a Manchester tram once admonished him: 'Dean, I tell you what it is, you spout too much.'

James Edward Cowley Welldon was born in 1854 in Tonbridge where his father, an evangelical clergyman, was on the teaching staff of the school. Brought up strictly, he secured a scholarship to Eton where he was captain of school and won a scholarship to King's College, Cambridge. There he carried all before him, became Senior Classic and Senior Chancellor's Medallist, was President of the Cambridge Union, and studied under Westcott and Lightfoot. He then went to Germany, to study German literature, and to Italy to study Dante, before returning to King's as a Fellow.

He remained there for five years until, in 1883, he was appointed Master of Dulwich College and ordained. The school was then at a low ebb but in the space of only two years he raised it, miraculously some said, to the very highest standard. On the strength of this, and aged only 31, he became headmaster of Harrow School, having been recommended to the Governing Body by Westcott.

He immediately dominated the school with his powerful personality and bull-like appearance but, although he lived with a permanent emotional conflict between his loyalty to Eton and his new commitment to Harrow, he came to be numbered among the great headmasters of the Victorian era. He changed the curriculum and knew how to win the loyalty of his staff and inspire the boys. He had, however, one notable failure.

Winston Churchill's career at Harrow was, from almost every point of view, lamentable. He did not like the place and, although Welldon was patient with his constant academic failures, he once 'swished' him for breaking some factory windows outside the school. Nonetheless, the two remained friends and after Churchill had, at the third attempt, scraped through the army entrance exams and been posted to India, Welldon sent him a letter of advice:

> I implore you not to let your wild spirits carry you away to any action that may bring dishonour on your school or your name. It is impossible that I should not hear of your follies and impertinences if you are guilty of them and you will recognise that you put a serious strain upon my friendship if you ask me to treat you as a friend when other people speak of you with indignation or contempt.

He went on to advise him to learn Latin and Greek and to read the whole of Gibbon. Churchill did not appreciate this advice and told his brother Jack that the letter did Welldon no credit:

> I still entertain the highest opinion of his brains and respect his judgement on nearly every subject – but his ideas have been warped by schoolmastering and contact with clerics both of which you should avoid.

None of which prevented Churchill from inviting his former headmaster to give the address at his marriage to Clementine Hozier in St Margaret's, Westminster, in 1908. This proved to be a notably percipient utterance in which the preacher seemed to foresee the bridegroom's future role as a statesman and the way in which he would lean on the loving support of his wife.

An incident involving another Harrow pupil showed Welldon in a much less favourable light. An Egyptian boy of high rank had suffered two black eyes at the hands of another boy who, when summoned to the headmaster's study, explained 'Please Sir, he said something bad about the British race'. Welldon responded, 'That is enough, my boy; you may go.' He had no doubt as to the innate superiority of the British race and that the British Empire owed its origin to Divine Providence. The Anglo-Boer War he welcomed, averring that wars were needed from time to time to keep the nation virile, and later he became Vice-President of the Eugenics Society which promoted selective breeding. A simplified form of English spelling would, he believed, help the language to become universally used.

The Puritan element in Welldon's evangelical upbringing never left him and he recalled hearing Charles Spurgeon, the great Baptist preacher, say that he thought a ball would be harmless if the men were to dance by themselves in one room and the ladies by themselves in another. Regarding himself as a social reformer, Welldon declared, 'I have been called to fight the trinity of evils by which the working people of Great Britain are demoralized – lust, gambling and drink.' He thought that Nonconformist and Roman Catholic schools should not qualify for state aid because, in his view, they did not produce such good citizens as those of the Church of England.

On the other hand, some of his views were surprisingly liberal. He thought that the school leaving age in the state sector should be raised to 16 – this at a time when many children left when they were only 12 or 13. He advised teachers and parents not to look for results too early – 'schools exist for boys, not boys for schools' – and he urged parents to take more interest in their children at boarding schools since this was not a natural environment for them. He forecast that the great day schools would make an ever-increasing contribution to the life of the nation. His own contribution to learning during his Dulwich and Harrow years included translations of Aristotle's *Politics, Rhetoric and Ethics* and numerous more popular volumes such as *The Hope of Immortality*.

In 1898 Welldon, only 44, was surprised to be offered the bishopric of Calcutta, which carried with it the position of Metropolitan of India, Burma and Ceylon. He had not previously set foot in the Indian sub-continent or acquired, even at second hand, any real knowledge of Indian church life, but his appointment was a not untypical example of the then current belief that capable Englishmen could manage anything in their country's colonial empire. He accepted the offer on condition that he could minister to native Indians as well as to servants of the Raj, but in the event survived for only four years.

On his arrival in Calcutta he was astonished to find that the cathedral congregation was just like a fashionable congregation in London, with few, if any, 'dark faces'. He travelled widely, preaching sermons to Christian congregations and giving addresses on moral subjects to others. These, given in halting forms of their own language emphasized the moral superiority of Jesus Christ and his gospel. The experience of Indian poverty greatly troubled him, though he concluded that death for a starving beggar involved him in less suffering than that endured by a dying English soldier who had more to lose. Many years later, and long after he had left India, he concluded –

So long as the loyalty of India to the King-Emperor and to the British Empire is maintained and, if possible enhanced, it is eminently desirable that India should be governed in conformity with the wishes of the Indian peoples; and the natives of India are naturally the best interpreters of popular feeling and the different sectors and classes of the peoples.

Meanwhile he had made himself unpopular by excluding from the garrison churches Scottish troops and chaplains. This was on the curious grounds that the buildings had been dedicated by Church of England bishops. He also became impatient with some aspects of the protocol that seemed to govern so much of the life of the Raj, though as one of its most senior officers he was not himself greatly inconvenienced by this. The crunch came, however, when he had a serious disagreement with the Viceroy, Lord Curzon, over the role of religion in the Raj. The official position was that the government was neutral and, while making provision for Christian ministry to its expatriate servants, applied no pressure to the native population to change their beliefs. The Christian missionaries were free to preach the gospel as and where they could. Lord Curzon believed that he was acting in accordance with this policy when he advised the Hindus not to forsake their faith but Welldon, who greatly admired the Viceroy, challenged him on the point – and lost. A bishop of evangelical convictions and belief that the Christian way of life was the highest and the best could not accept what he regarded as an official impediment to conversion, so he resigned. This coincided with a breakdown of health and he returned to England in 1902.

Appointment to a canonry of Westminster seemed an appropriate way of providing for his convalescence and he greatly enjoyed his four years at the Abbey, where he had his first serious encounter with Hensley Henson, the Rector of St Margaret's, who was also a canon. His position in a church which, as he put it, 'stands at the heart of a great nation and a great Empire' accorded well with his understanding of the role of an Established Church. A prolific writer, he gladly accepted an invitation to provide an Introduction to P. F. Warner's account of the Ashes 1903/4. The opportunity to have a modest part in the coronation of King Edward VII, which took place soon after his arrival at the Abbey, gave him considerable satisfaction. As the only episcopal member of the chapter he had the responsibility of consecrating the oil used for the anointing ceremony, and in the procession of regalia he carried the orb.

The Coronation was postponed from June until August because of the King's operation for appendicitis, and Welldon's account of the event confirms the general impression of a less than dignified ceremony. The dean, G. G. Bradley, was old and infirm and took hardly any part in the service. The Archbishop, Frederick Temple, was not only old and infirm but also nearly blind and, having placed the crown on the King's head back to front, knelt before him in homage and found it impossible to rise. The King, who was the most fit of the chief participants, helped him to his feet, but he fell back and this time the Bishops of Winchester and Bath and Wells tried to lift him. Once again he fell back and was eventually carried bodily to a chair. Afterwards Welldon heard the Bishop of London declare that he had never been so glad to hear the final Benediction pronounced at any religious service as he had been that day.

By 1906 Welldon was ready for a more demanding ministry and the Prime Minister, Campbell Bannerman, offered him the deanery of Manchester. This surprised him because, as he remarked, 'My acquaintance with the Prime Minister was only slight.' The city's medieval collegiate church had become a cathedral when the diocese was formed in 1847 but the role of the dean was more akin to that of the vicar of Leeds than to that of a leisured dean in a tranquil close.

Manchester's dean was an institution in the city and this suited the larger than life Welldon very well. He was expected to be known by the citizens and travelled by tram to facilitate this. He was, in the words of the new dignitary, 'a younger brother as it were of the Lord Mayor', and sat on a multitude of city committees. He spoke at innumerable meetings, and saw himself as a freelance evangelist called to establish contact with 'some of the lowly men and women who have lost touch with organized religion'. Boys who worked underground in the coal mines were invited to the deanery for Sunday tea, and guests on other occasions included women from the poorest lodging houses, hawkers and pedlars. During a railway strike he conducted religious services at five stations for the strikers and became an easily recognizable figure who never lacked a friendly word and an improving anecdote. At the great Whitsun walk, involving thousands of schoolchildren, he was at the head of the procession.

The cathedral, still known to most Mancunians as 't'owd church', is wide rather than long and, with 2,000 seats in the nave and a quarter of a million visitors a year, Welldon found it good for preaching. Except that his right to preach was confined to Easter Day and Whitsunday, though he was sometimes invited by the canons to use the Sunday afternoon service for experimental worship. From time to time this had a cantata instead of a sermon.

Special services provided Welldon with much greater scope. 'A cathedral should', he said, 'aim to make the largest number of worshippers at home within its walls', but he went on to warn that, 'a person who abandons a parish church for a cathedral may become not a more, but a less active member of Christian society.' On another occasion he said, 'A cathedral can give services and sermons, but not much more'. The city organizations were invited to both – 2–3,000 railwaymen marched to the cathedral, with stationmasters at their head, and accompanied by four or five bands. The butchers of Manchester and Salford also came, as did the Trades Union Congress, the non-militant members of the Women's Suffrage Movement, and theatricals, whom he often visited back-stage. The National Evangelical Free Church Council were invited as a 'conspicuous instance of charity' but were required to have a Church of England service. All enjoyed, or endured, a lengthy sermon, spiced with anec-dotes and improving stories, and delivered by a popular preacher who sometimes bellowed and sometimes spoke in a confidential whisper. Welldon was President of the Manchester Christian Social Union but a lecture which he gave to various audiences emphasized his belief that although Socialism was not iniquitous, it was impracticable.

Durham – a small city at the heart of a mining community – to which he moved in 1918 provided much less scope for Welldon's particular form of ministry and his appointment to the deanery in succession to Henson made little strategic sense. He was in any case well beyond his prime and although he showed some interest in the growing university and never refused an invitation to express his views at a meeting his leadership of the cathedral was undistinguished. He had, however, a high view of his office and when, after addressing a mass meeting of railwaymen at Stockton-on-Tees, one of his listeners asked, 'Who is worth more to the country – a dean or an engine-driver?' he replied, only half humorously, 'A dean is worth more than an engine-driver if only because the engine-driver would take people from Stockton to Newcastle, but a dean would take them from Stockton to Heaven.'

His sermons were replete with reminiscences, platitudes and what he considered to be good advice on matters of personal and social behaviour. Yet a mining disaster in one of the colliery villages would find him at the pithead, comforting families as the bodies of the casualties were brought to the surface and he was a welcome preacher in the parish church on the following Sunday. He also established good relations with the tenant farmers of the dean and chapter's extensive estates which, unlike those of the other capitular bodies, had not been surrendered to the Ecclesiastical Commissioners. Requests for rent reduction were, as he put it, 'always responded to with kindly feeling, if not always with acquiescence'. From time to time tenants were entertained to lunch in the cathedral library and whenever one of their number died Welldon wrote a sympathetic letter to the widow and her family. The dean and chapter were represented at the funeral. 'Very different this, sir, from the Ecclesiastical Commissioners', one of them told him. 'When we go to pay our rents to them we are drawn up in a queue as though we were on the dole.'

Unlike his bishop, Welldon was opposed to the revision of the Prayer Book in 1927/8 and believed that the problem of liturgical rebellion should have been dealt with by the bishops much earlier simply by depriving the rebels of their livings. On other matters he was, however, surprisingly open to reform and this sprang from his belief that an established, endowed church should display a liberal, comprehensive spirit. Thus he pleaded for the simplification of the Creed and suggested that an acceptance of the Bible and Apostles' Creed should be the only requirement for Church membership. Church unity in a federal form he regarded as an urgent necessity for missionary purposes, but also in order to confront 'a rigid despotic Roman Catholic Church' with something it could not ignore and with which it might be driven to collaborate. The ordination of women was something for which there could be no 'ultimate objections', and he added, 'I find it difficult to believe that when women become cabinet ministers they should not be entitled to become deacons and priests.' The arrival of the Church Assembly, more frequent meetings of diocesan conferences and other bodies was, he believed, 'evil' inasmuch as it was leading to centralization and distracting bishops and the parish clergy from their work of saving souls. Another distraction he denounced arose from preoccupation with 'the trivialities of rites and ceremonies' and he thought that a Collect for the Common Sense of the Clergy was a more urgent need.

The declining quality of the clergy, explained partly by the fact that they were not so well educated as in the past, greatly troubled him and, himself unmarried, he believed the answer lay in the encouragement of more of them to accept, at least for some years, the discipline of celibacy. This would, he explained, make them cheaper to employ and easier to assign to difficult work at home and abroad. Furthermore it would make it possible for men to speak to young men about purity; he did not see how they could do this if they were themselves enjoying the sensual delights of marriage.

Like some other clergymen of his time, Welldon became interested in eugenics and, in the 1930s, having noted that Hitler had adopted sterilization as 'the means of preventing the indefinite multiplication of unwanted children' went on to declare, 'A nation cannot fail to lose ground both physically and morally, if the worst citizens are encouraged – or even permitted – to impose upon the better citizens the well-nigh intolerable burden of feeding, clothing, teaching and medically treating the children whom they have brought into the world.' He also regarded warfare as a useful method of population reduction and agreed with Mussolini that it 'has been to manhood what maternity has been to womanhood'. Birth control was, he thought, the only real answer, and he was anxious lest its prohibition by the Roman Catholic Church might lead to a situation in England in which Protestants were outnumbered. An excessive number of foxes was, however, more tolerable – at least it was not to be reduced by hunting with hounds, which he regarded as a cruel sport.

In 1933 Welldon suffered a serious fall in the cathedral from which he could with only the greatest difficulty be raised. This left him crippled and his remaining appearances in the cathedral had to be in a bath chair. He retired to Sevenoaks before the end of the year and died there four years later.

17

The War Hero
Walter Matthews, St Paul's

Walter Matthews, who was Dean of St Paul's from 1934 to 1967 had a remarkable lot in common with his predecessor. He was an accomplished scholar, a Christian Platonist, a liberal churchman, an arresting preacher, a prolific writer and gifted journalist and at the helm of St Paul's during one of the two world wars of the twentieth century. But there was one great difference. Whereas Ralph Inge was shy, austere and forbidding, Matthews was warm-hearted, kindly and popular. These attributes are always welcome in a dean and never more so than at St Paul's during the years 1939–45 when the cathedral stood for a time at the centre of the German blitz on the city of London and came to symbolize the nation's defiance of the most dangerous assault in history on its independence and freedom. Matthews displayed great personal courage and at the same time provided the community over which he presided with inspiration, hope and sensitive pastoral understanding.

On 29 April 1939, by which time it was plain to all that the resolving of the Munich crisis in the previous September had only postponed a European war, the dean and chapter of St Paul's made a momentous decision. The St Paul's Watch, which had been formed during the 1914–18 war to protect the cathedral against enemy attack, was to be re-formed. Then it had found little to do, since air warfare was still in its infancy, but now there could be little doubt that the enemy threat to Wren's masterpiece would require dedicated and skilled resources to ensure its survival. Godfrey Allen, the surveyor of the fabric who knew every nook and cranny of the building, was appointed Commander of the Watch. He recruited other London architects, many professional people from the city, and volunteers from further afield and these were on duty in teams every night from 26 August 1939 until the end of the war in Europe. While it was recognized that the Watch would be powerless to deal with direct hits on the building by high explosive bombs, the danger of extensive fire caused by incendiary bombs was perceived to be no less serious, so members of the Watch were trained to deal with these by means of sand and water.

The main air attack on London took place between 5 September and 31 October 1940. During that summer and that autumn there were 100 consecutive nights of air raid alerts and, although most of the cathedral community were sheltering in the relative comfort of the crypt, the loss of sleep was disabling. Matthews wrote 'one became so sleepy that one drowsed on one's feet and on sitting down immediately lost consciousness'. On the night of 9–10 October a large bomb hit the east end of the choir and exploded in the space between the roof and the ceiling. This brought down masses of heavy masonry, wrecked the high altar, severely damaged the reredos, and completely destroyed one of the 'saucer domes'. All of which raised fears as to the stability of the dome itself, but these were dispelled following the making of tests and, in spite of the shortage of material and equipment, and continual air raids, the cathedral's works staff carried out essential repairs to the roof.

The bombing continued spasmodically throughout the winter and during the following spring. On 29 December a major fire raid on the city set the area around St Paul's ablaze and led to one of the war's most dramatic photographs which showed the cathedral's dome, surmounted by a cross, illuminated by fire and surrounded by dense smoke. The Prime Minister, Winston Churchill, sent a message 'St Paul's must be saved at all costs'. By this time, however, the water supply to the city had failed and Wren's chapter house, together with most of the surrounding buildings, including many Wren churches, had been gutted. But on the cathedral roof the Watch was dealing with some hundreds of incendiary bombs, throwing them to the ground or extinguishing them with sand and stored water. Afterwards Matthews pointed out to the authorities that much of the damage caused to the city that night would have been avoided had the other buildings been protected by Watches.

The greatest damage to the cathedral was sustained during the night of 16/17 April 1941 when a bomb pierced the roof of the north transept and exploded inside the building. Gaping holes were left in the roof and the floor, all the glass was shattered, and some monuments and furnishings were destroyed. Doubts about the safety of the roof required the daily services, maintained throughout the war with men voices, the choristers having been evacuated to Truro, to be held henceforth in the crypt. While grappling with these and many other associated problems Matthews was mourning the death of his eldest child. Michael, who had secured firsts in classics and law, as well as a cricket Blue, at Oxford, and served as a sub-lieutenant on HMS *Greyhound* – the first destroyer to reach Dunkirk during the great evacuation of the British army at the end of May 1940. While standing on the bridge of his ship he was killed by a bomb dropped by a German aircraft. His death was the great sorrow of Matthews's life and something from which his mother, a novelist, never really recovered. On the Sunday following the tragedy Matthews preached in the cathedral on the text 'He saved others; Himself he cannot save' (Matthew 27.2). The post-war restoration of St Paul's, which created immense financial problems, continued until the year before his retirement.

Walter Robert Matthews was born in Camberwell, South London in 1881. His evangelical parents took him to church and, after attending the local Wilson's Grammar School and working for a few years in a city branch of the Westminster Bank, he entered King's College, London, to read theology. There he was greatly influenced by the Principal, A. C. Headlam, who later became a notable Bishop of Gloucester, and he also came under the spell of R. J. Campbell, a prominent liberal theologian who occupied the pulpit of the City Temple. Matthews was not initially drawn to holy orders and when eventually he offered himself to the Bishop of London he was turned down for stating in the ordination examination that the story of the raising of Lazarus was probably not a historical event. At this point Headlam intervened and after Matthews had signed a compromise statement he was ordained.

A curacy at St Mary Abbots, Kensington, was combined with a junior lectureship in ethics and logic at King's College but he left the parish after one year because he was unhappy about ministering to the very rich. Neither were they happy with him, as an active member of the Liberal Party. He then served for a time at St Peter's, Regent Square, St Pancras, which had some rough parts in its generally rich parish, but when King's College lost most of its students following the outbreak of war in 1914 he was obliged to relinquish his teaching post and return to Kensington. This was for only a short time, however, as he was soon appointed vicar of Christ Church, Crouch End, in North London. This had a middle-class, intelligent congregation that greatly appreciated his services and sermons. But not for long, since he was at the end of 1917, and to his own great astonishment, elected dean and Professor of the Philosophy of Religion at King's College, London.

Others were astonished, too: and a postcard from a friend on the teaching staff, Clement Rogers, advised him, 'If you accept, we shall all resign.' His response was to send a telegram of acceptance, but the number of resignations was small.

The next 14 years were spent first in close collaboration with the Principal in rebuilding the life of the College from the depredations of war, and at the same time raising academic standards in the theology department, for which he was wholly responsible. This second task proved to be specially difficult, owing to a shortage of money for the payment of well-qualified professors and lecturers, but he persuaded a number of good scholars to combine their teaching with parish work, and the acquisition of Charles Gore, after his resignation from the Bishopric of Oxford, did much to enhance the college's reputation. Matthews was himself interested in the philosophy of religion but had published no more than a few essays and papers and immediately found it necessary to prepare a two-year course of lectures not only on Theism as a philosophy, but also on the elements of comparative religion.

He was in fact a highly effective teacher, as well as a guide and mentor to those in the department, the overwhelming majority, who were preparing for ordination, and by the time he left King's College in 1931 he was one of the leading members of the always small company of philosophical theologians. The most substantial of his 25 books, *God in Christian Thought and Experience*, published in 1930, confirmed his reputation as a thinker who could stand alongside William Temple, F. R. Tennant and John Baillie – contemporaries who were concerned to demonstrate the rational qualities of the Christian faith. It ran to seven editions, the last of which appeared in 1945. His views, and theirs, now seem distinctly dated – philosophy and theology have moved on – but during the 1920s and '30s their work represented an important attempt to show that Christian belief is intellectually respectable.

During the early years of his career Matthews described himself as a liberal and a modernist, and neither was inaccurate inasmuch as he was always open to new insights and ready to interpret Christianity in the language and thought forms of his day. Moreover he sat lightly to ecclesiastical authority and until the end of his day deeply regretted that the Church of England was unwilling to face the challenge of revising its sixteenth-century Thirty-Nine Articles of Religion. Yet on the core Christian doctrines he was essentially conservative. He had no problem with the concept of God or Trinity and, although he was unhappy with some of the Patristic definitions of the incarnation including that of the fifth-century Council of Chalcedon, which he described as unteachable, he believed that there could be no definition that did not emphasize equally the divinity and the humanity of Christ and present him as a unique being. He had no sympathy with the liberal-modernist view that the Kingdom of God would be realized in an ideal society on earth. 'Process theology' associated with A. N. Whitehead and some of his American followers was rejected on the grounds that it was not compatible with the Christian concept of creation. His position was closest to that of the early Cambridge Platonists, and, although his brave attempt to break new ground by using psychological categories to interpret Christian belief about original sin and Christ's sacrificial death was applauded, it won no significant support.

From 1931 onwards, however, philosophy had to be combined with the responsibility for two cathedrals. The three years he spent as Dean of Exeter were, he said, 'a paradisal interlude, standing out as happy beyond all others'. His bishop was none other than Lord Ernest William Gascoyne Cecil, a scion of the great house of Cecil whose eccentricities sometimes seemed to cross the borderline of madness. Matthews and his wife stayed with him for a few days before the installation and at tea one afternoon when the dean-elect was out on cathedral business Cecil surprised his guest by throwing powdered copper sulphate on the fire to turn the flames bright green. 'Nice colour', he remarked. Mrs Matthews was even more astonished when two rats appeared from holes in the floorboards to be fed with crumpets. The bishop assured her that they were intelligent and friendly. 'Love in a mist' they called him in the diocese, for he was exasperatingly unpredictable, but Matthews always spoke highly of him, recognizing beneath a very strange personality powerful signs of love and grace. Among those present at the installation was a former King's College London colleague, A. C. Headlam, who wrote:

> I feel I must come to see you on the last day when you are a reason-
> able human being. My experience is that when a man is installed as
> dean of a cathedral he becomes prejudiced and pig-headed.

Matthews became neither, though his open, liberal approach to the cathedral's witness created some controversy in a staunchly conservative diocese. Thus the staging of John Masefield's play *Good Friday* as part of the cathedral's 800th anniversary celebrations brought a public expression of disapproval from the bishop, though he changed his mind after he had seen it. The bishop again objected when Matthews invited two distinguished Free Church scholars – Wheeler Robinson and Scott Lidgett – to contribute to a course of lectures on 'The Kingdom of Christ and the Teaching of the New Testament'. He said that since the Free Churchmen had not subscribed to the Thirty-Nine Articles of Religion they were disqualified from preaching or speaking in the cathedral. More than half of the clergy in the diocese signed a petition against the Free Church lecturers, but Matthews pressed on with his course, which was very well attended, and he concluded that the petitioners were less concerned about the Free Churchmen than they were about the suggestion that they should be willing to think critically about religion – 'They are content with what they learned in their theological college, and that must lead to a crisis of belief in the Church.'

During his short time at Exeter Matthews preached in many of the churches in the diocese and made himself accessible to anyone who wished to consult him. And besides completing *God in Christian Thought and Experience* he wrote a satire in response to George Bernard Shaw's *A Black Girl in Search of God*, which he called *Gabriel in Search of Mr. Shaw*. When, however, W. R. Inge, having passed his seventy-fourth birthday, announced his retirement from St Paul's in 1934, Matthews was his obvious successor, though he accepted only with the greatest reluctance. On his removal journey from Exeter to London he paused at the Devon/Somerset border and wept.

Neither was his reception at St Paul's as cordial as might have been wished. Canon Sidney Alexander, who had been on the chapter since 1909 and caused Inge a great deal of trouble, was a powerful figure and disappointed that he had been passed over for the deanery. So he objected to the nomination of Matthews on the ludicrous grounds that his university degrees, which included a DD and a DLitt., were from London, rather than Oxford or Cambridge. This was quickly rejected and Alexander, as senior canon, was required, much to his chagrin, to carry out the installation. Archbishop Lang, who had a considerable hand in the appointment, thought that the influence of St Paul's had declined in recent years and told Matthews that reforms and a new spirit were needed. The Prime Minister, Ramsay MacDonald, summoned his nominee to Downing Street and in the cabinet room delivered what almost amounted to a lecture. He declared that St Paul's was not making the contribution to the life of the nation which it had in the past and that this was due to the last dean's involvement in journalism. Before Matthews could offer any comment or offer any defence of his predecessor he was shown out. The text of his first sermon was 'Owe no one anything, but love one another'.

The reformation of St Paul's, for which Primate and Prime Minister were looking, could not be easily accomplished. A revision of the statutes, which involved the bringing together of the ancient statutes contained in several different documents, had been completed shortly before Matthews's arrival and was of a distinctly conservative character. The independence of the college of minor canons was no more, but the canon in residence still had considerable authority during his month on duty and the role of the dean was akin to that of a dogsbody. It was soon made plain to the new dean that the canons were not willing to support changes but an early vacancy on the chapter gave him the chance to persuade the Crown to fill it with Dick Sheppard. Sheppard had won a national reputation as a dynamic and hugely gifted vicar of St Martin in the Fields, but his tenure of the deanery of Canterbury had been cruelly cut short by ill health. Now he was ready to resume his ministry, but with less responsibility, and for three years he and Matthews constituted a minority of two on the chapter. This ended in 1937 when Sheppard was found dead behind the locked door of his study. Yet, in spite of many disagreements extending over many years, Matthews remained on good terms with the canons and was greatly admired and loved by the wider cathedral community.

He inherited, like many another dean, some serious financial problems. A mid-nineteenth-century settlement with the Ecclesiastical Commissioners, following the surrender to them of the dean and chapter's immensely valuable estates, had been adequate for a time but inflation, exacerbated by the 1914–18 war, reduced it to a point where current costs could not be met. An attempt to gain an improved settlement failed and it became necessary to lease the chapter house to Lloyds Bank and the City Livery Club. Neither could members of the chapter manage on their official stipends and it was necessary to select canons who had either a private income or the capacity for substantial literary earnings.

Matthews, whose magnificent deanery required the service of five maids and a man, was hampered initially by the need to provide from his stipend a pension for his predecessor, but a compromise over this was eventually reached with the Ecclesiastical Commissioners. Even so, he needed to augment his income and from 1946 onwards he did this very successfully by means of a regular Saturday reflective article in *The Daily Telegraph*. When invited to undertake this demanding task he replied 'I will try it if you will double the pay' – which they did. Linked usually with the Prayer Book material for the coming Sunday, these articles appeared for more than 25 years and the fact that they remained interesting and illuminating for so long was an indication of their writer's fertile mind and wide-ranging interests. A collection of them published in 1952 is no less interesting today.

An early innovation at the cathedral was the introduction of a Christmas crib and tree. Both were firmly resisted by the chapter, but Dick Sheppard cunningly got King George V to present a tree from the Sandringham estate and this could not be refused. Crib and tree became immediately popular. The response to a New Year's Eve service was so great that it became unmanageable. A crowd of several thousands assembled outside the cathedral and Dick Sheppard attempted to address those who were unable to gain admission. He was, however, shouted down and pelted with empty beer and whisky bottles, with the result that the police forbade any more New Year activity in and around the cathedral.

The excessive length of the Sunday morning worship soon engaged the new dean's attention. The combination of mattins and choral Eucharist with a sermon lasted more than two hours and Matthews proposed that mattins with a sermon should be followed by an interval, after which there would be the choral Eucharist. Once again a majority of the chapter opposed change and in the end Matthews threatened to resign if they would not back him. The bishop, Winnington-Ingram, intervened on the side of the dean and in the end it was agreed that the new timetable would be adopted, provided that the old order was retained on the great festivals. The small attendance at daily sung mattins – sometimes no more than two or three in the winter – led Matthews to write a music-hall type song:

The Man Who Went to Mattins at St Paul's

Every morning when the bell so loudly calls,
On the stones my lonely footstep gently falls
   Through the empty, echoing aisles,
   And the chairs that stretch for miles,
Walks the Man who goes to Mattins at St Paul's.

There is an emptiness in benches and in stalls,
Through a wilderness the choir slowly crawls,
   And if Garbo* wants a rest,
   I really think she'd best
Join the Man who goes to Mattins at St Paul's.

O, I love to be within these ancient walls,
And if solitary worship sometimes palls,
   I won't resign my place
   As the world's church-going ace,
I'm the Man who goes to Mattins at St Paul's.

So could there be a tablet that recalls
My claim to be remembered in these halls?
   And just write upon the stone
   These moving words alone,
'He never missed a Mattins at St Paul's.'

Surprisingly, the chapter agreed to Matthews's proposal that mattins should be sung at 1 p.m. on Wednesday and Friday, thus encouraging office workers to attend during their lunch hour.

Beyond the cathedral he was President of the Modern Churchmen's Union but, although he never ceased to look for more rational expressions of the Christian faith, he remained orthodox on the fundamentals of the Creeds. His frequent attempts to secure the revision of the Thirty-Nine Articles of Religion were always rebuffed and when the report of an Archbishop's Commission on *Doctrine in the Church of England*, on which he had served, was presented to the Convocation of Canterbury in 1938 his renewed plea for revision of the Articles was rejected by a large majority. The experience of lecturing on RAF stations during the war led him to conclude that one of the reasons for the falling away from the Church was the lack of clarity in its teaching.

In April 1939 Matthews proposed that the Archbishop of Canterbury, Cosmo Gordon Lang, should go to Rome without previous warning and on his arrival, amid an organized blaze of publicity, try to persuade Pope Pius XII to join with him in a plea for peace. Lang consulted the other bishops who advised him not to go, and he expressed his own fear that he might be snubbed by the Pope. To

---

* Greta Garbo, a leading film star in the 1930s, often pleaded 'I want to be alone'.

which Matthews responded, 'Suppose you are snubbed in your effort to stop a world war who will seem the better in the judgement of history (to say nothing of the judgement of God) the snubber or the snubbed?' Lang decided not to put this to the test.

Less than a year later, February 1940, Matthews was on his way, at the request of the Ministry of Information, to the still neutral Norway, Sweden, Denmark and Holland. The purpose was to give lectures stating the British case against Germany and to gather information about the state of opinion in the churches and communities. The Ministry officials insisted that he should wear decanal dress, but it was not this that led to his receiving a mixed reception. The people were nervous, some were hostile and half the audience walked out of one of his lectures. During the war years the cathedral congregations dwindled but a Guild of Prayer, started at the time of the Munich crisis, attracted a large number of members who committed themselves to pray daily in St Paul's or elsewhere for specific subjects. The King and Queen made many informal visits, especially during the darkest period of the war. The cathedral's bells rang out to celebrate the liberation of Paris on 24 August 1944, and on VE day in 1945, although nothing had been planned and no signs or notices were displayed, an estimated 35,000 people attended nine services of thanksgiving held at intervals from morning till night. The King and Queen attended a special service on the following Sunday. Later the King of Norway awarded Matthews his country's Liberty Cross and the President of Czechoslovakia awarded him the Order of White Lion.

The return of peace demanded of Matthews much attention to the repair of the building and the renewal of the cathedral's life. But he was now free to travel abroad again for preaching and lecturing, which he did extensively. He also preached in the diocese a good deal and was a very popular after-dinner speaker in the city. The Council of Christians and Jews won his enthusiastic support, and members of the Lower House of the Convocation of Canterbury elected him as their Prolocutor. Chairmanship of meetings concerned with the revision of Canon Law – 'a misconceived project' – was, however, a great trial to him, and his involvement in central church government led him to conclude 'Our contemporary Bishops carry little weight: this is partly because they have nothing worth hearing to say.' He believed that they needed more time to read and think, and that the Church needed them to be 'leaders of armies and strategists' rather than simply pastors and administrators. He believed it was only a matter of time – a short time he hoped – before women were ordained to the priesthood. Interest in ethical questions led to his election as an Honorary Fellow of the Eugenics Society and he spoke at an annual meeting of the Society for the Legislation of Voluntary Euthanasia. Membership of an Archbishop's Commission on Artificial Insemination by Donor ended with him dissenting from its conclusion that this medical practice was always inherently evil.

Further financial problems led to the formation of the Friends of St Paul's in 1952 but not before opposition from the chapter had been overcome and a careful definition of the organization's limitations been agreed. Members of the wartime Watch were the first to join. During the 1960s the number of special services increased considerably and in 1965 the cathedral was in the world spotlight for the State funeral of Winston Churchill. Soon after this the Lord Mayor of London raised enough money to pay for the cleaning of the whole of the cathedral's exterior and, although Matthews found it necessary to answer criticisms from the general public, a surprising number of whom valued the grime, and those in the church who believed the money could have been put to better use, the final result was widely acclaimed.

Having reached the age of 86 in 1967, it was hardly surprising when Matthews announced that he was finding it difficult to cope with the responsibilities of office and proposed to retire. No other Dean of St Paul's, apart from R. W. Church, had been so loved and admired, and when the Queen added to the KCVO, which is a routine recognition of a decanal ministry at the metropolitan cathedral, appointment as a Companion of Honour this was universally acknowledged as fitting. He died in 1973.

18

The Socialist
Hewlett Johnson, Canterbury

Hewlett Johnson – 'The Red Dean' – who was at Manchester from 1924 to 1931, then at Canterbury until his retirement in 1963 at the age of 88, was the most widely known cathedral dean of all time, and also the most widely derided. Archbishop Geoffrey Fisher described his leadership at Canterbury as ineffective, yet, in spite of long absences, he was as competent as most of the other deans of his time and the large congregation that attended his funeral indicated that he was neither unappreciated nor unloved in his own city. During the war years when Canterbury was subjected to frequent German bombing he displayed outstanding courage. Certainly he looked every inch a dean. Tall, big-boned, endowed with a fine face and a splendid, domed head, framed by plentiful white hair, he was an imposing figure, and at the enthronement of Michael Ramsey in 1961 the sight of the dean and the Archbishop, who had a not dissimilar appearance, suggested a flashback to the Middle Ages.

Successive Primates were in fact often seriously embarrassed and sometimes annoyed when, as was commonly the case, the general public in Britain and overseas confused identities and attributed the dean's utterances about Communism to the Archbishop. Johnson became notorious because of his whole-hearted and uncritical acceptance of Communism as the best social and economic expression of the Christian belief that men and women are called to love their neighbours as themselves. And the Communism he embraced and promoted was not the visionary type of a Karl Marx but that which found expression in the totalitarian regime of Stalin's Soviet Union in the 1930s and '40s.

His book *The Socialist Sixth of the World*, published in December 1939, soon after the outbreak of World War II, brought him instant world fame. Seven hundred pages long, it was an account of a three-month-long stay in the Soviet Union as a guest of the Government, and sold several million copies in 22 editions and 24 languages. It informed its readers that the Soviet peoples were activated by a moral purpose and working for the common good, being motivated by Christian morality, even though they denied this. There was scant reference to the problems created by what he called 'the Soviet experiment' and none at all to Stalin's reign of terror which during the 1920s and '30s had decimated the Russian Orthodox Church and consigned millions to prison camps or firing squads. In 1951 Johnson was one of the first recipients of a newly created Stalin Peace Prize.

Later, his support of Chinese Communism and the rule of Chairman Mao Tse-tung was no less enthusiastic, and he was a welcome visitor to Cuba where Fidel Castro assured him of the great influence of his book in Latin America, and where he was pleased to meet Che Guevara. Yet Johnson was by no means unintelligent. He had an Oxford DD – awarded admittedly at a time when the requirements were nothing like as high as they are today – he was a brilliant preacher and speaker, and his fervent belief that the Christian faith required expression in Christian brotherhood could hardly be regarded as outrageous. It was simply that he became obsessed with socialism as the only answer to the world's problems and incapable of seeing its political outworking in other than madly idealistic terms. This, combined with certain unfortunate flaws of character eventually took him beyond the borders of absurdity. Victor Gollancz, a one-time friend and publisher, was cruel but not inaccurate in his assessment of Johnson:

> The dean was destroyed (for if his make-up had been only a little different he might have become a great man) by a number of tragic defects, many of which merge into one another. By spiritual pride: by intellectual arrogance, coupled with a brain not quite of the first order: by vanity: by the temptations – or rather by a lack of resistance when assailed by the temptations – inherent in a magnificent presence: by an absence of mental scrupulosity or pernicketiness: and certainly not least, by his ability as an actor. What an actor the man was!

Hewlett Johnson was born in 1874 in Kersal, at that time a fashionable suburb of Manchester. His father was the prosperous owner of Johnson's Wire Works and a devout man, while his mother was a deeply committed evangelical. His grandfather, Alfred Hewlett, was Vicar of Astley in Lancashire and known as the 'Spurgeon of the

North' because of his powerful preaching. When the family moved to a large house, requiring a considerable domestic staff, in Macclesfield, young Hewlett went to the local grammar school. There he displayed no great academic aptitude and when he was 16 left to study science, including geology, at Owen's College, which later became Manchester University. He also took up engineering and having secured a BSc also qualified as a member of the Institution of Civil Engineers. During this time he underwent a spiritual crisis which led to a period of agnosticism, but this was eventually modified as a consequence of his interest in psychical research.

Johnson spent three and a half years working for a firm of railway engineers and the contrast between the conditions of the ordinary workers and those of the managers provided fertile soil for the seeds of socialism that were to make spectacular growth when he became a priest. Meanwhile he moved to employment in his father's wire works before offering his services to the Church Missionary Society as a missionary engineer. The Society insisted, however, that he should first spend a year studying theology at Wycliffe Hall, Oxford, and the experience of this encouraged him to stay on and take a second class degree in theology at Wadham College. The effect of this was to move his beliefs in a direction much too liberal for the liking of the then highly conservative CMS and his offer for missionary work was rejected.

By now he was married to Mary Taylor who not only played an important part in the first 25 years of his ministry but also added her substantial private income to his own useful financial resources. Johnson was never short of money and, having lost the opportunity to become a missionary, he used some of it to launch a monthly magazine *The Interpreter*, designed to provide a forum for the presentation of the Christian faith in the categories of emerging twentieth-century thought. Edited by himself, and always subsidized, it survived for 20 years and attracted contributions from many reputable scholars, as well as a few Christian Socialists.

In 1905 Johnson was ordained and became a curate at St Margaret's, Altrincham – a parish in which the richest Manchester businessmen lived and where the vicar was an archdeacon. During the next three years Johnson made such an impact on the area that when the archdeacon moved to other work the leading lights in the parish petitioned the patron, Lord Stanford, to appoint him to the vicarage. Which he did, and Johnson embarked on a 16-year ministry of considerable vigour and distinction. His preaching, aided by his editorship of *The Interpreter*, was always stimulating, he had a flair for youth work and ran popular summer camps, and his journalistic skill also found expression in a lively monthly newspaper.

Neither were his interests confined to church work. He came increasingly under the influence of two Christian Socialists – Conrad Noel and Lewis Donaldson – and among his many interventions in Manchester's social affairs was a petition to the city council about insanitary slums. A significant pointer towards things to come was his chairmanship in 1917 of a public meeting called to welcome the Russian Revolution, with Bertrand Russell as the chief speaker. The effects of the war, especially the ever-increasing roll of casualties among his parishioners, also greatly affected him and extensive travel in Europe when the war had ended made him even more aware of the heavy cost of war. During the war he served as chaplain of a German prisoner-of-war camp located in the parish and this, too, increased his hatred of armed conflict. In a book on *Socialism and Social Credit* – a naive economic theory which interested him for many years – he wrote 'Capitalism had war at its heart from the first. If Capitalism began in petty commercial strife, it ends in war.' He looked forward to a time when service would replace profit, planning would replace personal whim, production would become both scientific and moral, having for its motive the provision of the means of wellbeing for all. It was a lofty ideal which he promoted by preaching and speaking in all parts of the country, but when in a Westminster Abbey sermon he praised the developments in post-Revolution Russia there were angry protests. Some of his wealthy parishioners in Altrincham were also becoming anxious.

It was perhaps this, as well as admiration for his many gifts, that led some of the more prominent among them to petition the Crown for his appointment to the deanery of Manchester when this fell vacant in 1924. Responsibility for his appointment is usually attributed to Ramsey MacDonald, the Labour Prime Minister at that time. In an interview with Johnson he said, 'It was not only my people of the Labour Party who asked me to appoint you, but the leaders of your own parish, rich and distinguished men . . . . Of course, we are only too glad to appoint you.' But there is evidence that the young William Temple, who had become Bishop of Manchester three years earlier, also played an important part in the decision-making. He had first come to know Johnson in 1918 as a member of the council of the church-reforming Life and Liberty movement, and then came to admire his parish ministry and his involvement in Manchester's civic life. The acquisition of an Oxford DD for some work on the Acts of the Apostles provided the necessary academic background.

Johnson accepted the post with alacrity and heeded the advice of the cathedral's head verger –

> Start well, start with a bang, Sir, work very hard for the first year, Sir, then you will be called 'the busy dean'. You can then take it quietly in subsequent years but the title 'the busy dean' will stick.

But it was never in his nature to take things quietly and a ceaseless round of activity during the whole of his deanship enhanced his reputation as one of Manchester's leading personalities. Unlike most deans he was not preoccupied with financial problems. The cathedral owned large areas of the city and there was money to spare to augment the stipends of city livings. Much of the property was, however, in working class areas where there were many public houses and much drunkenness. Johnson persuaded his chapter to reduce this problem by buying out the pubs and this proved not only to have social benefit but also to increase the value of the surrounding property. Johnson never came to believe that 'property is theft' and in due course built up his own modest portfolio. Nonetheless, the dean and chapter made land available at a low price for better housing for the poor.

Back at the cathedral he had the great west doors changed to glass, so that outsiders could see in and worshippers be reminded of their social responsibilities in the city. He took over the Sunday evening service, re-named it 'the Dean's Hour', and packed the building with people who wondered at his eloquence and were rewarded with a diet consisting of two basic ingredients – a new way of reading the Bible in the light of modern criticism, and Christian Socialism as a substitute for competition. Controversy was confined to complaints from the canons that the dimming of the lights for the dean's sermon was encouraging young people in the congregation to hold hands. Johnson replied that he saw no reason for such action to be discouraged. Banners and processions, after the manner of Conrad Noel at Thaxted, were introduced and a large choir, nearly 100 strong, was recruited. The choir boys were taken to enjoyable camps at Prestatyn and on one occasion the dean, clad in gaiters and apron, ran into the sea to rescue a boy from drowning. Similarly attired, he maintained and extended the practice of his predecessor, Bishop James Welldon, who visited the theatres and opera houses, especially at Christmas. Johnson spoke also to audiences from the stage in the neighbouring towns –

Blackburn, Oldham and Wigan – where he was a great hit and much enjoyed the publicity.

Closure of *The Interpreter* when he became a dean left him with time for contributions to the *Manchester Guardian* and other city newspapers. During the General Strike in 1926 he sided with the miners but on the whole kept fairly quiet about the issues. Less restrained was his praise for the new roads and improved railways in Italy and he congratulated Mussolini, 'our Socialist brother', on his achievements. These inspired the ex-railway engineer dean to challenge the London North West Railway Company's high charges for their sleeping coaches. A Manchester bus company was persuaded to provide coaches with sleeping facilities at lower prices and the effect of the competition had the desired effect of driving down the cost of the Socialist dean's journeys to London. In 1925 and 1927 he attended Peace Congresses in London and Paris, and from 1932 onwards was a frequent visitor to the Soviet Embassy in London as the guest of the Ambassador, Ivan Maisky.

In January 1931 he was, however, deeply affected by the death of his wife from cancer and William Temple, believing that he should move from Manchester, recommended him for appointment as Dean of Canterbury. This was supported by King George V who had been much impressed by his preaching at Windsor. Archbishop Lang of Canterbury approved and, once again, the Prime Minister, Ramsey MacDonald, gladly acceded. By midsummer he was happily in Canterbury, picking up the threads left by Dick Sheppard whose poor health had driven him to vacate the deanery after only two years. But the tranquillity of the cathedral close was soon disturbed. The attendance of the Dean of Canterbury at a garden party at the Soviet Embassy was recorded in the Press and provoked a brief public controversy.

No sooner had this died down than Johnson received as a guest at the deanery Mahatma Gandhi who was attending a Round Table Conference in London about the future of India and, at the suggestion of the missionary C. F. Andrews, had requested a 24-hour break in Canterbury. He brought with him his own goats, which were fed and milked, and having accepted an invitation to attend evensong was placed in a stall next to the dean. The angry canons refused to attend or to meet the great man in the deanery afterwards. Thus Johnson began to learn the difference between his role at Manchester, where his rule over a fairly small team went unchallenged, and at the Cathedral and Metropolitical Church of Christ in Canterbury where distinguished canons were much less easily persuaded and others in the close and the city had their own firm views about the cathedral's life.

This life included, at the time of Johnson's appointment, two major problems. The building needed £200,000 for urgent repairs and the King's School, standing in the shadow of the cathedral, was in dire straits – annual losses having brought a debt of £40,000, leaving available nothing for the repair of its badly decayed buildings. The first was solved relatively easily since George Bell, during his time as dean, had created the first ever Cathedral Friends organization which proved to be capable of raising large sums for the restoration and beautification of the building. The second was less easy and its solution had ramifications which were to plague Johnson for most of his time at Canterbury.

It hardly helped that he was known to be strongly opposed to public schools and that the chairmanship of the governing body of the King's School was accepted by him out of recognition that, for the time being at least, the revolution in England must be stayed. But critical to the school's future and to Johnson's loss of peace was the appointment of a new headmaster. The Reverend John Shirley came from Worksop College and immediately displayed his metal by insisting as a condition of his acceptance that he should be made a residentiary canon of the cathedral. This was made possible by the concurrent appointment of the eccentric Claude Jenkins to the Chair of Ecclesiastical History at Oxford and, having established a power base, Shirley became one of the twentieth century's outstanding headmasters and a persistent thorn in the flesh of his dean. Johnson's long absences on foreign assignments served only to increase Shirley's power.

The first of these assignments took him in 1932 to China where on behalf of a famine relief committee he investigated the effects of catastrophic floods. He covered over 1,600 miles of difficult, and sometimes dangerous, terrain in the company of a committee official and, besides a formal report, contributed an article 'Famine in China' to the *Manchester Guardian* and later wrote on the same subject to *The Times*. He also fell in love with China, and his admiration for its Communist rulers was eventually, and inevitably, to involve him in controversy. This first visit on a humanitarian mission was not without its problems. It required an absence from Canterbury of four months and, although Archbishop Lang felt unable to refuse permission, he made the point, strongly, that Johnson needed to give the impression that he intended to be a resident dean. Johnson responded by requesting a revision of the cathedral's statutes to give him greater freedom to pursue matters of concern in the nation and the wider world. No such revision ever took place but this made no difference to his travels, and in his first report to the chapter he emphasized the need for the cathedral 'to bring itself directly and indirectly into touch with a much wider circle even than the circle of the nation itself'.

The national circle soon contained 2.5 million unemployed and Johnson became active in denouncing an economic system that denied work to one in six of the employable population. The means test imposed on the many who turned for help to the National Assistance Board was the object of his great ire and in 1934 he promoted a modern Pilgrimage of Grace to provide some practical help for the poor. The idea originated with Mrs Bell, the wife of his predecessor but one who was now Bishop of Chichester, and involved the encouragement of people to undertake a pilgrimage to their local cathedrals offering there prayers and gifts for the unemployed. When Westminster Abbey refused to give a lead Johnson took the project under his wing, secured massive publicity, and won the support of 40 cathedrals and 15 other great churches. The King and Queen talked Westminster Abbey into participation and a substantial amount of money was raised – chiefly by the sale of half-crown pilgrimage tickets – and widely distributed. Johnson believed the publicity for the plight of the poor to be equally important.

As in many other cathedrals, the Canterbury statutes prescribed that the dean should preach in the cathedral only at the great festivals. This was intended to leave him free to pursue other interests or possibly to restrict his responsibilities to a bare minimum. But during the latter part of the nineteenth century an increasing number of deans began to feel frustrated by their exclusion from the cathedral pulpit and seized the opportunity provided by the new-style Sunday evening services, outside the scope of statutes, to make their voices heard. Johnson assumed responsibility for all the Sunday evening preaching at Canterbury and used the pulpit to express his own particular brand of Christianity. When absent, other socialist clergymen were invited to take his place.

Johnson also developed the cathedral's involvement in the arts, initiated by George Bell, and the first performance of T. S. Eliot's *Murder in the Cathedral* at the Friends Festival in 1935 was followed two years later by the first performance of Dorothy Sayers' *The Zeal of Thy House*. The cathedral's music was greatly strengthened by the recruitment of a younger team of organists and the highly gifted

Joseph Poole as Precentor. In 1936 eucharistic vestments were introduced for the principal celebrations on holy communion at the high
altar and when the money for these ran out Johnson unwisely
published in the *Church Times* a letter appealing for help. This drew
anguished complaints from extreme Protestant quarters and a reproof
from Archbishop Lang who at the time was struggling to maintain
some semblance of unity in the Church of England. On the whole,
however, Lang was appreciative of Johnson's efforts to improve the
cathedral's rites and ceremonies and told him 'Dean, it is not a change,
it is a revolution'.

By 1936 the dean was more concerned about a very different sort of
revolution. From the outset of the Spanish Civil War he supported the
Republican government against the Fascist forces led by Franco and in
March 1937 went with a group of Anglicans and Free Churchmen to
see for himself what was happening. This became only too plain,
when, soon after the party's arrival in Basque territory, they decided to
visit the town of Durango. As they were approaching the town it was
heavily bombed and almost completely destroyed by German aircraft.
Had they arrived just a little earlier it is more than likely that a new
dean of Canterbury would have been required. Thankful to be still
alive, Johnson went on to Madrid and on his return to Canterbury
appealed for £10,000 for a food ship for the Basque people and used
his Sunday evening sermon to denounce the Spanish and German
Fascists. This drew a letter of protest from Lang who, together with
two other bishops, attacked him in the Church Assembly. Undaunted,
he returned to Spain in the summer of 1938, taking with him a young
woman, Nowell Edwards, to whom he had become engaged the night
before leaving.

Between these visits, however, came his three-month stay in the
Soviet Union in 1937 which led to the writing of *The Socialist Sixth of
the World*. He was accompanied by Alfred D'Eye who went with him
on other visits to Eastern Europe and exercised a considerable
influence over him. He was a Marxist who lectured on history, politics
and economics for the Workers' Educational Association and, when
teaching in Kent, always stayed at the deanery where he assisted
Johnson with the facts and figures and intellectual arguments required
for his speeches and writings on Communism. Whether or not he was
a Soviet agent will never be known – he always denied this – but the
ease with which he moved in Communist circles, inside and outside
Russia, created deep suspicion.

On his return to England Johnson became closely associated with the Left Book Club and spoke all over the country about the virtues of the Soviet system. In a pamphlet, *Act Now! An Appeal to the Heart and Hearth of Britain*, published in the early part of 1939 and twice reprinted, he advocated collaboration with the Soviet Union and the embracing of Socialism to provide effective opposition to the menace of Hitler's Nazism. When in August 1939 the Soviet Union and Germany signed a non-aggression pact most of the leading left-wing leaders in Britain became disenchanted with Russia, but Johnson tried to justify the pact on the grounds that the Western powers had consistently rejected Russian overtures for friendship. The invasion of Finland by the Soviet army in November of that year was, however, plainly an act of unjustified aggression even to someone of Johnson's blinkered vision and for the first, and only, time in his life he criticized his Russian friends. His colleagues in Canterbury were not impressed and in March 1940 a letter appeared in *The Times*:

Sir,
In order to correct any possible misunderstanding, we feel compelled to make it known that we, the Canons Residentiary of Canterbury Cathedral, dissociate ourselves from the political utterances of the Dean of Canterbury, which, as reported in the public Press, have so often given the impression that he condones the offences of Russia against humanity and religion.

We have further thought it our duty to tell him that his political activities gravely impair the spiritual influence of the cathedral in the city and diocese of Canterbury, give grievous offence to many Christians throughout the world, and, in our view, are proving themselves to be incompatible with the proper discharge of the trust which has been committed to him.

We desire to make it known that we are at one with the Dean in believing that it is the duty of all Christians to further social and economic reform, but we believe it to be a dangerous illusion to hold that such reform will ever be achieved by the methods which have characterized the Soviet regime.

Johnson replied at some length, pleading liberty of conscience and assuring the readers of *The Times* that, far from neglecting his cathedral duties, he had attended 38 of the last 39 chapter meetings and, except when away, preached once a fortnight. Lang, who had tried unsuccessfully to act as a mediator, regretted that the canons had made their concern public: 'I only wish that the chapter had always been immune from that strange disease which I was accustomed to call "the cathedral blight" ', he wrote. Lang's relations with Johnson were in fact always most cordial and without trace of friction.

Meanwhile the defence of the cathedral and its community against the expected German onslaughts, resulting from the outbreak of war in September 1939, gathered pace. The crypt was turned into an air-raid shelter for the protection of the inhabitants of the city as well as of the close. This required the importing into certain parts of the building of sufficient soil to provide a three-foot deep protective layer against masonry that might crash onto the cathedral floor and penetrate the crypt ceiling. For several weeks the nave was like a building site. This led the Friends Council and others to protest and request that the protective work be undone, but the dean and chapter refused. In fact, the services were never interrupted, though after May 1940 they were held mainly in the crypt and, the choristers having been evacuated with their school to Cornwall, day boys were recruited from the city to maintain the choral tradition.

During the summer of 1940 Canterbury witnessed much evidence of the Battle of Britain being fought in the sky overhead and on 10 September, when it was reaching its climax, the order came for 15,000 people to be evacuated from the city. From this time onwards survival and the protection of the cathedral became Johnson's primary concern and, after Hitler's attack on the Soviet Union in 1941, his pronouncements on the merits of Soviet Communism provoked less controversy. During a lunch-time air raid in mid-October 1940 a large bomb – one of three to fall in the precincts – landed immediately outside the deanery front door. The thick walls of the building's façade collapsed into the crater, all the windows of the house were blown out and the interior was wrecked. Emergency repairs were carried out, but for the remainder of the war Johnson, and a number of his neighbours whose houses had been destroyed, and who came to live in the deanery, endured considerable hardship.

Another heavy raid on the night of 31 May/1 June 1941 was described by Johnson as 'terrifying and awe-inspiring, a large part of the city was ablaze, precincts' houses were again lost and many incendiary bombs fell on the cathedral roof'. These were effectively dealt with by trained fire-fighters who, as at St Paul's, were on duty on the roof throughout the war and in the end the cathedral, protected by sandbags, suffered only superficial damage. Not so the rest of the city which, by the end of the war, had suffered the deaths of 115 of its people with another 380 injured. A total of 445 high explosive bombs and 10,000 incendiaries caused the total destruction of 731 houses, serious damage to another 1,000 and slight damage to a further 5,000 properties. Throughout the onslaught Johnson stood as a pillar of faith and courage, and for most people in Canterbury this was far more important than his eccentric views on Communism. In April 1942 it fell to him to enthrone William Temple as Archbishop of Canterbury.

Three days after the German attack on the Soviet Union Johnson launched an appeal for a National Anglo-Soviet Medical Aid Fund and travelled the length and breadth of the country, appealing on its behalf. There was a huge response and besides £1.25 million a vast number of blankets and clothes were collected. He also prophesied that the invasion of the Soviet Union would lead to Hitler's downfall. The unexpected wartime alliance led to the reopening in 1943 of the banned Communist newspaper the *Daily Worker*, and at a meeting attended by 1,600 delegates Johnson was elected to honorary membership of its board, contributing articles until the end of his life.

On VE day 1945 he was on a visit to the Soviet Union and preached at a thanksgiving service in the British embassy in Moscow before accompanying Patriarch Alexi to the Orthodox cathedral. Later he had a 50-minute meeting with Stalin and Molotov during which the Soviet leader complained about the attitude of the British Press. Johnson explained to him that the newspapers were all owned by millionaires and that the only honest journal was the *Daily Worker*. He also offered the assurance that the great mass of workers in Britain had a lively and friendly feeling to the USSR, and, having observed many of the actions of the Soviet authorities, he felt them to be in closer accord with Christian teaching and morality than some of the actions of the Russian churches. He recorded that Stalin and Molotov responded with smiles.

This visit took him also to Leningrad and Stalingrad, where he was appalled by the war damage, and on to Georgia, Armenia (where he was present at the election and consecration of a new Catholicos), Czechoslovakia (where he met President Benes), Central Asia (where he spent a day with the Imam of Tashkent) and finally to Poland. There he was among the first British observers to visit Auschwitz and was particularly devastated by the scene at the German Institute of Hygiene in Danzig where the dismantled bodies of the victims of experiments were still piled high.

Soon after his return to Canterbury Johnson was off again – this time to America at the request of the Friends of American–Soviet

Unity. He spent 40 minutes with President Truman, then, in company with Dean Acheson, the Under-Secretary of State, addressed a mass meeting in Madison Square Gardens. This was followed by visits to Chicago, Boston, Toronto and Montreal. 1947 found him in Hungary, describing the elections as fair, and in Yugoslavia he spent a day with Tito. The same year saw the publication of his *Soviet Success* which drew a sharp response from Archbishop Geoffrey Fisher who always found Johnson's certainties irritating and the confusion in the public's mind between the dean and the Archbishop of Canterbury particularly galling. He issued a Press statement pointing out that the recent actions and utterances of the Dean of Canterbury had given rise to widespread misunderstanding in Britain and abroad – 'The Archbishop of Canterbury has neither responsibility for what the dean may say, nor the power to control him.' The attitude of the chapter was also hostile, but the vergers and workmen thought well of him and ordinary visitors to the cathedral were delighted by the impressive sight of a churchman about whom they had read so much in their newspapers.

In 1948 the US government refused him a visa when he sought to accept an invitation from the American–Soviet Friendship society, so he went instead to a World Peace Conference in Poland. A year later, however, he managed to get into America and gave 21 major speeches there and in Canada, including one to 20,000 people in New York where he appeared with the black singer Paul Robeson. Thereafter no year passed without visits to one or more countries, usually in Eastern Europe, where he often spoke at Peace Conferences, and sometimes further afield in Australia, China and Cuba.

Over the front porch of the deanery a three-foot-high board declared Christians Ban Nuclear Weapons. During a visit to China in 1952 he dined with the Prime Minister Chou En-lai and discussed political and social matters with Chairman Mao. He also picked up an allegation that in the Korean War, then raging, the American forces had used germ weapons, and on his return to London airport produced to 60 waiting journalists documents said to prove his allegation. There was an immediate storm of protest in the Press, while in the House of Lords Archbishop Fisher was among the peers who petitioned the Queen for Johnson's removal from office. In the House of Commons Winston Churchill, the Prime Minister, was content to observe that the dean was old and misguided. The two men were in fact born in the same year.

A visit to Hungary soon after the Soviet military intervention in

1956 led Johnson to the conclusion that the Hungarian Government had invited the Russian tanks to roll since there were those in their country who were determined to destroy Socialist gains and ready to promote German re-militarization. But the Suez crisis later that year was denounced from the cathedral pulpit as 'naked aggression'. Once more the deanery was besieged by the Press. 1956 was not a good year for Johnson. On Easter Day when Archbishop Fisher was processing out of the cathedral after evensong he was astonished to encounter the dean showing a Russian leader around the nave. Fisher was furious and as soon as he reached his palace penned a letter: 'You are the Dean of Canterbury Cathedral, the Mother Church of the Anglican Communion and to bring this man and all he stands for to Canterbury on Easter Day was provocative in the extreme.' Johnson explained that he had not wished to cause embarrassment, but the Russian party had arrived late and he thought it right to show them the cathedral in the time available, which unfortunately coincided with evensong.

The events of the year also brought conflict with the King's School which led the headmaster, Canon Shirley, to place the deanery out of bounds to the boys, and the governing body to indicate that they no longer wished the dean to chair their meetings. This was beyond their power and a compromise was reached when the Archbishop agreed, in his role as Visitor, to chair meetings on public occasions. Eventually Johnson resumed his place at all the meetings, but Shirley never ceased to oppose him in most cathedral matters. Both school and cathedral were, in the immediate post-war period, faced with serious financial problems arising from bomb damage and the loss of rents from city property which had been destroyed. A world-wide appeal for £300,000 for the cathedral was quickly achieved, thanks mainly to an American who contributed $500,000.

In all his conflicts and on his world-wide travels Johnson was greatly supported by his second wife Nowell. Young, beautiful and a talented artist, she was the daughter of his cousin and first visited the deanery when commissioned to paint his portrait. Her visits continued long after the portrait had been completed and, while some residents of the precincts presumed her to be a dutiful daughter looking after her widowed father, he normally introduced her as his niece. The inevitable gossip was heightened for a time when their engagement and marriage was announced but it proved to be a most happy partnership, blessed by the birth of two daughters. During the war years the young family lived in a delightful house in Harlech, Wales, which Johnson had acquired some years earlier. This was partly for reasons of their safety but also to free him for his heavy wartime responsibilities.

On her return to Canterbury when the war was over Nowell found herself subject to much of the hostility that the precincts' residents were now showing to her husband. The canons would not attend when he was preaching and one refused to receive holy communion at his hands. She shared his Communist convictions, always stood by him, accompanied him on most of his foreign tours and was usually alongside him on the platform whenever he was speaking, sometimes making her own contribution. These tours were exhausting but not without their compensations, for dean and wife were fêted wherever they went, accommodated at the best hotels and, having completed their duties, were often rewarded with a few weeks' holiday at an attractive resort. As he grew older these breaks, and the medical facilities included in them, became increasingly important to Johnson, for besides his travels he had a punishing Canterbury timetable, starting at 4 a.m. every day.

In 1962 he had a fall in his study which caused a broken collarbone and shortly before Christmas of that year the canons made a strongly worded request that he should retire. He was now 88. The announcement came on 31 December. In March he attended a Labour Party reception in Manchester and addressed a large *Daily Worker* meeting in the city's Free Trade Hall. Canterbury cathedral was packed for his final service on 27 April. By now he was the owner of a shop in Canterbury and a restaurant in a nearby village, and, in addition to his Harlech house and a London pied-à-terre, he owned a property in Canterbury which, on his retirement to it, he renamed The Red House. Off-shore investments reduced his income tax liability. On his ninetieth birthday greetings came from Krushchev, the Soviet President, and from Socialist countries throughout the world. In the same year he went back to China at the request of Chou En-lai and was received by Chairman Mao Tse-tung in the Hall of the Peoples.

During his final years he resumed his earlier interest in psychical research and often preached about life after death. He died in 1966 aged 92. In a somewhat turgid autobiography *Searching for Light* completed, with the aid of his wife and A. T. D'Eye, just three weeks before he caught pneumonia, he explained that the aim of his life and work had been to help 'create a World Brotherhood – modelled on the family in which I lived as a boy, a large happy family, not all equal in ability, but all equal in consideration and opportunity'. His funeral took place in the cathedral and his ashes were interred in the Cloister

Garth. Among the large congregation were the Archbishop and the Mayor of Canterbury, and also the First Secretary from the Soviet Embassy in London and the General Secretary of the British Communist Party – of which the 'Red Dean' was never a member.

19

The Master Glazier
Eric Milner-White, York

'The Dean of Kings and the King of Deans' they called him and certainly Eric Milner-White's 22-year reign at York (1941–63) was majestic, if not imperious. During these years his achievements in the key areas of the Minster's life – worship, furnishings and the care of the famous stained glass – were remarkable and few would dispute that he was one of York's greatest deans.

The secret of his success was the combination of an autocratic style of leadership, a wide-ranging knowledge of the arts which few were able to challenge, and a considerable private income which he was more than ready to use to pay for the projects close to his heart. Add to this a deep Christian devotion, expressed in books of prayers that enriched the spiritual life of the whole Church, and a celibate vocation that left the Minster without a rival for his love. It was a potent mixture that few other cathedral deans could ever be expected to produce.

His handling of the stained glass demonstrated, however, the perils inherent in such a style of decanal leadership. York's 128 windows contained the largest and most glorious collection of medieval glass in England. Milner-White arrived on the scene during the darkest of days of the 1939–45 war, just in time to see the last of the 80 best panels being removed to protective storage. His appointment to York and the attraction of this post to him (he had earlier declined Salisbury) undoubtedly owed much to the knowledge of stained glass which he had cultivated at King's College, Cambridge, where he was dean from 1918 to 1941.

In 1944, with the end of the war in sight, and bombing no longer a serious threat, he ordered some of the glass to be taken out of storage. This revealed to him that, as a consequence of earlier removals during restorations of the building, many of the two million pieces were no longer in their original places. The next 18 years were therefore devoted to the cleaning, conservation and re-ordering of the jigsaws. Milner-White assumed the role of master glazier and visited the work-shop twice or three times every day to supervise the work of a small team of skilled craftsmen, and to make decisions about the positioning of individual lozenges of glass. Sometimes he took small panels on his journeys to London and, to the mystification of his fellow passengers, would carry out cleaning in the railway carriage. Tedious debates in the Church Assembly also provided opportunities for work on the glass.

Many of his decisions were inspired, particularly those relating to the great east window, and he was not afraid to make radical choices involving the removal of panels to different windows. He also seized opportunities to add to the Minster's treasure house by acquiring medieval glass from redundant churches and stately homes. All of which he carried out with such confidence in his own power of judge-ment that he consulted no one. Yet, close at hand, was a member of the chapter, Canon Frederick Harrison, who was very knowledgeable and had written a book *The Painted Glass of York* (1927). Another expert, John Knowles, whose *Essays on the York School of Glass Painting* (1936) expressed unrivalled authority, was also ignored.

Thus some mistakes were made, principally but not exclusively in the windows of the chapter house, and these attracted severe criticism from some of the leading authorities in the field. After Milner-White's death several of the more manageable of the perceived errors were corrected. That acknowledged, it remains impossible to believe that any other Dean of York, before or since, could have achieved what he achieved, and today's visitors to York Minster, amazed and awed by its glass, would need little persuading that the wonder around them was worth a few mistakes.

Eric Milner-White (always known to his friends as Milner) was born in Southampton in 1884. His father, Sir Henry Milner-White, was a prosperous businessman, but the comfort and tranquillity of the house was shattered by the death of his mother when he was only six. His father's subsequent re-marriage provided him, however, with a step-mother to whom he became devoted and always regarded as his mother. From Harrow he went to King's College, Cambridge, where he took a double first in the history tripos and thence to Cuddesdon Theological College to prepare for holy orders. After curacies at Newington and Woolwich he returned to Cambridge as chaplain of King's and lecturer in history at Corpus Christi College. He also taught Divinity to the young Michael Ramsey who attended the King's choir school as a day boy. The link thus established lasted a lifetime and when, to Milner-White's great delight, he was responsible for enthroning Ramsey as Archbishop of York he said 'My child in the Spirit has become my Father in God.' A photograph of Milner-White was on the wall of the room in the Oxford convent where Ramsey died.

Milner-White, like Ramsey, was a High Churchman who valued the sacramental life of the Church and the best of its traditions, while remaining faithful to the particular ethos and traditions of the Church of England. In 1913 he became a member of the Oratory of the Good Shepherd – a dispersed community of celibate priests. A year later, however, the outbreak of war took him into the army as a chaplain and for most of the next four years he ministered with conspicuous bravery on the front line in France, winning a DSO and a Mention in Despatches. On one occasion he disregarded army regulations by abandoning his non-combatant status and taking temporary command of a unit whose officers had all been killed. On demobilization at the end of 1918 he returned to King's as Fellow and Dean, remaining there for another 23 years and retaining his Fellowship after appointment to York. He was made a canon of Lincoln in 1937.

Although Milner-White had a first-class mind and was a distinguished member of his college, he did not pretend to be an academic. He taught history to some of the weaker undergraduates but had no great interest in the finer points of theology. Worship and the arts were his forte and the music and glass of the world-famous chapel provided him with ample scope for both. One innovation, the result of close collaboration with the organist, was of lasting significance for King's and soon for the wider church – the Christmas Festival of Nine Lessons and Carols, which they adapted from the pioneering effort of Edward White Benson during his time as Bishop and Dean of Truro (1877–83).

On liturgical matters Milner-White was generally conservative but, writing of his wartime experience, he said, in language typical of his elegant style:

> Suddenly it became manifest to all that the 1662 book was out of date. It was plain, especially to chaplains in the field, that the country had no semblance of a popular familiar devotion . . . The Prayer Book did not seem able to reflect the lineaments of the Lord Jesus Christ, thereby failing to minister the love of God to souls desperately wistful.

Of critical importance for Milner-White was the highest standards of language, music and ceremonial. 'A metro-political cathedral can look at nothing which is not of the finest', he once said at York, and he believed that this applied to all cathedrals. Language was specially important to him, with a marked preference for that of the seventeenth century, and he explained, 'The aim of liturgy is not to evoke the interest of the passer-by, but to achieve a common prayer before God of which the Church cannot tire.' The well-known and much-used Bidding Prayer which he compiled for the Festival of Nine Lessons and Carols is a good example of what he meant by this. Another feature of great services at York was the fine printing of the service papers. He was not averse, however, to the language and format of detective stories – a collection of which occupied all the wall space of a room in the deanery.

The furnishings of the Minster naturally attracted Milner-White's attention and during his time there were many replacements and additions, including a nave pulpit in memory of Archbishops Lang and Temple, nave seats for choirs and clergy, a nave altar, an Archbishop's throne and altar rails for both nave and choir. Sir Albert Richardson, an architect in the traditional mould, was the most used designer, though the astronomical clock in the north transept was of necessity entrusted to the Royal Greenwich Observatory. For the renewal of the textiles he bought seventeenth- and eighteenth-century materials, often velvet, on the Continent and these, as with many other items, were paid for by himself, private donors or the Minster Friends.

The music of the Minster was always under his firm control, though he enjoyed a good relationship with successive, highly distinguished organists – Sir Edward Bairstow and Francis Jackson. His poetic *Lamentations*, for use in Passiontide, was set to music by Bairstow and soon entered the standard repertory of many other cathedrals. It was one of the twentieth-century's best choral works. The deanery housed Milner-White's ever-changing collection of mainly twentieth-century paintings, many of which were given away to art galleries when he had enjoyed them for a few years. His collection of early twentieth-century hand-made pottery, said to be the finest in the country, can now be seen in the Southampton and York city art galleries, while to the Minster he bequeathed a fine collection of Persian rugs. The ballet and rose-growing were other personal delights. His affluence was due to two interrelated factors. His father, who died in 1922, left him £40,000 – the equivalent of more than £1 million in today's money – and this was invested with the judicious advice of John Maynard Keynes, the great economist, who was also a Fellow of King's during Milner-White's time in the college.

At the end of the 1939–45 war Milner-White was one of a small group that established a York civic trust to ensure that the reconstruction of bomb-damaged buildings and the erection of the new ones was carried out in ways appropriate to a historic city. He soon became its most powerful voice and, working closely with the city council, helped to make central York the place of beauty it is today. The York Institute of Architectural Study also owes much to his vision, as does the University of York – he being the chairman of its academic development committee in the formative years.

Although always busy with one or other of his projects, and always active in the central government of the Church, he never ceased to regard the daily worship offered in the Minster as his highest priority. In an illuminating essay in a memorial book about Milner-White, one of the York choristers of his day, Robert Holtby (Dean of Chichester 1977–89) said 'Devotion in the Minster was the foundation for devotion to it.' His pastoral gifts were not strong, and he often appeared to be a somewhat aloof figure, and certainly formidable on the first encounter, but he was to be found daily at the altar and in his stall at mattins and evensong. And the depth of his devotional life was revealed in two collections of prayers which became very widely used in cathedrals and parish churches for intercession. Two other collections *A Procession of Passion Prayers* (1950) and *My God, My Glory* (1954) contain many beautiful prayers written by himself, and the fact that these are less easy to use publicly today may be attributed to the lack of poetry and rhythmic prose in contemporary worship. He once said that there would be no revival of religion until there comes a revival of poetry. His collections remain, however, a rich resource for private devotion.

Milner-White's death in 1963 marked the end of an era at York Minster, as did the retirements of his contemporaries C. A. Alington at Durham and E. G. Selwyn at Winchester. These were all men of very considerable ability who, in the society of their day, felt called to rule. Milner-White represented the very best of what a dean could be at that time. It was a noble contribution to cathedral life.

20

The Connoisseur
Walter Hussey, Chichester

No one did more to re-establish contact between the Church and the artist in the twentieth century than Walter Hussey. Some of the fruits of his endeavours are to be seen in outstanding works of religious art in St Matthew's Church, Northampton, where he was vicar from 1937 to 1955, and in Chichester Cathedral where he was dean from 1955 to 1977. The choral works he commissioned now belong to the standard repertory of all the English cathedrals and of other churches where the musical resources are up to their demands.

Although he was not himself either an artist or a musician, Hussey had an extraordinary aesthetic sense. Added to this was supreme confidence, more than justified, in his own judgements and an iron will that would never be satisfied until he had achieved his objectives. He also had the ability to win the admiration and the friendship of those who mattered in the realm of contemporary art and music, including most notably Henry Moore, Graham Sutherland, John Piper, Benjamin Britten and Leonard Bernstein. Sir Kenneth (later Lord) Clarke shared his vision and strongly supported his efforts to bring the artist back into the service of the Church.

Yet these considerable achievements apart, his ministry as a dean was disappointing – some said disastrous. By the time he reached Chichester, the Anglo-Catholicism in which he had been nurtured, and which for the whole of his life took him to the altar daily, had been replaced by a form of liberal Christian Platonism. Art and music, rather than the redemptive message of the gospel, now nourished his soul and the effect of this was to leave him largely indifferent to the character and needs of a Christian community. Chichester Cathedral, all glorious within and without, became a cold, unhappy place.

Hussey's work began at St Matthew's Church, Northampton, a large and impressive example of Victorian Gothic architecture where his father, the first vicar, had ministered for 50 years. Young Walter was born during this time and at Marlborough College had John Betjeman as a fellow pupil. When his English master suggested that one of his essays, on Thomas Hardy, was not original work he immediately gave up school English. Thereafter his chief interest was in music, for which he had no great talent, and to a lesser degree painting and sculpture. In later life he was neither an intellectual nor creative in his thinking, but he was highly intelligent and very discerning in his evaluation of the ideas of others and in his assessment of character.

At Keble College, Oxford, he took a third in politics, philosophy and economics. Then came Cuddesdon Theological College followed by a curacy at St Mary Abbots, Kensington. It was during his ministry there that his serious interest in art was stimulated. The Royal Academy bored him, so he turned to the National Gallery, the Tate and Bond Street galleries where he was greatly affected by some of the contemporary art. This became a consuming interest during his early years in Northampton where in 1937 he succeeded his father. At first responsibility for a lively parish and the outbreak of war stood in the way of his giving this any practical expression but the prospect of celebrating in 1943 the Golden Jubilee of the church's consecration provoked what he called 'a wild and ambitious dream' which envisaged five projects – a piece of music written for the occasion, a top-class organist to give a recital, a recital by a fine singer or instrumentalist, a concert by a leading symphony orchestra, a work of painting or sculpture to be commissioned.

His first choice of a composer was William Walton who seemed disinclined to collaborate. Then he heard a radio performance of Benjamin Britten's *Sinfonia da Requiem* and also a broadcast talk on music by Britten, so he wrote to him, care of his publishers, and said that he had a bee in his bonnet about a closer connection between religion and the arts and wondered if he would be prepared to compose something for the St Matthew's Golden Jubilee. Britten replied that he had the same bee in his bonnet and said that he would visit Northampton to judge the capability of the choir. Fortunately this proved to be of an acceptable standard, and Britten chose a section from the eighteenth-century poet Christopher Smart's long poem *Rejoice in the Lamb*. This was subtitled 'A Song from Bedlam', which in fact it was, for, although Smart was deeply religious and had flashes of insight, his mind was seriously unbalanced and for long periods he was held under lock and key. The poem in praise of creation includes a delightful passage about 'My Cat Jeffrey' which

Hussey was at first hesitant about including, but Britten insisted and got his way. Asked about his fee, Britten said he did not want one provided he could have performance rights and the proceeds of the sale of sheet music. Hussey gladly agreed and also gave him £25.

The new work was completed in good time for 21 September, St Matthew's Day, and Britten, who conducted the final rehearsals and the first performance, got Michael Tippett to compose a fanfare to greet the Bishop at the beginning of the service. Hussey persuaded the band of the Northamptonshire Regiment to provide the instrumentalists. The two composers wore cassock and surplice and processed with the choir. Afterwards *The Times* music critic wrote enthusiastically about the anthem and commended Hussey for commissioning a modern work of religious art. A few days later George Thalben-Ball of The Temple Church gave an organ recital and the celebrations also included Sir Adrian Boult conducting a broadcast performance by the BBC Symphony Orchestra. Benjamin Britten returned with Peter Pears to give a song recital – something they repeated in future years.

Meanwhile the creation of a piece of sculpture was going well, though it could not be completed and dedicated until February 1944. During 1942 Hussey went to the National Gallery to see an exhibition of pictures by war artists and was greatly impressed by drawings of people sheltering in underground stations during air raids. These were by Henry Moore, a little-known artist who worked mainly in sculpture, and on his return home Hussey discussed the exhibition with the Principal of Chelsea College of Art which had been evacuated to Northampton. By chance, Moore was shortly to visit the college to judge a students' competition and the Principal agreed to ask him if he would be prepared to create a sculpture for St Matthew's. Moore responded positively and, after Hussey's father had offered to pay for a statue of the Madonna and Child to mark the church's jubilee, he produced five models. Hussey took these to the National Gallery to discuss with Sir Kenneth Clarke and Jasper Ridley, the chairman of the Tate Gallery, and Clarke said of the one chosen, 'It is the most exciting sight I have ever seen.'

Hussey then took the model to his church council, along with supporting letters from Clarke, T. S. Eliot and Eric Newton, a prominent art critic. Bishop George Bell of Chichester also wrote about the need for the churches to give a lead in the revival of the association of religion and art and hoped that St Matthew's would set the ball rolling. The church council accepted the gift unanimously and, after further discussions between Hussey, Moore and Clarke, the statue took shape – a seated figure, slightly over life size, and in simple, primitive almost, style. Moore said of it, 'A Madonna and Child should have an austerity and a nobility, and some touch of grandeur (even hieratic aloofness) missing in the "everyday" Mother and Child idea.'

The day of the unveiling by Sir Kenneth Clarke got off to a bad start inasmuch as it was bitterly cold and the train bringing the London guests, including Moore himself, Clarke, Graham Sutherland and William Walton, was delayed by a bomb falling on the railway line. The service started an hour late, to the great displeasure of the Bishop of Peterborough, Dr Blagden, who was in any case unhappy about the statue. For several months large numbers visited the church to see it and among the many letters in the local newspaper some were bitterly hostile. But the London art critics were full of praise for what proved to be one of Moore's greatest works. Not so the President of the Royal Academy, Sir Alfred Munnings, a fierce opponent of all modern art, who at the Academy's annual banquet several years later took the opportunity to denounce it as 'a graven image'. A lively debate in the national Press followed.

The statue's installation in the north transept of the church led Hussey to believe that something – a painting rather than a sculpture – was needed in the south transept to balance it. Moore suggested Graham Sutherland for this and Hussey took the opportunity to discuss the possibility with him after the unveiling of the Madonna and Child. Sutherland agreed to paint a crucifixion and a box was placed near the statue for gifts for the commissioning of works of art for the church. Benjamin Britten and Peter Pears gave another of their concerts to swell this fund. Photographs of Sutherland's final sketch, endorsed once again by Kenneth Clarke and Eric Newton, went to the church council and drew from one member the comment: 'This is one of the most disturbing and shocking pictures I have ever seen; therefore I think it should go in the church.' The rest agreed and at the unveiling by Sir Eric Maclagan, the former Director of the Victoria and Albert Museum, the choir sang 'Lo, the full and final sacrifice' – an anthem, composed for the previous year's Festival by Gerald Finzi, which soon entered the repertory of other churches and cathedrals.

Again there was controversy – some found the picture frightening – but less than that created by Moore's statue and all the London critics approved. The *New Statesman* described it as 'astonishing and quite without parallel in this island at the moment'. Edmund Rubbra,

Lennox Berkeley, Kirsten Flagstad, W. H. Auden and Norman Nicholson were among the other contributors to the annual Festival, and by the end of his time at Northampton Hussey was on terms of friendship with many of the leading figures in the arts world. He was often in London.

The end came in 1955 when a letter arrived from the Prime Minister, Winston Churchill, offering him the deanery of Chichester. This proved to be the last of Churchill's Crown appointments, the suggestion having been made by the Bishop of Peterborough and the Archdeacon of Northampton and warmly endorsed by Bishop George Bell. It seemed to be an imaginative appointment and Chichester Cathedral today provides powerful testimony to the courage of those who made it. Hussey at that time had a uniquely creative mission. Moreover, he had some of the traditional assets of a dean – an impressive appearance, a cultured and sonorous voice, and behind him 18 years' experience as a parish priest, including five as a rural dean. It was to be expected that he and Bishop George Bell, another pioneer in uniting religion and the arts, would get on specially well, though in the event their ministries overlapped by only three years and Hussey did not even merit a mention in Bell's official biography.

He lacked, however, the warmth and sensitivity to human need required of the leader of any community, most of all of one claiming to express the values of the Christian gospel. Unmarried, he was at Chichester a lonely figure, not given to hospitality, though the sign identifying the deanery was beautifully designed. Preachers travelling from parishes in the diocese as far distant as 80 miles from the cathedral were not offered so much as a cup of coffee. Students from the nearby theological college fared somewhat better. The cathedral acquired the reputation of being an unwelcoming place for its increasing number of visitors and from time to time complaints about this were voiced in Sussex newspapers. Hussey seemed to regard the building primarily as a historic monument – itself a work of art and a place for other works of art. He preached only infrequently and his sermons had little identifiable Christian content, being confined mainly to the role of beauty in religion. He nonetheless preached a notable sermon in Westminster Abbey at the memorial service for Benjamin Britten.

The running of the cathedral was left largely to the Archdeacon of Chichester, Lancelot Mason – a difficult and stubborn man who was disappointed not to have been appointed to a deanery and more than ready to wield power at Chichester. Hussey, who hated confrontation, never openly challenged him. He was, however, unyielding in his determination to secure the best in contemporary art for the adornment of the cathedral and, both at Northampton and Chichester, he never failed to get his way, even if this sometimes took a long time to achieve. He was equally adroit in obtaining the necessary funding.

An opportunity to demonstrate his skills came during his early years at Chichester, though not over a work of modern art. A fine early fifteenth-century stone screen, separating the nave and the choir, had been taken down in 1859 and replaced by a second-rate wooden screen. A controversy over a proposal to bring back the stone screen was already raging when Hussey arrived, so he decided to wait for a time. On the death of George Bell in 1958 he suggested that the restored screen might be an appropriate memorial to a greatly admired bishop and this not only made everyone happy but also brought in the money needed for the work involved.

When this was completed he decided to deal with a nineteenth-century carved wood reredos behind the high altar. Although this had later been painted it still made the sanctuary gloomy so Hussey discussed the situation with Basil Spence, the architect of the recently completed Coventry Cathedral. When Spence's suggestion was unacceptable, he talked to John Piper who undertook to design a tapestry to hang on the stone screen previously obscured by the reredos. This would consist of seven separate panels – the three in the centre representing the Trinity and the flanking panels representing symbols for the elements and the evangelists – all to be woven by Pinton Freres of Aubusson in France who had been responsible for the Sutherland tapestry at Coventry.

Piper talked to the Friends of the cathedral about it and they agreed to provide the necessary money, but at the last minute the archdeacon complained about the lack of a specific symbol for God the Father. Eventually he was placated and the high altar – a simple stone table by Robert Potter – stands against a background of striking originality, the vivid reds and blues of which are visible through the choir screen as soon as the visitor enters by the west doors. These doors – another of Hussey's projects – are of glass which admits more light to the nave and provide less of a barrier to the outside world. Piper's tapestry was, and is, widely admired but it aroused more protests than anything else initiated by Hussey during his time as dean. The panels are taken down during Lent.

In the chapel of St Mary Magdalene, at the east end of the south aisle and visible for the whole length of the building, is another Robert Potter altar over which hangs a dramatic painting, *Noli me*

Tangere by Graham Sutherland. This portrays the Risen Christ when warning Mary 'Touch me not', and its appearance led to some hostile letters in the local newspaper. On the whole, however, the reaction was favourable. An altar frontal in St Clement's chapel, *The Lens of Divine Light* by Cecil Collins, scraped through the chapter by a single vote in 1973. The commissioning and completion of a window by Marc Chagall – one of the twentieth century's most important painters – provides another good example of Hussey's method and tenacity.

Only too well aware that Chichester was weak in stained glass, he was greatly moved by an exhibition of Chagall's paintings held in Paris in 1967. On his return home he immediately wrote to Chagall, expressing admiration for his use of colour and asking if he would be prepared to create a window for Chichester. Chagall's wife replied that her husband was interested but was too busy at the moment to accept new commissions. Hussey was not, however, willing to be put off and his persistence was rewarded by an invitation in late 1976 to visit the great painter who was now aged 89. Arriving at his remote cottage in France very late in the day and soaked by a storm, Hussey persuaded him to visit Chichester. This he did and, after further discussion, produced a design illustrating Psalm 150, 'O praise God in his holiness . . . Let everything that has breath praise the Lord'. The dominant colour is blazing red and typical Chagall figures symbolizing the different arts lead to a central figure symbolizing the worship of God. The cost, just under £18,000, was raised by Hussey from a number of trusts, so avoiding conflict with a current appeal for the major restoration of the building, and the window was unveiled in October 1978, just a year after Hussey's retirement.

As at Northampton, the commissioning of visual art was accompanied by the quest for new music. For the Southern Cathedrals Festival in 1965 Hussey got Leonard Bernstein to compose for a suite of Psalms in Hebrew – *The Chichester Psalms* – and once again artist and patron became friends. The 900th anniversary of dedication of the cathedral saw the beginning of the Chichester Festival which, over a period of three weeks, brought leading orchestras and soloists to perform in and around the cathedral. The American Wilhelm Albright composed a Mass for a Festival Eucharist and William Walton a Magnificat and Nunc Dimittis for a Festal evensong. The Festival became, and remains, an important annual event in the cultural life of southern England. Moreover, Hussey's successors have been inspired to commission other notable works of contemporary art, confirming the belief that medieval buildings can accommodate art from different ages provided it is of the highest quality.

Hussey retired to London where he was able to enjoy his many friendships in the world of art. He died in 1985 and, although he had always pleaded poverty, his shrewd buying and selling of paintings and sculpture, combined with gifts from artist friends enabled him to leave over £1 million. His own collection was bequeathed to art galleries in Northampton and Chichester.

21

The Reconciler
H. C. N. (Bill) Williams, Coventry

H. C. N. (Bill) Williams who went to Coventry as provost in 1958 was the ideal choice for the leadership of a cathedral due to be consecrated in early 1962 and the rebuilding of which after wartime bombing had caught the imagination of the Christian world. He combined wide vision, boundless energy and dynamic leadership skills and at Coventry found the freedom to exercise these gifts in a unique situation where the bishop, Cuthbert Bardsley, although a more conservative churchman, was ready to support his enterprises.

A South African by birth and early education, Williams often said that he felt cramped in England after the open spaces of Africa and that he needed a world-wide ministry. He came to England in the 1930s to read theology and prepare for ordination at Hatfield College, Durham, but after a three-year curacy in Winchester returned to South Africa in 1941 to be chaplain, then principal, of St Matthew's College, Grahamstown.

In 1950 he was back in Winchester as vicar of Hyde, and four years later was appointed Rector of St Mary's, Southampton. The ancient parish church, and several other churches in central Southampton, had been destroyed by wartime bombing and William was entrusted with the formidable task of rebuilding St Mary's and leading the reorganization and renewal of church life in the city centre. This he accomplished with marked success during a short four-year ministry. As the new church rose from the rubble (it turned out to be much too large for future needs), special efforts were made to engage its mission with that of the community's renewed commercial and industrial life. Specialist chaplains were appointed to minister in the shopping centre, the factories and the docks, and it was undoubtedly his capacity for inspiring others that led to his appointment to Coventry long before his ideas had become firmly rooted in Southampton.

When he arrived in Coventry the new cathedral was already taking shape. The beautiful fourteenth-century parish church of St Michael, which had been the cathedral since the formation of the diocese in 1918, was almost completely destroyed during a ferocious air attack on the city in November 1940. Only the tower, spire and some of the outer walls remained. Its sole defenders had been the Provost, R. T. Howard, a 65-year-old layman and two young men in their early twenties equipped with hand pumps and sand. On the following morning the provost stood in the smoking ruins and declared that the cathedral would be rebuilt. Two charred timbers were erected in the form of a cross and three nails were joined together to form a mobile cross that would later be taken to all the parishes of the diocese, and much further afield, as a symbol of both reconciliation and resurrection. The daily services were now held in the crypt and special services involving large congregations, sometimes 2,000 strong, were held in the ruins, open to the sky. The first performance of the Coventry Mysteries since the reign of Elizabeth I was staged there.

A reconstruction committee was formed in 1941 and the design of the new building was entrusted to Giles Gilbert Scott, the architect of Liverpool Cathedral, who was instructed to retain the old ruins. He submitted his plans in 1946 and these were of a church built round a central altar, with a special chapel of unity (which was the idea of the saintly, eccentric Bishop Neville Gorton) and a Christian Service Centre. The committee was happy with the plans, but they were rejected by the Royal Fine Art Commission, whereupon Gilbert Scott resigned.

A commission chaired by Lord Harlech then held a competition, with a rule that the building should be in the English Gothic tradition. Two hundred and nineteen anonymous entries were considered by the commission and the design submitted by Basil Spence was the unanimous choice, though it caused loud public controversy. The foundation stone was laid in 1956 and the building was completed at a total cost of £1,350,000 of which war damage compensation provided £1 million.

The year of Williams's arrival in Coventry saw the appointment simultaneously of a highly talented team to share in the leadership. Joseph Poole, the Precentor, had a remarkable flair for the arranging and staging of services; Edward Patey, who later became Dean of Liverpool, had much experience of youth and education work; Simon Phipps, who was to become Bishop of Horsham, then of Lincoln, came to lead an Industrial Mission; Stephen Verney, who combined strong pastoral gifts with deep spirituality and later became Bishop of

Repton, was made diocesan missioner with responsibility for the spiritual preparation for the cathedral's consecration and the involvement of the parishes in the diocese. Eventually the staff grew to be 70 strong and included a high-calibre director of drama and one of the best youth officers in the country, as well as a team to deal with the visitors.

The consecration of the cathedral on 25 May 1962 was a spectacular occasion, seen world-wide on television, and was followed by a festival which included the premier of Benjamin Britten's *War Requiem*, conducted by the composer, and a performance by the Berlin Philharmonic Orchestra. A nearby theatre staged opera and ballet, and the proclamation of the cathedral's resurrection was heard far and wide. The response was remarkable. Visitors came from all quarters of the globe and long queues formed to gain admission to the building. Four million were admitted during the first 18 months and, although entrance was free, the cathedral's income from sales in its bookshop and restaurant was sufficient to finance the large staff. The services also attracted crowded congregations.

Although many architects and most liturgists were critical of the rectangular shape of the building – 'expresso-bar Gothic' one called it – the overwhelming majority of the visitors were deeply impressed by what they saw and experienced, as indeed the greatly reduced number who followed them have been. The outstanding feature of the cathedral is not its basic architecture but the extraordinarily high quality of much of the art it contains, the credit for which goes to Bishop Gorton, who knew the world of contemporary artists and commissioned the most notable items, which he was destined not to see. Graham Sutherland's great tapestry of Christ in Glory, Jacob Epstein's sculpture of St Michael defeating the dragon, and John Piper's baptistry windows are major works of twentieth-century art. And there are many others by important artists such as Elisabeth Frink.

Williams was in the early days lavish in his praise of the new cathedral and wrote guide books extolling its virtues and assisting visitors to appreciate its religious significance. But before long he was complaining that it was difficult to use, as it was bound to be for anyone seeking to express the insights of the Liturgical Movement in the worship. The Gilbert Scott design would have been much more to his liking and, had he been provost at the time, he would doubtless have fought the Royal Fine Art Commission over their rejection of it. The building also proved to be very inconvenient for the staging of drama and ballet – which he wished to use in the worship – and he described Sutherland's tapestry as 'like a poster'. Its powerful dominance of the east end makes the altar virtually invisible.

In spite of these reservations about the building, Williams was, however, in no doubt as to its purpose. Shortly before the consecration he wrote:

> The single objective of the ministry of Coventry Cathedral is to establish a creative relationship with the community in which it is set. There are many community structures which the parish system cannot begin remotely to influence. Among those are industry, the arts, commerce, social service, local government, science, technology. The ministry of Coventry Cathedral is so organised as to experiment on the widest possible front to find 'points of entry' into these definable community structures and to learn the fundamental principles they raise about human relations of the future.

This line of thinking was in close accord with that of various working parties of the Western European members of the World Council of Churches who had concluded that local churches were now severely limited in their mission potential and that the chief unit of mission should be the region or *zone humain*. Williams's distinctive contribution was the suggestion that a cathedral provided an appropriate base for such an approach. And he sought to prove this by embarking on an extensive programme of activity designed to engage the life of the cathedral with that of the city and the wider Midlands region. Because the cathedral had been a spectacular victim of wartime conflict, he also believed that it had special responsibilities and opportunities for witnessing to the importance of international reconciliation.

Thus he initiated a programme of activity larger in scale and scope than ever before conceived by any provost or dean. The carefully staged Sunday morning Eucharist devised particularly for Coventry was in some ways more conservative than that of some parish churches at the time but included elements which eventually became normal almost everywhere – lay involvement, an offertory procession, exchanging of the peace, and coffee afterwards. Occasional Sunday evening services were designed for various groups in the city – commercial houses, banks, statutory social services – and intended to be a summing up of the cathedral's day-to-day involvement with these groups. A Tuesday lunchtime service, advertised by 10,000 programmes distributed throughout the city, attracted a regular congregation of 700 rising to as many as 2,000 in the summer when visitors joined in. Great care was taken to ensure that diocesan services expressed the needs and aspirations of each organization, and at every point the genius of Joseph Poole was evident.

Simon Phipps, the senior industrial chaplain, made it plain that he and his team were not offering a pastoral ministry to individuals, but rather a prophetic ministry to the structure of industry – asking questions and listening, not pontificating. Every evening of the week two to seven groups of people from industry met in the cathedral's undercroft rooms to discuss current issues. A stores chaplain did, however, do much pastoral work among shop-workers, and organized a lunchtime club for them, with refreshments. Regular contact was maintained with the social services and a cathedral representative served on the committee of the local Ministry of Labour. Several services a year were held for old people's organizations and a meeting place for immigrants, including a community of Sikhs, was provided in the undercroft. The organist and choir provided a high standard of music for all the main services, but it was recognized that the music should always be appropriate to the occasion and accessible to the very varied congregations. The schools of the city and county were encouraged to bring their choirs and orchestras to perform in the cathedral and professional advice was offered to the organizers of the annual miners' music festival.

International work was a major part of the cathedral's life. A Centre of Christian Reconciliation was built by 16 young Germans as a gift from the German Church, and a youth hostel accommodating 40 provided an opportunity for British and foreign young people to share in residential courses. A group of young people went from Coventry to Dresden to share in the rebuilding of that city. In the space of five years over 100,000 foreign students visited the cathedral and shared in some way in its life. Imaginative use was made of the Cross of Nails which Williams took with him on lecture tours in Germany, America and other parts of the world. This led to the formation of many local Cross of Nails communities dedicated to work of reconciliation.

The involvement of large numbers of young people in the international work was not unrelated to the Cathedral's ministry to young people in the city and diocese. Open youth work in the evenings attracted large numbers from the streets, while a lecture society was of sufficient quality to attract young professionals. Up to 200 students and sixth formers attended Christmas and Easter courses and week-end courses were held for parish youth leaders. A large educational department was established to handle school visits. As many as 100,000 children a year were taught in classes before being taken on a tour of the cathedral. A library was established for use by religious education teachers and the diocesan clergy.

A chapel of unity was conceived as a pioneering venture in ecumenical work long before Williams appeared on the scene and by the 1960s he was very disappointed that it had become separated from the Christian Service Centre which was an integral part of the original scheme. He was also keen that the whole of the building, rather than a small part of it, should be seen as a focus of unity. Other churches were encouraged to hold their own major services in the cathedral and preachers from all denominations were often invited to occupy the pulpit at the regular services. The chapel of unity became a meeting point for prayer and study.

When St Michael's Church became Coventry's cathedral it retained its parish and local pastoral responsibilities. This continued after the consecration of the new cathedral though by this time the number of people living in the immediate vicinity was greatly reduced. Nonetheless, there were 1,000 names on the electoral roll, admission to which was only allowed on the understanding that the individual would offer service to the cathedral's mission. A chaplain was appointed to minister to the regular congregation and to integrate families with children into its life. The team of 70 clergy and laity responsible for this huge enterprise met for a morning every week, for a whole day every month and for a week away every year. The senior staff met the Bishop once a month to discuss general policies and long-term objectives.

While the scale of the early Coventry mission and ministry remains well beyond the capacity of every other cathedral today – including Coventry itself – many of Williams's pioneering ideas and experiments now constitute a standard feature of English cathedrals. His book *Twentieth Century Cathedral*, published in 1964, was widely read and thus inspired a new breed of deans and provosts to seize the pastoral and mission opportunities provided by their building's prominent place in the community and, in the case of the older cathedrals, an ever-increasing flow of visitors from all parts of the world. It is not too much to say that the vigorous life and warmth of welcome experienced uniquely in most English cathedrals today is due to the pioneering ministry of Bill Williams. He is one of the two most significant figures in the twentieth-century history of the cathedrals; the other being Frank Bennett of Chester in the 1920s.

Like many visionary prophets, Williams was not easy to work with. There was a paranoid element in his personality which made him excessively jealous of Coventry Cathedral's reputation and liable to explode in anger at the slightest hint of criticism. It was fortunate that the members of his initial chapter were able enough to stand up to him and that Cuthbert Bardsley, who understood and admired him, was able to exercise his own notable ministry of reconciliation between Williams and those who served with him. Bardsley readily forgave him for his refusal to have anything to do with a great episcopal Mission to Coventry based on the cathedral. Welcome periods of relief were also offered by his increasingly frequent absences on 'Cross of Nails' business overseas. Once the vision was translated into the cathedral's life he felt the need to spread his wings wider than Coventry and the absurd offer of the suffragan Bishopric of Jarrow was rightly declined. His love of mountaineering fitted his life and personality well.

One unforeseen, but perhaps predictable, result of the cathedral's international ministry was that the city and diocesan communities came to feel neglected. The sheer scale of the operation was inimicable to the minute particulars of parish life. The more conservative elements in Coventry also felt excluded by the cathedral's new architecture and style. Into this situation came Lawrence Jackson, himself destined to become a cathedral provost, who had been appointed vicar of nearby Holy Trinity, Coventry, another magnificent medieval church, which had escaped the wartime bombing. Recognizing that it was futile to try to compete with the cathedral, Jackson offered, as an alternative, a traditional ministry of the highest order. This filled the local gap and, as an honorary canon, Jackson could have been regarded as providing a necessary, complementary, extension of the cathedral's ministry. But Williams never quite saw it that way and relations between provost and vicar were correct, rather than cordial.

By the 1970s the flood of visitors to Coventry had subsided, with serious consequences for the financing of the cathedral's many-faceted ministry. Williams's pioneering colleagues had also left the scene and in the end retrenchment and reorganization could not be avoided. Colin Semper who succeeded Williams in 1982 carried this out, before moving to be a canon of Westminster in 1987, but much of the best of the Williams vision has survived, including the commitment to international reconciliation. He died in retirement in 1990.

22

The Prophet
Ernest Southcott, Southwark

A dynamic parish priest who has spent a large part of his ministry creating or remodelling a local church in accordance with his own, personal insights and experiences is never going to find the transition from a vicarage to a deanery easy. What could be decided and begin to be implemented in the parish within 24 hours may well take weeks, months or even years to complete the obstacle course constituted by cathedral canons, statutes and customs. It is also the case that forms of worship and Christian community that work well in a parish sometimes lose their power when translated to a cathedral in which size and constituency are very different. If the parish priest who is installed as a dean happens also to belong to the rare breed of prophet he is certain to find in his new role more formidable obstacles and causes of frustration than in almost any other place on earth. The massive, ancient structure for which he is responsible and on which his new ministry is based expresses stability, continuity and resistance to radical change. There are more ways than one of stoning a prophet.

The appointment of Ernest Southcott as Provost of Southwark in 1961 was therefore bound to highlight these problems in a particularly dramatic form. Like many others, he was greatly inspired by the wartime work in Paris of Abbé Michonneau, described in *Revolution in a City Parish* published in English in 1949. For the previous 17 years he had been the vicar of St Wilfred's, Halton – a parish consisting of five estates of mainly pre-1939 housing inhabited by the Leeds working classes. There he had during the immediate post-war era pioneered a new pattern of parish life which attracted a great deal of interest and some emulation. This was assisted by a widely read book *The Parish Comes Alive* and his ready acceptance of invitations to speak in almost all the theological colleges to those preparing for ordination.

Those who heard him lecture or preach could hardly be unaware that they were in the presence of a singular personality. He was a striking figure. Standing several inches over six foot, his appearance was gaunt and the combination of jet-black hair dark skin and hooked nose suggested Native American blood. He was born in 1914 in British Columbia. Rarely was his body or his mind still and he was consistently unpredictable. After completing his education in Canada, he came to England to prepare for holy orders at the College of the Resurrection, Mirfield, where he was for a time a novice monk. This brought contact with the biblical theology and liturgical movements. Curacies in two tough artisan parishes in County Durham also made him conscious of the wide gulf between the church and the working classes and of the need to link worship and mission.

Appointment as vicar of Halton in 1944 provided him with an ideal opportunity to put his beliefs into practice. His predecessor had built a fine new church and created a strong sacramental tradition, but there was infinite scope for more pioneering ministry. During the next decade there developed a pattern of church life centred on the Sunday morning parish communion, followed by breakfast (both new ideas at the time) and the public administration of baptism, after careful preparation of parents and Godparents (more new ideas). A weekly parish meeting, open to all, was held for the working out of the local demands of mission, there was an intensive ministry to the sick, teaching programmes and support of other community action. Integral to all this was the development of the house church. Southcott argued that if the church was to be the church, and if the Eucharist was to demonstrate and cement the church's identity as the Body of Christ, it must meet outside church premises for the Eucharist to experience and share with others its divine calling. This would also demonstrate the holiness of the secular. Thus Halton was divided into six areas under lay leadership. Church members gathered regularly in living rooms and kitchens for the Eucharist and encouraged non-churchgoers to join them. They also undertook pastoral work in the locality. What became commonplace in the 1970s, and was taken in a different direction by evangelicals in the 1980s and '90s was considered highly controversial in the 1950s. When he was Bishop of Durham Michael Ramsey forbade the celebration of the Eucharist in private houses on the grounds that it was forbidden by Canon Law, except in cases of sickness.

The combination of all these activities created a hectic parish life, soon increased by the arrival of interested observers from many different parts of the world anxious to learn from the Halton experience. Some were amazed, but there could be no doubting that the church was alive and that experiments of some significance, with firm theological roots, were promoting the Christian mission in new ways. Dr John Moorman, a scholarly High Church Bishop of Ripon, was, however, less certain. Invited to spend a day and a night in the parish, he quickly found himself caught up in a whirlwind of activity – sharing in worship in the parish church, meeting church and community leaders, and attending the house churches. Retiring thankfully to bed in the vicarage soon after midnight, he was disturbed at about 2 a.m. by the sound of the vicar returning from the last of the day's house churches. Four hours later the bishop was called in order to be present at an early morning house church and breakfast, after which he escaped, puzzled and exhausted. But he had seen and experienced enough to convince him that Southcott was an outstanding parish priest who loved his people and was himself greatly loved by them, so he made him an honorary canon of Ripon Cathedral.

The bishop was not, however, the only one to feel exhausted. After 17 years of ceaseless activity, driven by an intensely spiritual dynamo, most of the parishioners, particularly those in positions of leadership, were feeling the need of a rest. And Southcott was displaying dangerous signs of burn-out. How best might his insights and gifts be used once he had been given space for renewal? Although he was, at the time, unaware of it, the first suggestion came, surprisingly perhaps, from Number 10 Downing Street.

In 1959 Mervyn Stockwood, after a short but spectacularly successful ministry at Great St Mary's, Cambridge, was appointed Bishop of Southwark. A new suffragan Bishop of Woolwich was also required and the Prime Minister's Secretary for Appointments put it to Stockwood that Southcott was the man for this job. Stockwood was determined, however, to nominate one of his former Bristol curates, John Robinson, who was now Dean of Clare College, Cambridge, and told Archbishop Geoffrey Fisher:

> I admire Southcott, but I doubt if he has the theological competence for this particular work. Moreover he is, by nature, so intense I should, for temperamental reasons, find it difficult to work with him. And I think he might overwhelm the clergy.

Truth to tell, there was not room for the two of them on the same stage, but before long they were required to work in close proximity. Hugh Ashdown, the Provost of Southwark Cathedral, was appointed

Bishop of Newcastle and the Crown nominated Southcott as his successor.

If the vicar of Halton's future ministry lay in the cathedral sphere – which most of his friends doubted – Southwark was clearly the right choice. Created a cathedral in 1905 from the former Augustinian priory church of St Saviour and St Mary Overie and located in what was until the late 1990s a squalid setting near London Bridge railway station, it is a modest building, though it has a magnificent Early English choir and retrochoir and a successful Victorian Gothic nave. Moreover it is the burial place of Lancelot Andrewes, one of the Church of England's saints. Yet, overshadowed by the mighty St Paul's, just across the Thames, it seems to be the Cinderella of cathedrals. This lack of grandeur and proximity to the rough and tumble of commerce was, for Southcott, a positive advantage since the task of the church was, he believed, 'to reveal the transcendent in our midst', wherever this might happen to be. The existence of a parish was, for him, another advantage and the absence of stuffy formality and constricting tradition suggested considerable freedom to share in the promoting of what came to be called 'South Bank Religion'. Unusually for a cathedral of its size, it had six residentiary canons, though two of these had what amounted to full-time diocesan posts. But all lived at some distance from the cathedral which discouraged attendance at daily services and inhibited the development of any sort of community life. Southcott was the nearest, ten minutes' walk away, through Dickensian wharves and alongside the river.

Into this markedly different church and setting Southcott brought the insights he had gained during his 17 years in Leeds housing estates, the validity of which he held with the deepest passion. Again the cry went up 'Let the liturgy be splendid'. The traditional Prayer Book sung Eucharist celebrated at the high altar was replaced by a concelebrated Eucharist involving the whole chapter at the head of the nave, with Series 2 – a new experimental rite. Representatives of the parishes in the diocese were invited to read lessons and lead intercessions. Others, including groups from schools and universities joined the services. Alcoholics, prison governors and black people from the diocese of Madagascar, as well as parish people carried the bread and wine in the offertory procession. The service ended not with the formal dismissal, but with the cry 'Coffee', for Southcott believed that meeting after the Eucharist was an integral part of the gathering. All of which considerably enlivened the Sunday morning worship and endless discussions took place in chapter about the possible re-ordering of the cathedral's interior to take account of the new liturgical arrangements, but, as with most of the new provost's projects, there was no money available for its financing.

The thinly attended Sunday afternoon evensong was replaced whenever possible with special services for particular groups of people, but the big event, and altogether new, was 'Sunday Night in Southwark' which provided a neutral place for discussions of current issues. These involved politicians, actors, educationalists, ecclesiastics and celebrities of every sort, and attracted large crowds to share in the lively debates. 'The Church Must Meet' was one of the Halton principles and deemed by Southcott to be equally important in Southwark. A new cathedral council, one of the first, brought the laity into the decision-making processes, but Southcott longed, in vain, for a regular parish meeting-style assembly involving the whole of the congregation and people from the diocese. After the manner of the house church, the cathedral should also be honeycombed with small groups concerned with world poverty, the arts, drugs and so on. 'Why should not a cathedral be a place noisy and bustling with life?' he asked. 'It would', he answered, 'seem to me to be immoral to spend a quarter of a million pounds on a building next to the cathedral to serve as a mission and lecture hall (a long hoped-for development) when the cathedral itself can become a multi-purpose building – flexible and adaptable, with moveable seats.' Part of this vision was realized in Southcott's time, but after his departure many millions of pounds were raised for the provision of fine ancillary buildings, including a restaurant.

He spoke often of what he called 'the two-sided vocation of a cathedral'. It must be the mother church of the diocese, used for big liturgical occasions, and it must also be the home ground for specialized groups, among whom he hoped there would one day be a college of worker priests. In the event this did not materialize but closely associated with the cathedral was a pioneering ordination course which provided part-time training for priests who would exercise their ministries while remaining in secular employment. This was the brainchild of Mervyn Stockwood and John Robinson, and run by Stanley Evans, one of the residentiary canons, with Southcott's enthusiastic support. He was himself much involved, as chairman of the executive committee of Parish and People, in the 1960s reform movement.

Beyond the cathedral he played a significant part in the life of the Southwark community. His position as provost of Guy's Hospital, expressing the historic link between the church and the hospital, provided many opportunities for healing work and he hoped that the cathedral would one day become a centre for training in pastoral care. He was also chairman of the Southwark Council of Social Service and much involved in the setting up of 'Crisis at Christmas' for the benefit of London's homeless. In spite of the passion and boundless energy that he poured into everything he did, he came to recognize that the office of Borough Dean of Southwark, a new role with responsibility for four former rural deaneries, really required a full-time appointment.

Another particular interest is the cathedral's historic association with Shakespeare – the site of the Globe Theatre is nearby – and this led him to hope that the cathedral might become a centre of 'creative drama'. There was a lot of the actor in his own personality and friendship with Sydney Carter and Donald Swann led to the first performance of *Lord of the Dance* at a Sunday morning Eucharist in May 1960. Enthusiastic encouragement of Sam Wanamaker led, many years later, to the rebuilding of the Globe Theatre where Shakespeare had often performed and in which he had had some financial interest.

Southcott always worked more easily with laypeople than with his fellow-clergy and gave himself unstintingly to the pastoral care of the cathedral parish, appearing on doorsteps at all hours of day and night. And he was greatly loved in the back streets. But with the chapter, which at the time was made up of an unusually gifted company of priests, his position was different. They each had their own special interests outside the cathedral and his integration of these with their capitular responsibility required both sensitivity and good organization. Southcott possessed one in abundance but was entirely lacking in the other. His enthusiasms, frequent changes of mind, forgetfulness, and failures to communicate could be, and often were, exasperating. On one occasion the London *Evening Standard* advertised him as preaching in three different churches at the same time on the same Sunday. Neither could anyone have been less skilled than he in the art of cathedral politics and, although he longed to be close to his bishop, Mervyn Stockwood always kept him at a distance. Stockwood had in fact little time for the cathedral apart from when he wanted to use it for a diocesan event, and Southcott's emotional separation from his colleagues was always a source of personal pain.

In the end it all became too much. The burned-out prophet became in desperate need of understanding and intensive love and, although his wife, Margaret, and his family offered everything they could, it was not enough. A distressing psychological breakdown became inevit-able. Among the few people permitted to visit him during a prolonged period in hospital was Denis (now Lord) Healey who was MP for South-East Leeds and became Defence Secretary and Chancellor of the Exchequer in successive Labour Governments. In his autobiography Healey acknowledged Southcott's powerful influence on him: 'Ernie's Christianity was numinous and he impressed me more than any priest I have met.' He had also changed the face of Southwark Cathedral.

When eventually he was deemed to be sufficiently recovered he was appointed vicar of the less than glamorous parish of Rishton in Lancashire where, for a few more years, he sought to recreate the excitement of his Halton ministry. He died suddenly, aged 62, but not before he had again won the admiration and love of his discriminating parishioners.

23

The Modern Churchman
Edward Carpenter, Westminster

Edward Carpenter, who was at Westminster Abbey from 1951 to 1985, first as a canon then from 1974 onwards, as dean, was an erudite and engaging churchman of a sort no longer bred. He was in the mould of his most eminent Victorian predecessor, A. P. Stanley, whom he greatly admired – a scholarly historian, a man of liberal mind, an eloquent preacher, a reformer, a lover of people and, above all, one who shared Stanley's vision of the Abbey as 'a religious, national and liberal institution'.

His 23 years as a canon were, because of this, a time of much frustration. He was not unhappy, for he loved the Abbey, but he was for most of the time condemned to serve in ultra-conservative chapters in which new ideas were constantly rejected. Thus when he became dean, at the age of 64, he was very much 'an old man in a hurry' and effected more changes in the Abbey's day-to-day life than any of his predecessors since Stanley. Exempt from compulsory retirement, he stayed until he was 75 and remained convinced that continuity required constant reformation.

Most of the old formalities that gave the impression of stuffiness were dispensed with and visitors, whether attending a service or simply passing through on a guided tour, were more warmly welcomed – often by the dean himself. This was not always easy, as the advent of wide-bodied jet aircraft in the 1970s sometimes led to the Abbey being overwhelmed by overseas tourists. An American who had been nearly trampled to death, then found his pocket picked, took some convincing that a pilgrimage to the shrine of Edward the Confessor was 'a spiritual experience'. But the dean tried.

A lifelong pacifist, Carpenter believed that the Commonwealth, together with the United Nations, was a vital instrument of peace, so the High Commissioners in London were invited to read a lesson at evensong on their national independence days, and attend a social gathering afterwards. A high point in his year was the annual Commonwealth Day Observance attended by the Queen, the High Commissioners and their staffs, and conducted by the leaders of all the main religious faiths.

Inter-faith relations was another high priority which took him into active membership of the Council of Christians and Jews. The Dalai Lama was accorded greater loyalty than most Christian leaders and this sometimes led to problems. Members of the chapter were surprised to learn from a Sunday newspaper that the heavily guarded Tibetan leader would not only be staying at the deanery but also give Buddhist teaching in depth in the Abbey. In the event he spoke about peace. The strictly vegetarian deanery household was thrown into a turmoil when His Holiness required bacon, liver and sausages for breakfast.

Although Carpenter had a first-class mind and rarely considered a matter without reference to its history, he was essentially a romantic and an idealist. This often led him to look upon life with an almost child-like simplicity. The fact of sin and the necessity of compromise were for him almost too painful to contemplate; the Sermon on the Mount provided the ethical basis for political as well as personal conduct. Cruelty in the natural order also greatly troubled him and he was active in animal welfare societies.

His theological outlook was shaped by the early twentieth-century Modernist movement, which viewed much of the Bible and most traditional Christian doctrine with a marked degree of scepticism. He remained a leading member of the Modern Churchmen's Union long after its post-1939–45 war decline. This gave him a certain affinity and a good deal of sympathy with the *Honest to God* radicalism of the 1960s but, inasmuch as he had been largely unaffected by the Biblical Theology and Liturgical Movements, his position was different and he became something of a 'period piece'.

A fine, albeit somewhat prolix, preacher, he rarely referred to the Bible in his sermons and often selected a text from Cicero or Plato and illustrated his points with copious quotations from his beloved Shelley or the almost equally revered Dr Johnson. Poetry was always very important to him and during his time as dean 11 memorials were added to Poet's Corner – as many as in the previous 250 years. He also felt free to replace bloodthirsty and obscure Old Testament lessons with something he believed to be more edifying, and on more than one occasion prefaced the reading of a New Testament lesson with the comment 'St Paul got things wrong'.

In constant demand for sermons elsewhere and always ready to accept invitations – he loved rail travel – asking him to preach involved certain hazards. His diary was not always well ordered, leaving him booked to be in the pulpit of different churches at the same time. Or he might lose his way while walking from the station and arrive breathless long after the service had started, with the vicar in despair. Having arrived, his sermon could be quite unrelated to the subject on which he had been asked to speak, but would be recognized as a tour de force delivered by a man whom it was a delight to meet over a cup of coffee afterwards.

Carpenter's unpredictability and informality made his relations with the royal family less easy than the close friendships enjoyed by his immediate predecessor, Eric Abbott, and certainly by Dean Stanley whose wife was a lady-in-waiting at the Court. He was never invited to lunch at Buckingham Palace and this, not because he was unappreciated but probably because he did not quite conform to royal expectations. Entirely unselfconscious, he treated everyone alike and on those occasions when duty took him to Buckingham Palace for some function he would weave his way through the London traffic on his ancient bicycle, clad in a shabby suit and coloured scarf, and on arrival forget that his trousers were tucked into his socks. In conversation he could seem abstracted and abruptly depart from the subject under discussion. When the dean and chapter entertained Queen Elizabeth, the Queen Mother, on the occasion of her eightieth birthday, the dean proposed her health with moving eloquence but then absent-mindedly seized her carefully prepared gin and tonic and downed it himself. Her Majesty was greatly amused and the dean was in no way disconcerted. The decision of the Prince of Wales to have his ill-fated marriage in St Paul's (made for architectural reasons) was a deep disappointment to him, not because he desired the limelight – he was much too humble for that – but because it seemed to be a denial of the Abbey's historic role.

Edward Frederick Carpenter, the son of a local builder of modest means, was born in 1910 at Addestone, near Weybridge. He went from Strodes School, Egham, to King's College, London, where he took a first in history, followed by an MA with distinction and later a PhD. His chief interest at this time was in late seventeenth- and early eighteenth-century Anglicanism and he wrote biographies of Bishop

Thomas Sherlock, Archbishop Thomas Tennison and Bishop Henry Compton. While at King's he came under the influence of liberal theology and transferred to the theological faculty to prepare for ordination.

He was a curate at Holy Trinity, Marylebone, from 1935 to 1941 and while there met and married Lilian Wright, a student at the Royal Academy of Dramatic Art, who played a vital part in his future ministry and eventually introduced him to the Baha'i faith. After a further curacy at St Paul's, Harrow, he was appointed vicar of Great Stanmore, Middlesex. There he had six idyllic years, relishing every aspect of the work of a parish priest and making an impact that was remembered half a century later by those who had been his young parishioners. Among those who were impressed was the then Prime Minister, C. R. Attlee, who had a house in Stanmore, and in 1951 he took the opportunity to appoint Carpenter to a vacant canonry of Westminster.

This was not a popular move at the Abbey. He was young, he had been to a redbrick university, and undoubtedly he was a Socialist. Attlee had totally disregarded ecclesiastical advice. Carpenter's early years in the Little Cloister were not easy. For a time he was cold-shouldered, and there seemed nothing for him to do, but eventually his own warm humanity melted the hearts of his colleagues and he found his feet. The fact that he had time on his hands meant that he was able to pursue his studies and write books. He also became involved in a great number of liberal movements and organizations, joining forces with his friend John Collins, of St Paul's, in the campaign for the abolition of capital punishment, the campaign for nuclear disarmament, and the anti-apartheid movement.

He was present at the Coronation in 1953 and carried to the altar the orb – a prophetic symbol, perhaps, of his own future global concerns. There was a young family to bring up and he and Lilian delighted to keep open house: so open that once when returning from an early morning service in the Abbey he met two stocking-footed burglars leaving by his front door and, either innocently or absent-mindedly, expressed the hope that they had had a good night. In 1959 he was, in the absence of any other willing candidate, appointed treasurer of the Abbey and held this post for 15 years until he became dean. It was not an office for which he was temperamentally suited, but he carried it off by getting the Receiver General, who ran administration, to hand him the accounts and budgets at the beginning of chapter meetings. These, although previously unseen, he presented with the aplomb and apparent expertise of a high-powered financier, leaving the Receiver General to field any questions.

The office of archdeacon, to which he was elected in 1963, was much more to his liking, and this, not simply because it was essentially a sinecure, but because it gave him a pastoral relationship with the 26 parishes of which the dean and chapter were the Patrons. He greatly enjoyed visiting them, preaching, encouraging their clergy and musing on their historic links with the Abbey. Later, when he became dean, they were invited to Westminster for half a day – for a tour of the Abbey, tea and evensong. The parish priests were encouraged to come more frequently and to spend the inside of a week in the precincts, while responsible for hourly prayers in the Abbey.

Having been appointed to Westminster when only 41, it was natural that he should sometimes wonder if the remainder of his life was to be spent in the service of the Royal Peculiar or if he might be asked to move elsewhere. With the right kind of administrative support, he would have made an exciting bishop and become a much-loved pastor of a diocese. Succession to Bishop Barnes at Birmingham would have been an imaginative choice by the Crown, but the route to the episcopate was barred by Archbishop Geoffrey Fisher as Carpenter discovered when undertaking research for Fisher's biography. Among the papers at Lambeth was a copy of a letter from the Primate to the Prime Minister in which he advised that under no circumstances should Canon Edward Carpenter be preferred to a bishopric, since he was interested in many things and ought to become a professor of history.

When the rectory of St Margaret's, Westminster, which is annexed to a canonry of Westminster, fell vacant in 1956 Carpenter asked if he might be considered for transfer to this post. He would have been an ideal choice and taken seriously the preaching opportunities and the church's link with the House of Commons, but the dean, Alan Don, told him in the nicest possible way that a Socialist could not be appointed to so fashionable a church. A quarter of a century later, when St Margaret's was facing bankruptcy and closure, Treasurer Carpenter, whose affection for the church never wavered, came to the rescue with the proposal that it should be reincorporated into the Abbey, from which it had been separated in 1837. He was much involved in the drafting of a Parliamentary Bill to make this possible.

His disappointment over St Margaret's was, however, as nothing compared with the anguish he felt over his failure to be appointed Dean of St Paul's in 1967. Carpenter was in no sense an ambitious man, but the deanery of St Paul's was the one post in the Church of England, outside Westminster, in which he believed he could make a significant contribution. Moreover, the retiring dean, W. R. Matthews, had written to him expressing the hope that he would be his successor and indicating that he would recommend him to the Crown. The only other serious candidate seemed to be John Collins, who was senior canon of St Paul's, and the two friends would have been content if either had been appointed. But in the event Martin Sullivan, the junior canon, was chosen and, since his gifts were largely confined to after-dinner speaking, insult was added to injury. Both Carpenter and Collins were devastated and for the next 11 years St Paul's had totally inadequate leadership.

Meanwhile, the Abbey community was still recovering from the strenuous celebration of the 900th anniversary of its foundation by King Edward the Confessor in 1065. Three members of the chapter (Eric Abbott, Max Warren and Joost de Blank) were invalids, another (Michael Stancliffe) was rector of St Margaret's, so it was left to Carpenter to plan and implement a programme. Which he did with gusto, crowding in as many events as 365 days could carry. A great variety of people were drawn into the Abbey's life and the celebration was deemed to have been a huge success, but everyone, apart from Carpenter, was left exhausted. He also managed to edit a large new history of the Abbey, *A House of Kings*, which remains an invaluable resource for both the scholar and the general reader.

When Eric Abbott, who had been ill for several years, retired in 1974 the Chapter made strong representations to the Crown that Carpenter should be his successor. No one knew more about the Abbey or embodied its spirit more than he, and it was hard to believe that any other priest in the Church of England was better equipped for this special post. The Labour Prime Minister, Harold Wilson, had no difficulty in concurring and indeed attended the installation, though the length of the new dean's sermon required him to leave early to deal with urgent matters in the House of Commons. Thus began an 11-year reign that proved to be a happy experience for everyone involved in the Abbey's life and a fitting climax to an outstanding ministry.

Inevitably perhaps, his love for people and sheer goodness proved to be a disability when he was called upon to administer discipline. It was too easy to take advantage of his incapacity to recognize sin and he sometimes tolerated conduct that ought not to have been tolerated. But the open house deanery and the sight of the dean bustling about the cloisters or risking his life (he had very impaired sight) by cycling across Westminster and the West End to visit someone who was ill exuded goodwill. It even made it possible to forgive a 4 a.m. telephone call from California, made by a dean who was apparently unaware that clock time in London was different.

Carpenter could himself manage on very little sleep and, having simply added his decanal responsibilities to the multitude of commitments he had accumulated over the previous 23 years, it was hardly surprising that he could never turn to the writing of a book much before midnight. During his time as a canon he had published several books, the most substantial of which *Cantuar* (1971) – was a valuable compilation of brief lives of all the Archbishops of Canterbury. Then, shortly before moving to the deanery, he undertook to write the official biography of Archbishop Geoffrey Fisher. This was a strange alliance, since he had little in common with Fisher and had often been highly critical of his Primacy, but as he became immured in the task he developed a liking for his subject, amounting almost to admiration, and became so fascinated with Fisher's life and times that he found it impossible to lay it down. He took it with him into retirement and 19 years after signing the original publisher's contract, the 820-page volume was permitted to see the light of day. It was more in the expansive style of a Victorian biography than of an analytical modern study but will always be an important quarry of twentieth-century Church history.

Dean Stanley spent much of his time at Westminster exploring and documenting the royal vaults and in 1977 Carpenter was given the opportunity to follow modestly in his somewhat macabre footsteps. The smell of gas in proximity to the Stuart vault caused anxiety lest an escape from the public supply was accumulating and threatening an explosion. There had recently been disastrous instances of this in some blocks of flats. Royal permission to open the vault was obtained and late on a quiet evening in July the dean and chapter and a few historians descended into the cellar-like room to view the scene described by Stanley – the lead coffins of King William III and Queen Mary, of Orange, and of Queen Anne and her consort, Prince George of Denmark, intact but that of Charles II caved in and revealing the decayed remains of the once 'Merry Monarch'. Carpenter, the historian, was deeply moved and returned immediately to pen an account of what some others had experienced as a disturbing event. There was no gas.

During his latter years as treasurer and throughout his time as dean, the Abbey and St Margaret's church underwent major restorations that transformed their exteriors, leaving them gleaming white as if newly built. The original appeal for £5 million had to be doubled and eventually raised to £20 million. This was efficiently handled by the Duke of Edinburgh and a sequence of city magnates, without much effort from the canons. But the dean was required to present the Abbey's public face at a multitude of fundraising occasions, where his enthusiasm and evident commitment had a powerful influence.

Following his retirement it 1985 he remained active, retaining his links with liberal causes and continuing to deliver erudite sermons and speeches. His lifelong support of Chelsea Football Club was reflected by the football included in his official coat of arms. By the time death liberated him from the sad indignities of Alzheimer's disease in 1998 he had lived through the greater part of the most turbulent and dangerous century in human history. And the dean of unorthodox faith had always been a beacon of hope and love.

24

The Urban Regenerator
Derrick Walters, Liverpool

That Britain's largest cathedral – Liverpool – should have been built during a time, 1904–78, when the Church in these islands suffered its greatest numerical decline may be attributed to faith or folly. But the story of the erection of this vast Gothic-style edifice is one of remarkable tenacity and generosity in a century beset by two world wars and undergoing a social revolution that militated against the monumental. It was in fact started by a leading evangelical bishop, F. J. Chavasse, at a time of supreme confidence when it was believed by many that the gospel would be preached to the entire world during their generation, and that the new century would be 'the Christian century'. That so noble a church should have been designed by a 22-year-old architect, the Roman Catholic Giles Gilbert Scott, is also a cause for wonder.

The new cathedral was fortunate to be served by a sequence of four unusually gifted deans. Until the establishment of a dean and chapter in 1931 the role had been fulfilled by the bishop, though shortly before the consecration of the first part of the building in 1924 (the Lady Chapel was dedicated in 1910) Frederick Dwelly, vicar of a Southport parish, was appointed 'Ceremoniarius'. Seven years later he succeeded to the deanery.

Autocratic and eccentric, Dwelly was endowed with a supreme sense of theatre. Unhindered by later liturgical theories and fads, his flair for movement, gesture and colour provided the building with forms of ceremonial which are still in use. He was followed by F. W. Dillistone, a learned scholar who had already been chancellor for four years. Earlier, he had spent some years in India and saw the cathedral as a base for mission that required strong links with the city and the diocese. In the end, however, he found the demands of the deanery incompatible with his vocation as a scholar and retired to an Oxford Fellowship to write more books.

Dillistone's successor, Edward Patey, was different again. He had been a member of the chapter that launched the re-built Coventry Cathedral on the world and took to Liverpool challenging ideas about the task of the Church in the late twentieth century. A man of vision and imagination, he used the immense spaces of the cathedral to devise memorable special services for local, regional and national organizations. Thus the service to commemorate the centenary of the Liverpool YMCA included dramatic examples of its activities, with a wartime canteen and a football match in the nave. Although he had some doubts concerning the value of church buildings, it fell to him, in the way that these things often do, to labour for many years to raise the £1 million required for the completion of the building and to arrange the final consecration in 1978.

This effort and the consequent exhaustion left some gaps in the cathedral's community life. Choral services were at this time held only on Sundays and sung by an amateur choir. Some of the original furnishings were beginning to look shabby. The interior of the building was often empty for surprisingly long periods and seemed gloomy and lifeless. Relations with the city council needed attention and, as Patey himself said at the time of his retirement in 1983, his successor should be someone who could sort out the cathedral's chaotic finances.

Outside the cathedral, the finances of the city were even more chaotic. The decline in Liverpool's role as a major port, combined with the ruthless policies pursued by Margaret Thatcher's government and the negative tactics of the Labour 'militant tendency' city council, had brought Merseyside almost to its knees – economically and socially. Widespread unemployment and urban decay caused simmering discontent, which boiled over in 1981 in major riots in Liverpool's Toxteth area. The consequent publicity was far removed from that of the halcyon days of the Beatles era.

Where might a dean be found who could make a significant impact on a weary cathedral and a community in crisis? Improbable as it must have seemed at the time, in the beautiful, tranquil close at Salisbury. The choice of 51-year-old Rhys Derrick Chamberlain Walters who had for the last four years been canon treasurer of Salisbury Cathedral, as well as diocesan missioner, proved to be brilliantly successful and he became one of the great deans of the twentieth century, serving at Liverpool from 1983 until cancer drove him into retirement in 1999.

He was born in 1932 in Glamorganshire, where his father was a trade union official, and he never lost his Welsh classless charm. Endowed with a warmth and humanity that enabled him to get on with everyone, but also a courage and determination that would brook no obstacle to the realization of his vision. He attended the Gowerton Boys Grammar School and went from there to the London School of Economics to read sociology. Preparation for ordination at Ripon Hall, Oxford, was followed in 1957 by a brief curacy in Swansea, which led to appointment as Anglican chaplain at University College, Swansea – a ministry for which he was ideally suited.

In 1962 Walters moved to Derby diocese to become vicar of Totley, near Sheffield, and five years later was appointed vicar of Boulton – a large suburban parish near Derby which housed many employees of Rolls Royce and British Rail Engineering. This was more than enough to keep him fully occupied, but the bishop wished to set up a diocesan communications office with Walters as part-time communications officer. He could not have chosen better and, although the dual responsibility was often taxing, an impressive communications operation was established. The co-ordination of religious broadcasting for BBC Radio Derby was taken under its wing and good use was made of the officer's considerable communications skills.

His gifts then came to the notice of Bishop George Reindorp who had been translated from Guildford to Salisbury in 1973 and who in the following year appointed him as his diocesan missioner – a post combined with responsibility for the small Wiltshire parish of Burcombe. Lay training was, he believed, the key to effective mission and for the next nine years he went about the largely rural diocese, enthusing the laity and running stimulating courses that prepared many of them for a newly instituted Bishop's Certificate. In 1979 he left his parish to become a canon residentiary of the cathedral and, besides the lay training, displayed another skill as Treasurer. Four years of this were long enough to indicate a decanal future.

Having arrived at Liverpool and surveyed the scene, Walters declared, 'So much time and money has been invested in the building of a great cathedral, now we must be involved in the rehabilitation of the surrounding city,' and in a newspaper interview he said, 'While our primary role is to let the cathedral help people in their encounter with God, you can't ignore the context in which we're working. It is desperately important that we create new jobs in the city because that's what gives people a sense of pride and meaning.'

A modern dean has, however, no prescriptive right to leadership in the sphere of urban regeneration, and only very rarely the necessary skill. Although he claimed to be a Socialist, Walters brought to the task Conservative economic convictions that were as unfashionable in most parts of Liverpool as they were in the upper echelons of the

Church of England's hierarchy. He did not always see eye to eye with his own bishop – David Sheppard – on these matters, though the two got on well enough. Certainly, 'Wealth creation and job creation are an essential part of the church's ministry' was not a message the city councillors were pleased to hear, but eventually his ability to get money for major social projects and his determination to see them carried out won their confidence. Significant numbers were coming off the dole. The Walters approach also coincided with the Government's public/private partnership policy and he became an ambassador of the city to Whitehall and an 'honest broker' between the Government and the city. He was trusted by both sides and so became a funnel for initiatives and grants.

On first acquaintance he seemed more like a businessman than a church dignitary. Always immaculately dressed in a grey, double-breasted suit, with a white tie, visitors to his office were often surprised to find the equipment of a high-powered chief executive – a television screen flashing the FTSE 100 Index, the very latest in computers and a long conference table. A copy of *The Economist*, rather than the *Church Times*, lay on his desk and he spoke of strategic planning, investment, contracts and margins. Yet visitors quickly went on to discover that all this was inseparable from burning Christian convictions and a passionate commitment to what the cathedral stood for. Never short of ideas, not all of which proved to be viable, he made stimulating company.

His first major social project was on the cathedral's own doorstep. Although it occupied a magnificent site on The Mount, the great building had always been surrounded by urban squalor of the worst kind, including some of Liverpool's most appalling housing. This had been noted as far back as the 1930s but a series of development schemes had to be abandoned for want of agreement and much bitter wrangling among the city and county councils who owned the land. The impasse was broken by Michael Heseltine, a dynamic Government Minister, who was despatched to Liverpool by the Prime Minister to deal with the problems highlighted by the Toxteth riots. He promised government financial support for the redevelopment of the cathedral's environment and, after a strongly fought design competition, work began in 1983 – at about the same time as Walters arrived at the deanery, then located five miles from the cathedral.

From the outset the scheme was beset by problems, many related to the character of the site, but progress was made and in 1986 houses forming a close for the cathedral clergy were completed. It was not quite like Salisbury but the benefits from having the chapter living near the cathedral, rather than scattered in the city's suburbs, soon began to be felt. At this point, however, a severe economic recession, affecting the whole country, brought a loss of confidence in the housing market and, with few buyers in prospect, the developers pulled out of the scheme leaving the area no more than a large building site.

Walters and his chapter took over, bought out the developers' interests with the aid of a bank loan, obtained £2.4 million in Government grants and brought the scheme to a highly successful social and economic conclusion. Besides the close, there is an attractive courtyard, social housing and rented lodgings for 400 students of the Liverpool John Moores University. The Derrick Walters Building houses the university's media and critical arts department, while Redmond House, paid for by a media mogul, is occupied by an International Centre for Digital Content. Walters strongly supported the Foundation for Citizenship which provides five public lectures a year on current social issues and he had the vision of cathedral and university enjoying a close relationship, as at Durham.

Next came a project in Toxteth where the riots had been largely located in Falkner Road, within a 1970s housing estate of inadequate design and replete with social problems. The response of the city council was to demolish the estate, leaving a 65-acre derelict site, with no plans for its redevelopment. Walters, whose wife Joan worked as a schoolteacher in the area, produced a scheme, with the council's approval, enlisted the support of Merseyside Task Force, and formed a consortium which included the cathedral's own charitable Estates Company. Government financial backing was obtained and the result was one of the largest inner-city regeneration schemes in the country. Eleven sites were allocated to different functions – public and private housing, a maternity hospital, parkland and an enlarged factory that became the largest local employer.

This was followed, in 1996, by the chairmanship of a Chavasse Park Development – a major project incorporating, at a cost of £91 million, a Discovery Hall illustrating the creation of life and the milestones in the progress of science, a Media Factory relating to information technology, a public park with a covered performance facility for over 3,000 people and a spectacular suspension bridge. Again, this was to be a public/private partnership, with the promise of significant funding from the Millennium Commission, and Walters hoped to spend the first years of his retirement working on it, but severe legal problems over the site could not be solved and, sadly, the project had to be abandoned. It would have created 2,000 jobs. Nonetheless, Walters was involved in development schemes requiring £230 million of investment and in 1994 he was appointed OBE.

To all these projects he brought vision, skill and energy – qualities needed no less in the renewal of the cathedral's life. Shortly before he retired, Edward Patey appointed a young and highly gifted musician, Ian Tracey, as organist and master of the choristers. He and Walters immediately struck up what became a close friendship and partnership in the renewal of the cathedral's music. Lacking the support of a choir school, Tracey recruited choristers more widely from the city's schools, gave them intensive training, and attracted lay clerks from the colleges. Soon evensong was being sung on five weekdays and many more worshippers were attracted to the Sunday services. His appointment as chorusmaster of the Royal Liverpool Philharmonic Society, together with other city and university posts, helped to make the cathedral a major centre for music in the North West.

Walters was always open to new forms of worship and the imaginative special services continued, a particularly notable example being a memorial service, televised worldwide in 1989, for 95 Liverpool Football Club supporters who had been crushed to death in a stampede during a match at Sheffield. But his personal preference was for the 1662 *Book of Common Prayer* and the King James Bible and this because of his great sensitivity to language and poetry. He also took preaching very seriously and his sermons expressed both his increasing search for truth and his warm humanity. Paintings were commissioned for the chancel, the west end and the chapter house, and Elisabeth Frink's sculpture 'The Welcoming Christ' was placed above the west door. An embroidery exhibition was opened in the triforium and new choir stalls were introduced. The administration was, naturally, reorganized and the dean and chapter's financial reserves quadrupled.

These signs of renewal needed, however, to be accompanied by an infusion of pilgrims and visitors to bring the great building alive. Here Walters was fortunate, soon after the installation, to have the chapter reinforced by the appointment of two new canons who shared his vision and were endowed with no less energy. Kenneth Riley knew Liverpool backwards, having begun his ministry in the city, been Anglican chaplain of Liverpool University and most recently vicar of one of its largest parishes, as well as rural dean. He also had a deep interest in music, drama and film, and when he had done a stint as treasurer became precentor. Walters and he saw the urgency of establishing a visitor centre and refectory to encourage more visitors and to enhance the experience of those who came. Both were created with great flair in the two least-used parts of the cathedral itself and were opened in September 1984.

Strong management and much voluntary help brought immediate success, and it soon became necessary to establish a second dining area to cater for larger organized groups. During his ten years as a canon, Riley made a significant contribution to the process of renewal led by Walters, before moving to become Dean of Manchester and deeply involved in the development of the community life of that city. Nicholas Frayling came from a tough South London parish and, after four creative years as precentor, became rector of Liverpool and subsequently Dean of Chichester. The arrival in 1995 of Noel Vincent, who had worked with Walters on communications in Derby and subsequently spent 13 years at the BBC as a religious programmes producer, brought to the chapter another kind of expertise that was turned to good use. It was always a strong team.

The ministry of Walters, within and without Liverpool Cathedral, was a staggering achievement and reinforces the belief that a long tenure of a deanery can work wonders if its occupant has unusually creative gifts and a strong, collaborative chapter. Walters was in fact – and in his own judgement – a medieval dean at heart. He saw the cathedral as the centre of its local community, providing employment, training apprentices, building houses and workplaces, involved in education, fostering the arts, offering worship, questing for and proclaiming the truth – standing as a testimony to 'the things that cannot be shaken', and as a sign and a servant of the Kingdom of God. The final years of his own life involved much uncomplaining suffering as he battled against cancer and he died aged 68 in 2000, just one year after his enforced retirement. At the memorial service Professor Peter Toyne, the Vice-Chancellor of Liverpool John Moores University and a close friend and collaborator, said:

> He used his influence with people of influence to influence the lives of those with little or no influence. He had a rare gift to make the most unlikely people work together, which no one before him had ever been able to do. No cathedral can have done more for the city in which it is so magnificently set.

The world of Derrick Walters was as different as can be imagined from that of William Buckland whose portrait is first in this gallery of deans, yet the two priests were united in believing that they were called not only to the leadership of a great Church, but also to advance the welfare of humankind.

25

The Missionary Leader – Looking Ahead

In spite of spectacular developments in the second half of the twentieth century, the English cathedrals were in its closing decade faced with a number of serious problems. Some of these were in fact created by the success of the developments, others were related to a general decline in the strength of the Church of England itself. Not all have been solved and the new century brought several new challenges.

The first signs of serious cathedral stress appeared nationally in 1988 when the dean and chapter of Hereford announced that it proposed to offer for sale its copy of the thirteenth-century Mappa Mundi. The financial predicament of this small cathedral, located some distance from any large centre of population and lacking sources of substantial income, was so acute that there seemed no alternative to the sale of a great treasure. The need to conserve a historic chained library served only to exacerbate the crisis. A national outcry followed and a wider awareness of the fact that five clergymen were responsible for the protection and display of an important piece of the country's heritage which they were at liberty to sell to the highest bidder. The dean came in for much criticism, but no one made any realistic proposals as to how the problem might otherwise be solved. In the end a happy solution was reached by a munificent American benefactor and a grant from the National Heritage Memorial Fund. But such a solution could not be relied upon for dealing with similar problems in other cathedrals, and an increasingly vociferous heritage lobby expressed widespread concern.

Financial and administrative problems at Exeter and St Paul's next attracted unwelcome publicity, and some time later the Bishop of Salisbury carried out a Visitation of his cathedral which also hit the headlines. Although his cathedral was generally regarded as among the best run in the country and the dean had valiantly led a £5 million appeal for the restoration of its famous spire, the bishop was far from sympathetic to many of the dean and chapter's activities. 'Come out of your comfortable cloisters', he called, and recommended that commercial activity and the levying of entrance fees should be abandoned in favour of subscriptions from all the parishes of the diocese. This was seen at the time to be impracticable – not least by the parishes.

Far exceeding any of these incidents in the publicity they attracted was, however, a long-running and damaging conflict within the chapter at Lincoln. Although this did not surface until the early part of 1990, it had been a growing problem throughout the long decanate of Oliver Fiennes (1969–89) and brought about a breakdown in his health. Alerted to this by some of her Lincolnshire friends, the then Prime Minister, Margaret Thatcher, consulted the evangelical members of her entourage and, with surprising speed, the Provost of Bradford, Brandon Jackson, was translated to Lincoln with instructions to 'sort things out'. The effect was akin to that of petrol being poured on an already blazing fire. The conflict between the new dean and the sub-dean, Rex Davis, began as a result of an investigation into an exhibition of the cathedral's copy of the Magna Carta in Australia, which had been organized by Davis and yielded a loss of £60,000. It quickly turned, however, into a publicly staged struggle for power.

The Bishop of Lincoln, Robert Hardy, intervened and in a 20,000-word admonition censured the dean and, having rebuked all the canons for their 'reprehensible' and 'shameful' behaviour, called on each one of them to 'consider his position'. This served only to highlight the lack of power available to bishops in the running of their cathedrals and the Archbishop of Canterbury, George Carey, fared no better. Lacking nothing other than spiritual and moral authority, he made a brave attempt to break the Lincoln impasse and called on both the dean and the sub-dean to resign, 'for the greater good of the cathedral and the wider Church'. This call was reinforced by 124 votes to four in the Lincoln diocesan synod and a majority in the general chapter, but neither man was prepared to go and the bishop announced that he was unwilling to worship alongside them in the cathedral on Christmas Day 1996. During the following year, Jackson resigned, but Davis remained for another six years until he reached compulsory retirement age. It was not until the end of 2003 that Jackson's successor, Alec Knight, was able to announce that, with the appointment of three new canons residentiary, Lincoln could at last make a new start.

This sad saga highlighted also the lack of authority possessed by a dean – an old issue often illustrated in the preceding pages, but always a surprise when brought to the notice of most churchgoers, and incomprehensible to those involved in secular administration. A dean, first among equals, requires the consent of the chapter for any changes in the life of the cathedral he or she may wish to initiate. At first sight this may not seem unreasonable in a Christian community bonded by love and mutual respect, but 'experience over many centuries has proved it to be a serious obstacle to reform or even minor improvement. Reasonable debate and acceptable compromise have too often been hindered by obstinacy and personal vendetta.

Equally, canons residentiary often feel deeply frustrated. Having previously exercised strong leadership as rector of a large parish or in some other appointment, a canon may discover that the new role offers hardly more freedom than that of a curate and has no defined responsibilities. This may in the past have suited a scholar who had no wish to be disturbed from his studies by administrative chores, but today these are fairly rare birds, and in any case cathedrals now require some involvement of all the chapter in their wide-ranging activities.

The absence from chapters of the skills necessary to the handling of multi-million pound budgets and the management of fairly large staffs also became increasingly evident. Bursars, accountants and the like were being employed but were excluded from policy-making and other important decisions. At another level, the absence of precentors from many chapters, and the treatment of organists as no more than employees, hardly accorded with the constant and legitimate claim that the primary purpose of a cathedral is the offering of worship.

These problems were felt in different ways by all the 42 capitular bodies, though less severely by the smaller parish church cathedrals which had retained some important elements of their previous parochial status. By the early 1990s there was broad agreement among the deans and provosts that corporate action was needed, if only to forestall unwelcome intervention by the General Synod, which was known to have limited sympathy for cathedrals and was becoming restless over the damaging publicity that some of them were creating.

With only one negative vote and a single abstention the Deans and Provosts Conference therefore asked the Archbishops of Canterbury and York in 1991 to set up a commission, 'to examine the working of the English cathedrals' and, 'if necessary propose such legislative changes as may be required for their continuing to contribute to the mission and ministry of the Church in the twenty-first century'.

Assured that the cathedrals would meet the financial cost of the proposal, the Archbishops responded with commendable speed and in 1992 appointed a 13-member commission under the chairmanship of Lady Howe of Aberavon, who had wide experience of the workings of public institutions. The other members embraced most of the expertise and experience required and the commission set to work with a will, handicapped only by the surprising lack of an organist in their ranks.

The urgency of the task and the dedicated labours of the commission enabled the work to be completed within two years. Every cathedral was visited by delegates from the commission and submissions were received from nearly 400 bodies and individuals who felt drawn to offer opinion or advice. The 262-page report published in October 1994 contained a wealth of material about the life of the cathedrals, discussed the chief areas of concern, and concluded with 104 recommendations ranging from evangelism to trading, and including 33 related to governance and management. It was emphasized that the commission had found, 'much to praise, including an impressive adaptability and openness to change', and there was an assurance that the cathedrals were not in crisis and that any problems were capable of being resolved within the evolving tradition that had marked them for centuries.

Most of the recommendations were of a general kind and concerned with good practice in matters such as Friends organizations, shops, education and accountancy, and required no structural changes, though some would need extra personnel and cash. Accountability was an altogether different matter and a council was proposed to act as a watchdog over the cathedral's life. The diocesan bishop would be in the chair and 20 or more members represent the different communities of interest served by the cathedral. Its concerns would include long-term planning, the annual budget, approval of published annual accounts, and any other matters on which a report might be requested. In extreme circumstances the council could petition for the removal of the dean.

Next came membership of the dean and chapter. A qualified administrator should have full voting rights, along with up to three independent lay members appointed by the bishop, after consultation with the council and with the dean. The dean should be the, 'executive chairman', responsible for day-to-day leadership and decision-making, and with a casting vote at meetings. On the critical matter of clerical appointments, deans would continue to be appointed by the Crown, but the diocesan bishop would be consulted and members of the chapter permitted to 'comment'. The proposed dean would have the opportunity to meet his future colleagues before deciding whether or not to accept. Canons would continue to be appointed by the diocesan bishop (in a few cases by the Crown), but only after consultation with the dean, the canons and possibly the council. Special attention would be paid to candidates' aptitude for working in a team.

The final major recommendation concerned tenure of office and it was proposed that freeholds, held to the age of 70, should be abolished and replaced by appointment for a term of years or left open-ended. All were to be terminated after a period of notice by either party: in the case of canons the dean would make a recommendation to the bishop, who would then decide. Aggrieved canons could appeal to a tribunal. In the case of deans, the recommendation would be made by the bishop and confirmed, or not, by the Archbishop. Again, a tribunal would hear appeals. There was no suggestion as to how incompetent or uncollaborative bishops might be removed from the role of Visitor.

The report was met, initially, with hostility by a large proportion of the deans and provosts who appeared to have forgotten that it was they who had asked for a commission to be appointed and that it was not, therefore, to be regarded as something imposed from on high. The comprehensive character of the recommendations, which had been unforeseen, was undoubtedly daunting and seemed unnecessary to busy men who were confident of their own ability to keep their cathedrals on course and working efficiently. It was generally acknowledged that the cathedrals were flourishing as never before and constituted one of the Church's few success stories; why, therefore, choose this moment in their history for what amounted to a root and branch reform?

The appointment of canons residentiary for fixed terms might well be helpful but the extension of this proposal to deans and provosts was seen as a dire threat. So also did the recommendation that, 'other than in exceptional circumstances, the diocesan bishop should chair the council'. This was said to conflict with the juridical role of the bishop, but in reality the opposition was an expression of the age-old resistance to episcopal interference. Not everyone saw the need for councils or for lay canons on their chapters. The deans and provosts elected to the General Synod were, therefore, charged to keep a wary eye on the legislation required to make any of the commission's recommendations prescriptive, but after much heated discussion and formal debate a new Cathedrals Measure passed into law in 1999.

This incorporated most of the recommendations, but with significant modifications. The bishop must not chair the council, but nominate a layperson to this role. He may himself attend council meetings and speak at them, but not vote. The council is to consist of the lay chairman, the dean and 11–19 other members drawn from the chapter, the honorary canons, the cathedral congregation and the wider church and community. It must meet at least twice a year to receive (not approve) reports and accounts, and to make proposals, but it has no power to petition for the removal of the dean. Matters of concern may, nonetheless, be drawn to the attention of the bishop or, if money is involved, to the Church Commissioners. It may, in consultation with the bishop, revise the statutes.

The commission's proposals for the chapters were largely accepted, except that the dean retains a freehold until the age of 70. No more than four canons residentiary can be appointed and these may hold office for a term of years or on a freehold like that of the dean – the decision in each case to be made locally. The choice of canons is still made by the bishop, but only after consultation with the chapter, and the duties of each canon is to be clearly defined. Not less than two, and no more than seven, people, of whom two-thirds are laity, must be appointed to the chapter by the Bishop on the recommendation of the dean. The cathedral administrator may also become a full voting member. The chapter is required to formulate, after consultation with the bishop, proposals for the general direction and mission of the cathedral and submit them to the council for advice. A finance committee must include laypeople with appropriate expertise.

The leadership role of the dean remains largely unchanged, though there can be no alterations to the forms of worship without the dean's consent, neither can the budget be settled unless the dean agrees. The dean has a second or casting vote when there is disagreement and is to be a member of every committee. Diocesan bishops are now expected to be more involved in the life of their cathedrals than ever before during the last 1,000 years, and provision is made for this, but the degree to which bishops become involved is certain to vary from cathedral to cathedral, and the power of Visitor to do more than exhort and admonish remains severely limited – to the great satisfaction of the deans.

It is too soon to tell what the results of these reforms are likely to be, even in the fairly short term, and they are bound to be experienced differently according to circumstances and the personalities involved. In general, however, the response to them has been favourable. The appointment of laity to the chapter is acknowledged to have brought valuable insights and expertise, even where some canons have found it difficult to accept their contribution. Finance and investment committees are also proving their worth and in deteriorating financial situations their skills are indispensable.

Accountability has, predictably, brought a considerable increase in paper work and bureaucracy which the introduction of information technology has done little to alleviate. In some cathedrals the effect is said to be too time consuming and productive of an administrative, rather than a visionary, approach to policy-making and problem solving. But the reforms are not entirely to blame for this, since recent years have seen much government legislation relating to child protection, employment rights, disability, health and safety, data protection and auditing. Additional staff has often been needed to handle the new demands. The appointment of chief lay administrators to chapters, with full voting rights, has had a mixed reception, though the dean's leadership role is more widely acknowledged.

The removal of freehold tenure is evidently allowing greater flexibility in the appointment of canons and consultation between bishops and chapters over these appointments is seen to be beneficial. There is, however, said to be an acute shortage of suitable candidates and in some instances bishops, having consulted chapters, then disregarded their views, which is obviously worse than not seeking them in the first place. It is almost normal for posts to be advertised.

The most difficult area of reform is, as was anticipated, that which relates to councils, and problems have arisen over different understandings of their role and responsibilities. In some places busy lay members have resigned because they felt they were wasting their time on matters of little consequence. In others, groups of able members have sought to usurp the authority of the dean and chapter over the day-to-day running of the cathedral. But there are also reports of valuable collaboration and constructive partnership, and happily there have not so far been instances of crisis requiring a council to take action against a dean and chapter by means of reports to a bishop or to the Church Commissioners.

Meanwhile intense financial pressure, with potentially dangerous consequences, is now being felt by all the cathedrals, and most of all by those whose work has, for a quarter of a century or more, been substantially sustained by income from visitors. The Howe Commission reported that 19 cathedrals were in deficit and that if legacies and appeals were excluded this figure would rise to 30. The largest annual deficit then was £486,000, and another seven cathedrals had deficits in excess of £180,000. The position now is even more serious. In January 2004 the secretary of the Association of English Cathedrals said, 'I do not know one cathedral that isn't facing a critical financial situation.' Evidence of this is not difficult to find. In April of the previous year York Minster reported a deficit of £600,000 on its annual £3.5 million budget and announced that it would shortly impose admission charges and close its historic library. The Archbishop intervened to save the library but, having seen the Minster's accounts, considered that there was no alternative to admission charges. Chester, for many years one of the most visited of the cathedrals, announced a deficit of £200,000 and the axing of three of its staff. Bradford was said to be bankrupt, having found it impossible to pay more than a small proportion of the contractors' bills for the building of a £5 million 'Life Force' exhibition centre that attracted few visitors. At Winchester an important theological library was closed when the dean and chapter, faced with acute financial problems, placed several of its close properties on the commercial letting market. A cash crisis at Ripon was said to be threatening the future of the choir.

Several factors have combined to create or exacerbate the financial problems. In recent years investment income has fallen and Church Commissioners' grants to many cathedrals have been reduced. The cost of educating choristers in independent residential schools has escalated considerably, and major restoration programmes encouraged by English Heritage grants have often over-run initial estimates. Even modest salary increases for labour-intensive organizations, such as cathedrals, are bound to add significantly to costs. But most serious for the major cathedrals has been the dramatic fall in visitor numbers following the terrorist attacks on New York and Washington on 11 September 2001. Fear of further attacks in other parts of the world continues to keep at home those Americans and Japanese tourists most likely to visit English cathedrals. There are also signs of changes in the pattern of tourism involving the British public. Thus a not untypical annual loss of 150,000 visitors (about 400 a day) each of whom may contribute in various ways an average of £1.50, is bound to have a major impact on a cathedral's finances.

International crises and currency value fluctuations are not new and have often affected visitor numbers for relatively short periods, but the current situation seems likely to be prolonged and this has driven some cathedrals to put back the clock and re-impose admission fees or introduce more or less compulsory 'donations'. When viewed in the light of the early twentieth-century battles to abolish such obstacles to entry – seen by Dean Bennett of Chester and others as essential to a cathedral's mission – this is bound to create disquiet and raise some fundamental questions about the nature of the cathedrals' future work.

All of which needs to be examined in the context of the general and accelerating decline in the numerical strength and influence of the Church of England during the last 50 years – a feature of all the major churches of Western Europe in the same period. In England this decline can be traced from the early years of the nineteenth century, but from 1960 it became more obvious – except to most Church leaders – when the reduction in regular church attendance was accompanied by a dramatic falling away of those who once went to their local church for baptisms, weddings and funerals. The closing decades of the twentieth century also witnessed a profound cultural change which has left the church even more isolated from the younger generation. In 2003 at least one in seven church buildings was vandalized and violence against clergy became common.

The statistics of decline are now so well documented that it is unnecessary to reproduce them here, but the scale of the problem for the Church of England is indicated by the fact that the regular congregations in 50 per cent of the 16,280 churches (all of them designed to seat 200 or more) number no more than 20, and in the next 30 per cent only 70. Only one in five babies is now brought for baptism, one in four couples are married in church. That such a decline in membership and consequent influence in society should have taken place without there being some decisive action to evaluate causes and produce remedies beggars belief. But this is the sad reality and indicates both weak faith and defective leadership.

The cathedrals have bucked this trend and are one of the Church of England's few twentieth-century success stories. Now they must decide how they can respond to the acute crisis facing the rest of the church. In recent years attempts have been made to forge stronger links between cathedrals and their dioceses, but with only limited success. The Howe Commission called for redoubled effort in this direction and it might seem obvious that the present situation demands integration and sharing of resources.

At the present time, however, such a move would be full of danger, with the real risk of cathedral communities being weakened and dragged down by their sinking dioceses. By the end of 2003 this was becoming more than a theoretical possibility. A joint group appointed by the Archbishops' Council and the Church Commissions proposed a reduction of £500,000 in cathedral grants in order to help finance network missions and also the ending of the Commissioners legal obligation to pay directly the stipends of full-time canons. Strenuous opposition to this by the deans, supported by the bishops, led to its rejection by the General Synod.

The end of November 2003 also found no fewer than seven of the 42 cathedrals without a dean. Salisbury had by this time been vacant for 15 months and another two months were to pass before it was announced that the appointment was going to one of the cathedral's own canons. Wells had been vacant for eight months, York and St Albans each three months. In every case the outgoing dean had given several months' notice of his intention to retire or to move to another post. There were rumours that delay was being caused by the new consultation procedure, that some bishops were being 'difficult' over choices, that there was a shortage of suitable candidates, that able priests were reluctant to become enmeshed in administration and finance. In a letter to the *Church Times*, however, the Prime Minister's Secretary for Appointments explained that an unusually large number of vacancies among the deans and bishops had caused 'strategic and planning' delays. Which can only be taken to mean that the appointments system has broken down and is in urgent need of reform.

Until the Church as a whole has entered into a period of serious reform and adopted new mission strategies appropriate to the challenging situation in which it now finds itself, the cathedrals should fight tooth and nail to retain their independence and, if necessary, find extra money to make this possible. More than ever before the Church of England needs what the cathedrals can do best – offer particular forms of worship at the highest level, provide a wide-ranging programme of Christian education, keep an open door for people of every sort of religious faith and maintain creative contact with many of the secular institutions of its region.

But however well they may function, cathedrals obviously cannot do more than play a relatively small part in the rekindling of faith of the English nation and it must be accepted that for the time being they are engaged in what amounts to a constructive holding operation. Their longer term role should, nonetheless, involve integration in a new strategy of mission embracing the whole Church. What form might such a strategy take, and how might the cathedrals become part of it?

There can be no progress in this direction without effective leadership, that is to say, leadership of the missionary, rather than the administrative sort. As I argued in my book, *The Bishops* (2002), the episcopate needs to be liberated from its present pastoral-management role in order that it may inspire and lead the reorganization of the church for mission. Such a change, while radical, would be no more than the recovery of the bishop's original, apostolic function.

Mission requires also recognition that the territorial parochial system, devised for a static agrarian society, no longer enables the Church to engage with most people in the most important aspects of their lives. For many, the parish is the place where they sleep rather than where they live. Community for them is experienced primarily in a network of relationships that cross geographical boundaries. Vocational, educational, leisure, social work, political, youth and many other associations provide a sense of belonging and common purpose that is often lacking even in small villages and rarely experienced in large urban areas. A Church concerned to engage with people where they are, which is essential for mission, must seek to establish a corporate presence in these spheres, as in a former age it became established in every rural or small town community where every aspect of an individual's life was expressed and contained.

This is not a new conclusion. The worker-priest movement in France in the 1940s and '50s and Industrial Mission in England and elsewhere, at about the same time, recognized its validity, and for even longer chaplaincies have been established in the armed forces, hospitals and some schools and colleges. During the 1960s a West-European working party of the World Council of Churches undertook much research in this field and produced a powerful report on *The Missionary Structure of the Congregation*, which urged churches to reshape their lives so as to engage with the many different communities, small and large, of the modern world. This report was widely discussed, conferences were held, books were written, but nothing of significance happened: the churches remained locked in their medieval, residence-based pattern of ministry. Most of the modest experiments in alternative methods were abandoned when financial pressures became acute.

Forty years later, however, there are signs of movement in this direction, originating from an unexpected quarter. During the late 1970s a few strong evangelical churches, led by Holy Trinity, Brompton, experimented with what became known as 'church plants'. Some members of their congregation were detached to engage in mission work in places where church life was at a low ebb. These met with success and small, vigorous new church communities were formed, but they were met with hostility, not only because they were located in an existing parish which did not share their outlook, but also because they ignored geographical boundaries and made contacts more widely.

Nonetheless, the number of church plants began to grow, reaching about 40 per year in 1990 and by the turn of the century totalling 370. A report, *Breaking New Ground*, to the House of Bishops in 1994 concluded that the structures and Canons of the Church of England were flexible enough to permit bishops to encourage church planting in their dioceses. A further report, *Mission-shaped Church*, appeared in 2004 with an enthusiastic commendation by the Archbishop of Canterbury. Of considerable significance, it provided a wealth of material about the development of different kinds of 'plant' in various parts of the country and argued, theologically, that while these will continue to grow alongside parish-based churches they should not be regarded as ancilliary to these but rather as authentic churches in their own right.

The report did not, however, tackle the question of how best the Church might engage with secular power structures, neither did it – for understandable reasons – consider what major alterations to the Church of England will be needed for the change to a mixed economy of parish and network churches. Tinkering with the present system will not be sufficient.

Chief among these alterations must be the way in which the full-time clergy are deployed. Here another neglected report, *A Strategy for the Church's Ministry* (1988) – the work of John Tiller, a former chief secretary of the Advisory Council for the Church's Ministry – remains relevant. This proposed that residential parishes should be served by local, unpaid priests working with a lay eldership, while a corps of well-trained, full-time clergy should be employed by the diocese, some in specialist roles relating to secular institutions, but most providing missionary, educational and pastoral skills to the parishes. It is not difficult to envisage such a system being extended to incorporate network churches or to believe that these informal faith communities require this kind of skilled ministerial assistance.

The present dioceses of the Church of England vary considerably in geographical size and in their populations, but for the sake of illustration, and subject always to local adjustment, let it be assumed that each has about 300 parishes and 400 churches, served by, say, 225 stipendiary clergy, 50 non-stipendiary and locally ordained clergy and

200 readers. Under a new dispensation the number of churches to be kept open and in use for regular worship would be subject to constant review, care being taken to ensure that no recognizable community is left without a church building. There is evidence that weekday services are becoming more popular and in some places these might replace regular Sunday worship.

The number of stipendiary clergy must then be gradually reduced to about 100, with entry and training standards raised very considerably. Of these 100, about 20 would be deployed in specialist secular chaplaincies, another 20 allocated to large and strategically placed parishes, leaving 60 to provide resources for the parishes and networks. The kind of clerical or lay leadership required for these smaller units of church life is bound to be varied and cannot be forecast, but both would normally be locally recruited. It may be anticipated that a large number of non-stipendiary priests will be required for local ministry and, with 50 of these and 200 readers, plus a number of Church Army evangelists already active there already exists a pool of talent and experience from which to draw. Better use of retired clergy, half of whom (about 4,000 nation-wide) are still active, would further increase clerical resources. In the long term, however, it is likely that new patterns of mission and ministry will produce new forms of leadership and that ordination will be seen as an act of confirmation, rather than initiation, into priesthood.

Strong centres for this mission-orientated form of church life would be provided by the cathedral and, say, five other large churches in key geographical location in the diocese. Each must enjoy the degree of independence necessary for a flexible response to changing circumstances in their areas. The stipendiary clergy would be divided into six groups and based at one or other of these churches. The leader at each centre, apart from the cathedral, would be an area dean.

The cathedral would retain its role as the chief focus of the bishop's ministry and the place where large-scale diocesan, civic and community services are held. The cathedral chapter would consist of a dean and two full-time canons, together with an appropriate number of qualified laity. These would be augmented by the stipendiary clergy allocated to diocesan or area duties who would be responsible for many of the diocesan and community services and activities held at the cathedral. Thus the dean and chapter would be left responsible for the day-to-day running of the cathedral, liaison with the other five major centres in the diocese, and three other long-established tasks:

First, continue to ensure that worship of varying kinds is offered at the highest level. In this context, sermons are to be regarded as not less important than music, inadequate preachers being as out of place in the pulpit as tone-deaf singers are in the choir. Besides its corporate worship, the cathedral must be recognizable as a place of prayer and reflection.

Second, maintain a theological resource centre for the whole diocese. It is unrealistic to expect that the dean and canons should be professional theologians, though one of them might be, and the others ought to be capable of undertaking research at a reasonably high level. Additional contributions could be made by a part-time canon theologian and through contact with university departments of theology and religion. A good library is at least as important as a good organ.

Third, continue to secure the preservation and embellishment of the building and maintain close relations with the world of arts.

This picture of a cathedral playing a vital part in the life of a Church which has been revived and is responding to God's call to share in his mission to the world, may perhaps be no more than the creation of an old man who dreams dreams, and is therefore of little value. But if this be so, a picture of no less challenging vision is required if the Church's decline is to be arrested and the Christian gospel freshly proclaimed. Either way, the dean of the future must be first and foremost a missionary leader.

Bibliography

Philip Barrett's monumental study of English cathedral life in the nineteenth century, *Barchester* (1993), is a delight and never likely to be surpassed. It combines meticulous scholarship with an attractive literary style and is essential reading for anyone who wishes to understand how the cathedrals entered the modern world. The author's premature death has robbed us of a promised companion volume on their twentieth-century life, and this is a serious loss. Surprisingly, perhaps, Anthony Trollope's classic Barsetshire novels shed little light on cathedral life in the Victorian era, though the modern dean will always treasure Archdeacon Grantley's reassuring remark to his father-in-law, Mr Harding, who felt too old to become Dean of Barchester – 'Where on earth can a man have peace and rest if not in a deanery?'

The more illustrious of the nineteenth-century deans were commemorated by full-length biographies and nearly all of them found their way into the *Dictionary of National Biography*, but their twentieth-century successors on the whole fared less well and were limited to a newspaper obituary or a page in their cathedral Friends journal. Deans are not what they once were.

The following list of biographies and autobiographies is provided for readers who may wish to know more about some of the deans whose lives are briefly treated in this present volume. In some instances no such work exists, so wherever possible relevant books by the absentees have been included, together with a few other volumes about the development of cathedral life in modern times. Official cathedral histories, most notable those of Canterbury and St Paul's, contain a wealth of information about deans and chapters.

Second-hand booksellers should be able to help, but anyone with access to the Internet can do no better than visit www.abebooks.com.uk.

Life of Henry Alford, edited by his widow, 1873

A. C. Benson, *Edward White Benson, Life*, 2 vols, Macmillan, 1928

E. W. Benson, *The Cathedral, Its Necessary Place in the Life of the Church*, 1878

F. S. M. Bennett, *The Nature of a Cathedral*, 1925

—— *On Cathedrals in the Meantime*, 1928

Life and Letters of Dean Butler, 1897

Mary Church (ed.), *Life and Letters of Dean Church*, 1894

George A. B. Dewar (ed. with a memoir), *Letters of Samuel Reynolds Hole*, 1907

R. Farrar, *Life of F. W. Farrar*, 1904

Adam Fox, *Dean Inge*, John Murray, 1960

Robert Tinsley Holtby (ed.), *Eric Milner-White, a Memorial*, 1991

Robert Hughes, *The Red Dean*, 1987

Walter Hussey, *Patron of Art*, Weidenfeld & Nicolson, 1985

W. R. Inge, *Diary of a Dean*, Hutchinson, 1945

—— *Vale, an autobiographical farewell to St Paul's*, Longnaus Green, 1934

Hewlett Johnson, *Searching for the Light*, Michael Joseph, 1968

W. R. Matthews, *Memories and Meanings*, Hodder & Stoughton, 1969

Stephen Platten and Christopher Lewis (eds), *Flagships of the Spirit*, Darton, Longman & Todd, 1998

Rowland E. Protheroe, *Life and Letters of Arthur Penrhyn Stanley*, 2 vols, 1893

E. W. Southcott, *The Parish Comes Alive*, Mowbray, 1956

W. H. W. Stephens, *Life and Letters of Dean Hook*, 1880

C. J. Stranks, *Dean Hook*, Mowbray, 1954

T. E. Taylor, *Joseph Armitage Robinson*, James Clarke, 1991

Bishop Welldon, *Forty Years On*, 1915

—— *Recollections and Reflections*, Cassell, 1915

David Williams, *Genesis and Exodus: A Portrait of the Benson Family*, Hamish Hamilton, 1979

H. C. N. Williams, *Twentieth Century Cathedral*, Hodder & Stoughton, 1964

Mission-shaped Church, a Church of England Report, Church House Publishing, 2004

Index of People

Index of Places